I, MILLENNIAL

TOM BALLARD

I, MILLENNIAL

ONE SNOWFLAKE'S SCREED AGAINST BOOMERS, BILLIONAIRES, & EVERYTHING ELSE

SCRIBNER

SCRIBNER

First published in Australia in 2022 by Scribner,
an imprint of Simon & Schuster Australia
Suite 19A, Level 1, Building C, 450 Miller Street, Cammeray, NSW 2062

Sydney New York London Toronto New Delhi
Visit our website at www.simonandschuster.com.au

SCRIBNER and design are registered trademarks of The Gale Group, Inc.,
used under licence by Simon & Schuster Inc.

10 9 8 7 6 5 4 3 2 1

A catalogue record for this
book is available from the
National Library of Australia

9781761100635 (paperback)
9781761100642 (ebook)

Cover design by Barney Sullivan
Typeset in 12/16.5 pt Sabon by Midland Typesetters, Australia
Printed and bound in Australia by Griffin Press

The paper this book is printed on is certified against the
Forest Stewardship Council® Standards. Griffin Press holds
chain of custody certification SGSHK-COC-005088. FSC®
promotes environmentally responsible, socially beneficial
and economically viable management of the world's forests

For Mum and Dad:
the best two Boomers a kid could ask for.

Thank you for loving me, and for giving me money.

and

For Cecilia:
Welcome to the world. Sorry about everything.

CONTENTS

'Communion goes beyond walls 🛡️🛡️🛡️'
— @britneyspears, Instagram, March 2020

Prologue

kids these days

I started the decade on ketamine.

In the early hours of 2020, I sat slumped on the couch in a friend's sharehouse in Carlton North and groaned as the horse tranquilliser washed over my brain. The ket had enlisted the evening's cocaine, MDMA, vodka Red Bulls and amyl nitrite and formed a supergroup that was now performing live in my skull, and they were playing all the hits.

Not gonna lie – I was cooked.

I took a sip of my gin and tonic and tried to focus. A friend was addressing the room, recounting her story about a creepy interaction she'd once had with Harvey Weinstein. I was doing my best to concentrate, because that's the polite thing to do when someone is telling you a #metoo, even at 5 am on New Year's Day. But I was struggling. The supergroup was loud and getting louder, and the lounge room was somehow upside down and back to front and reality was being warped and folding in on itself. I needed to wee, and also, it was becoming very clear that nobody here was going to have sex with me.

I gave up and tuned out. My head lolled back, and I stared up at the ceiling, drifting in and out of the now, wondering what was going to become of us all (specifically, me).

I was a month and five days into my thirties.

Meanwhile, **Australia was on fire**. While my friends and I had been coordinating our drug orders earlier that evening, four thousand people had been huddling together on the Mallacoota foreshore under a blackened sky, surrounded by flames, listening as the town's gas cylinders exploded in the heat. The country had been burning for months; our driest spring on record had turned into a Black Summer. December had brought tens of thousands of lightning strikes, 60 km/h winds and the hottest day in Australian history, and now two hundred bushfires were blazing across the country. Fires in the Blue Mountains and East Gippsland had become so fierce they'd generated *pyrocumulonimbus*: giant thunderstorm clouds that could cause their own lightning strikes, gusts of wind and hail blackened with soot. These fucking fires were *creating their own motherfucking weather* – weather which could, in turn, start and spread more fires.

It was very bad.

And another bad thing was on its way.

As Australia burned – and as I crawled home from that sharehouse to my apartment (where I would spend the next three days in bed, feasting on UberEats and Pierce Brosnan Bond movies) – a seafood market in Wuhan was being closed for 'environmental sanitation'. A string of new pneumonia-like cases had been reported around the city, but not to worry, probably nothing. Confused merchants watched as public security officers dressed in protective gear sanitised the market's fish tanks and collected samples. A few days later, a regular at the wet market became the first reported death from the mystery illness. By the end of January, the Chinese government had closed off the city and there were ten thousand confirmed cases worldwide, from South Korea to the US. The World Health Organization declared a 'public health emergency of international concern' due to

Severe Acute Respiratory Syndrome Coronavirus 2 (SARS-CoV-2), purveyor of the COronaVIrus Disease of 2019, or COVID-19.[1]

As the pandemic has unfolded over these past few years, **it's felt like the whole world has joined me in that New Year's Eve k-hole and we've all been trapped in there ever since.** Right off the bat, things just kept getting scarier and more surreal with every update: Now we can't touch our faces.

Now we're all wearing masks.

Now people are punching each other in supermarkets. Now my brother's wedding has been called off.

Now I'm alone in a hotel room in Brisbane, my week of stand-up shows cancelled, going a bit crazy. Now the borders are closing. Now I'm definitely not moving to London. Now the lockdowns have started. Now I'm going fully crazy. Now the President of the United States is suggesting that maybe drinking bleach is a good thing to do, health-wise. Now the police are handing out thousand-dollar fines and using drones to patrol locked-down suburbs. Now the Melbourne Comedy Festival is cancelled. Now the Olympics are cancelled. Now news cameras are panning along endless dole queues as international celebrities sing 'Imagine' to us from inside their mansions. Now the guy from *My Kitchen Rules* is trying to sell you a magical Dalek that can cure the virus for just $14,990.

Now a Nobel Prize laureate and former Australian of the Year has confused Googling with tweeting.

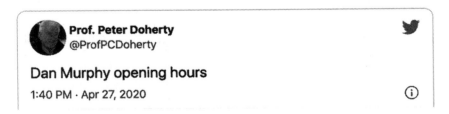

Prof. Peter Doherty
@ProfPCDoherty

Dan Murphy opening hours

1:40 PM · Apr 27, 2020

---

1   Guessing you're across this.

Now there's a second wave. Now we're in a recession for the first time since I was a toddler. Now George Floyd has been murdered and *everything's* getting cancelled. Now the government has managed to find hundreds of billions of dollars out of nowhere and we're suddenly lifting people out of poverty and ending homelessness. Now we've stopped doing all that and billionaires have doubled their wealth and all the talk of radically changing everything to create a new and better normal has been forgotten, and it's back to business as usual.

This is us now: **we live in an age of fire, pestilence and chaos.** As we try to survive and make some sense of it all, the powers that be promise to make things better and tell us to hang on to hope.

It's all going to be okay, everyone; after all, We're All In This Together.

SMDH AT HOW RANDOM THE WORLD IS RN

I was born in November 1989 – the same month the Berlin Wall was singlehandedly demolished by David Hasselhoff.

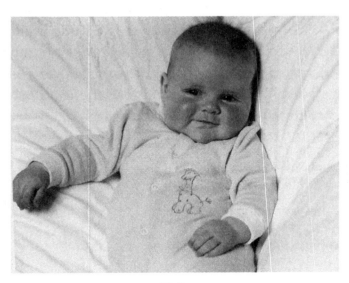

Hello

The toppling of the Wall heralded the dissolution of the Soviet Union, the end of the Cold War and the fall of communism, and everyone was very excited about the possibilities of change and freedom and the future. Earlier that year, a neoconservative at the US State Department by the name of Francis 'Oops' Fukuyama had written a much-lauded essay entitled 'The End of History?', in which he argued that the world was now witnessing 'the end point of mankind's ideological evolution and **the universalization of Western liberal democracy as the final form of human government**'. The political economic system of capitalism was here to stay forever, and everyone could see #TheWestIsBest. From now on, humanity and politics was just going to be about 'the endless solving of technical problems, environmental concerns, and the satisfaction of sophisticated consumer demands'. Sounds sick, Frank, great work everyone 👍👍👍.

Three decades later, I think we can agree that History is still very much Going, and it appears to be wielding some Big Dick Energy. In just my lifetime, History has brought us burst bubbles and recessions, globalisation, genocides, oil spills, 9/11, the War(s) on Terror (did we win?), the emergence of billionaire Silicon Valley psychopaths, the *Big Brother* turkey slap, a Global Financial Crisis, a failed Arab Spring, the Syrian Civil War, ISIS, super-powered creepy surveillance states, Brexit, pReSidenT dOnAld trUmP, a resurgent alt/far-right, Jeffrey Epstein 'committing' 'suicide', the collapse of public trust in civil institutions, a crippled labour movement, widespread alienation and loneliness, a broken democracy, a relentless assault on minority rights, a climate crisis, a global refugee crisis, a mental health crisis, an obesity crisis, a cost of living crisis, a housing crisis, a horse meat crisis, 'fake news', QAnon, Ebola, drones, and strawberries stuffed to the brim with fucking needles.[2]

---

2   Okay that one's gone away but it was pretty intense there for a bit.

In Australia, we've churned through seven Prime Ministers in just 15 years. Somehow, we've ended up with a demented billionaire class with too much power, a ghoul-ridden political class that produces nothing but scandals and cringe, and a dumb media class that consistently says and does dumb things that make us all dumber (which is a problem, because we're pretty dumb to begin with). We all gasp at the mistakes and lies and shitfuckery of the people at the top, and then they pretty much get away with it, and we all move on to the next thing and the old outrages are sucked down our collective memory hole. As we post and meme our anger and dismay, as we lob grenades at one another from the trenches of the endless culture war, as the scope of our political imagination gets smaller and smaller, as we're told about Royal Commissions and inquiries and reports and reviews and proposals for reforms that never go anywhere, we feel increasingly powerless and cucked.[3]

And now, just as some piss-icing on this melted turd cake, we've copped a global pandemic, featuring a highly contagious and lethal disease that came from either a bat or a lab, which has exposed and magnified all the cracks in the way we go about doing everything.

I dunno, maybe this 'final form' of human government isn't so great after all. There are shitloads of technical problems and environmental concerns that haven't been solved, shitloads of new ones are popping up every day and billions of demands are going unsatisfied. Crucially, *contra* Fukuyama, **the 21st century has made it clear that things don't automatically get better.**

---

3   The 2022 federal election certainly pushed Australia in a more progressive direction, but it's fair to say that *we were coming off a very low base*. Seeing the back of the demonic Morrison Coalition government was very nice, but Anthony Albanese's 'pro-business, pro-employer' Labor Party won government on a record low primary vote, promising to cut taxes for the rich, keep the poor languishing in poverty and open new fossil fuel projects to please their donors.

So it's still #auspol, and therefore bad.

The moral arc of the universe doesn't necessarily bend towards justice; sometimes it bends the wrong way, and sometimes it bends so far that it snaps, and God or Allah or Whoever just says 'Oh fuck it don't even worry about it actually' and walks away to do literally anything else.

Right now, a better future feels impossible. We really have no idea where we're headed as a country or as a species, but it's hard to imagine that it's going to be anywhere great. I mean, *Soylent Green* is set in 2022.

And nobody has been feeling this more keenly than the incoming captains of this sinking ship: my generation, **The Millennials.**

OK, I'LL BITE: WHAT'S A 'MILLENNIAL'?

Yes, generational categories are, in many ways, bullshit. They have their origins in the fields of demography and sociology, but these days they're mainly used by marketing agencies to sell us shit we don't need, or by journalists fishing for clicks with (actual) headlines like 'Millennials are killing the golf industry', 'Millennials are killing the movie business', 'Millennials are killing paper napkins', and 'Are Millennials killing wine? An exposé'.

So while there's a lot that this kind of generational framing *can't* tell us – and in the coming pages we'll come to see The Bigger Truth about our crappy status quo – I've still chosen to include it throughout this book. I believe we can still make some broad, general claims about generations, because our identities, politics, cultural touchstones and material realities are heavily informed by when we were born, and we do find ourselves being able to broadly relate to others who are experiencing the world and certain life stages at roughly the same time as we are.

Plus, I'm not going to change anything now because we've already done the cover.

The definitions of these categories vary. The Australian Bureau of Statistics (ABS) used to combine 'Generations X and Y' into one generational definition – those born between 1966 and 1986 – because it said that these groups 'have many characteristics in common'. This would put my older brother Gavin, just three years my senior, in the same generational category as ex-Prime Minister

Scott Morrison (born 1968) and celebrity chef Gordon Ramsay (1966). This is weird, and I don't like it. The ABS also used to categorise me and every other Australian born between 1986 and 2006 as a member of what they called 'iGen', which is gross.[4]

Australian market research company Roy Morgan defines 'Millennials' as those born between 1976 and 1990. This is also unacceptable, because it would place me in the same generational category as comedian Charlie Pickering, who literally represented Gen X on Channel Ten's *Talkin' 'Bout Your Generation*, and if we cannot trust the veracity of our light-hearted TV game shows, then surely all is lost.

For our purposes, **the Millennial generation is made up of those born in the 15 years between 1981 and 1996.** That's following a definition used by the likes of the Pew Research Centre, Gallup Polling, Australian think tank The Grattan Institute and my sense of self. And it makes sense: **'Millennials' are those who came of age around the dawning of the new millennium.** Our ranks include the likes of Hamish and Andy, Lleyton Hewitt, Mark Zuckerberg, Yassmin Abdel-Magied, Guy Sebastian, Sarah Hanson-Young, Flume, Ellyse Perry, Grace Tame, Ian Thorpe, Patty Mills, Ruby Rose, Nikki Webster, Lorde, FriendlyJordies, Sharri Markson, Nick Kyrgios, Delta Goodrem, Bo Burnham, Courtney Barnett, Chris Hemsworth, my brother, and moi.

The other generations break down like this:

GENERATION	BORN	AGED TODAY	GENERAL VIBE	E.G.
GREATEST	1901 – 1927	Mid-90s+	Currently very chill	Ruth Cracknell, Gough Whitlam, Vincent Lingiari, Slim Dusty, my gran Nola.
SILENT	1928 – 1945	Mid-70s to early 90s	'Back in my day . . .'	John Howard, Rupert Murdoch, Bob Hawke, Ita Buttrose, Father Bob Maguire, Dawn Fraser, Dick Smith, Graham Kennedy, Maggie Beer.

---

4   'iGen' makes me think of Kraft Foods' 2009 attempt to rebrand Vegemite as **'Vegemite iSnack 2.0'.** This horrific name had been selected as the winner out of 48,000 submitted entries based on 'its personal call to action, relevance to snacking and clear identification of a new and different Vegemite to the original'.

Two months after the rebrand had prompted a national outcry, Kraft Foods abandoned the change, sombrely admitting in a statement that the new name 'has simply not resonated with Australians', despite its obvious call to action and relevance to snacking. Truly, this was a deeply shameful period in our country's history.

GENERATION	BORN	AGED TODAY	GENERAL VIBE	E.G.
BABY BOOMERS	1946 – 1964	Late 50s to mid-70s	Facebook	Julia Gillard, Kerri-Anne Kennerley, Donald Trump, Ernie Dingo, Tony Abbott, Noni Hazlehurst, Paul Kelly, Pauline Hanson, Anthony Albanese, Judy and Neil Ballard, and, quite incredibly, Keanu Reeves. Yes – Neo/John Wick is a Boomer.
X	1965 – 1980	Early 40s to mid-50s	*'Whatever.'*	Kurt Cobain, Wil Anderson, Nicole Kidman, Adam Goodes, Julian Assange, Poh Ling Yeow, Pat Rafter, Tim Rogers, Schapelle Corby, Scott Morrison, Bill Shorten, Natalie Imbruglia.
Z (AKA 'ZOOMERS')	1997 – 2012	10 to mid-20s	Righteous fury + flossing	Greta Thunberg, Tayla Harris, Bindi Irwin, Malala Yousafzai, Billie Eilish, Jungkook from K-Pop sensation BTS, my boyfriend, and no doubt a thousand YouTube, TikTok and SoundCloud personalities who I simply refuse to learn anything about.[5]
ALPHA	2013 onwards	Under 10s	Bless	My niece 😍 😍 😍

So – Australian Millennials are now 'adulting'. The oldest Millennials are now entering our forties, and the youngest of us are in our mid-twenties. Most of us happen to be in our early thirties. Many of us are married with kids, while others are still freaking out at the fact that our friends are now parents, because we know that they're idiots.

---

5   Zoomers clearly share a lot in common with Millennials – e.g. a big uncertain future – but these little upstarts have recently begun to solidify their own generational identity, and have even developed the gall to mock us, their elders, who they should respect and admire. (According to TikTok, we Millennials are embarrassingly obsessed with red wine, 90s nostalgia and Harry Potter. Fair play.)

   If you're a Zoomer reading this thinking 'Pfft what could Ol' Grandpa Ballard possibly have to say that's worth listening to?', I say stick around. The same wicked problems facing my generation do/will apply to you too, only worse.

The median Australian is aged 38 and is therefore a Millennial. (The median First Nations person is a Zoomer, at age 23.) We're 5.4 million strong, making up approximately 21.5% of the Australian population – almost exactly the same size as the Boomers. (Gen X account for 19%, Zoomers 18%.) Over two-thirds of us live in metropolitan Australia. A fair chunk of us were born in Asia. One in three Millennial dudes has a uni degree; for women, it's one in two.

We grew up watching *Degrassi, Round the Twist, Ship to Shore, Cheez TV, The Secret World of Alex Mack, rage, Video Hits* and *Rove Live.* We have swum through oceans of reality TV. *The Simpsons* is a fundamental part of who we are. We began to see some glimpses of our adult lives on screen in *Please Like Me* and *Girls.* We read *Harry Potter, Goosebumps, Looking for Alibrandi* and *Tomorrow, When the War Began.* We've seen *The Lion King, Toy Story, Space Jam, The Castle, The Matrix, Shrek, Mean Girls, Anchorman* and the *Fast & Furious* movies many times. We've known three different Supermen, three Spidermen, five Jokers and six Batmen. Our lives have been soundtracked by The Wiggles, Britney Spears, Blink-182, Avril Lavigne, Eminem, Powderfinger, Beyoncé, Coldplay, Bloc Party, Taylor Swift, Crazy Frog, Kanye West and, for a short and unfortunate period, Jet. We had an embarrassing emo phase there for a while. We're more familiar with Alien Ant Farm's 'Smooth Criminal' than Michael Jackson's, and almost 100% of us graduated from primary or high school to the sounds of Vitamin C's 'Graduation (Friends Forever)'.

We mainly get our news through Facebook and TV news. We are extremely online – over 90% of us are on social media – even though we know it can be a toxic hellscape. We are turning away from God; more than 46% of us marked 'No Religion' on the latest Census. We are woke hipsters in skinny jeans, globalist yuppies, proud bogans in hi-vis and cyber-bullying 'digital natives'. We have been moulded by Tamagotchis, MySpace, Napster, MSN Messenger, *Grand Theft Auto*, iPods, iPhones, Samsung Galaxies, YouTube, selfies, emojis, Tumblr, Reddit, Tinder, Netflix and clickbait. We've ingested millions of ads into our central nervous system over the course of our lifetimes, including that one with the guy in the milk bar who just wants milk that tastes like real milk and the 'NOT! HAPPY! JAN!' Yellow Pages one.

And we are a generation *on edge.* We were experiencing record levels of anxiety, depression, loneliness and suicide *before* the pandemic; since then, it's only gotten worse.

We're a lot of fun. Nice to meet you.

GIVE US A BREAK

The whole 'Everything Getting Worse' thing is a major source of concern to Australian Millennials (and to Zoomers and Alphas), because we're not going to be dead for ages. We're quite pissed off about it, tbh. See, we were given the impression that there was some kind of **intergenerational bargain** going on – a general understanding that each generation is supposed to leave a better world to the next – but apparently we're not doing that anymore. As long as Millennials have been around, we've been watching the world go to hell in a handbasket, and we've seen our individual lives grow harder and harder, as more of us are denied the means to secure ourselves a decent life on a planet that isn't on fire.

This would be bad enough, if it didn't also come with the experience of being constantly ignored, dismissed and patronised by the very Baby Boomerocracy that is ripping us off. Ever since Millennials started giving some constructive feedback about our predicament, we've been told by our parents, our political leaders and the media that we have no idea what we're talking about and we've actually never had it so good and also we're the worst. Perhaps you've read about just how much we suck in *Time* magazine (a 2013 cover profiled 'Millennials: The Me Me Me Generation') or in books like *How Not to Become a Millennial: Learning from America's Largest Sociological Disaster* or *Not Everyone Gets A Trophy* or *The Dumbest Generation*.[6] Everyone knows that Millennials are lazy, entitled, screen-addicted, selfish and clueless snowflakes who, like, talk weird? and do nothing but whinge and demand hugs and take photos of our food. We don't know how good we have it, and even if things *are* bad for us, it's not because of history or the movements of powerful macroeconomic forces

---

6   Subtitle: *Don't Trust Anyone Under 30.*

outside of our control – it's because of our poor attitude and our brunch.

'The younger generation now tells me how tough things are – give me a break,' then-75-year-old former Vice President Joe Biden declared at a book event in 2018. 'No, no, I have no empathy for it, give me a break.'

For Biden, the biggest problem facing young people today is our lack of a **can-do mindset**. 'Here's the deal, guys,' he told the room, 'we [old people] decided we were going to change the world, *and we did*.'[7]

In response to this gaslighting, my generation has embraced a burning sense of intergenerational resentment. We've retaliated with our own literary missiles (titles include *A Generation of Sociopaths: How the Baby Boomers Betrayed America, Millennials Strike Back* and *Please Just F* Off: It's Our Turn Now*), as well as a plethora of side-eye, think pieces and memes, from Old Man Yells At Cloud to referring to COVD-19 as the 'Boomer Remover'. On my late-night comedy show for the ABC, *Tonightly with Tom Ballard*, we regularly engaged in generational warfare discourse, especially during 'Boomer Week': a special five-day orgy of cheap, taxpayer-funded jokes and sketches made at our parents' expense.[8] After *Tonightly* was cancelled (for being too funny), I went on to write a furious stand-up show, *Enough,* which included a passionate routine that began, 'Any Baby Boomers here tonight? No? Cool, let's talk about them: *when are they going to die?*

---

7   When running for president the following year, Biden told a room full of wealthy donors in Manhattan that if he were to be elected, 'nothing would fundamentally change'.
     Clearly, Joe had changed the world enough, and now he was tired.

8   Reporter Bridie Connell, in Serious ABC Journalist Voice: 'Owning an entire house may seem to you or I like something that the Queen of England does. But in the Boomer community, it's perfectly normal to own the property you live in, effectively making you your own landlord.'

'Seriously; Boomers are hanging around like a John Farnham farewell tour. When are they going to shuffle off this mortal coil and *GIVE ME A HOUSE?!*'

And everybody laughed and laughed.[9]

WHA' HAPPENED??

This intergenerational culture war has been super fun and entertaining, but I think it's time to wrap it up. It's getting us nowhere. By this point, the question *'Do young people today really have it harder than their parents?'* has been answered: yes, we definitely do, and pretty much everyone knows it. In 2021, the ABC's *Australia Talks* survey – the biggest and most rigorous opinion poll ever conducted in this country – found that 65% of Australians think it's harder for young people to get by now than it used to be, and **59% think that young Australians will be overall worse off than their parents.**[10]

The real question now is **why?** *Why* has that intergenerational bargain been broken? How the fuck did we get here? How did the world get so deranged? And what – if anything – can we possibly do about it?

These questions have been rattling around my head for some time. They've changed me. I have always identified as a

---

9   When this routine was filmed and shared on ABC TV's Facebook page, the comments lit up with feedback from Boomers like Beryl ('And everyone wonders why there is no respect these days!') and Warren ('Tom if I was your parent I would leave you NOT a thing!!!').

10 *Australia Talks* is a collaboration between the ABC, the University of Melbourne and data science company Vox Pop Labs. Your typical Newspoll or Essential poll surveys about 1,000 people; the 2021 *Talks* survey had 60,000 respondents, and the results were statistically weighted and controlled for sample selection effects. It's the closest thing we have to actually knowing what 'mainstream Australia' thinks about stuff right now, but of course its results are almost entirely ignored by the corporate media because it comes from the GayBC.

Sky News geniuses don't need no fancy 'data' to know what the Quiet Australians think; they prefer to listen to their guts, and release the results of their research via their buttholes.

'progressive'; I was born to Labor/Green-voting parents who were unionists and members of Amnesty International, and as a kid I tried to heal the world by doing the 40 Hour Famine, running for student council, and joining a local, awkwardly named anti-homophobia youth group (YUMCHA = Youth United Making Changes against Homophobic Attitudes).[11] Throughout my early twenties I was a classic bleeding-heart SJW, signing petitions and going to refugee rights rallies and tweeting snarky comments about religious homophobes and watching *The West Wing*. I knew that politics generally sucked, but hey, at least Kevin Rudd and Obama were The Good Guys, and they'd do Good Things. I also knew for sure that the Greens were awesome, all conservatives were racists and politics would be much better if everyone was just *nicer* to each other. Simples.

But then 2016 broke my brain. Pauline Hanson returned to the Senate on a wave of Islamophobia; Broken Britain voted to leave the European Union; I spent six weeks filming *First Contact,* an immersive SBS documentary series about white/Black race relations in Australia, alongside One Nation co-founder David Oldfield; the whole Baby Boomer vs. Millennial 'the only reason you can't afford a house is because of smashed avocado' discourse had begun in earnest; and in November, Donald Trump was elected to be the 45th President of the United States. I can still remember travelling home to Warrnambool on a V-Line train that afternoon, watching

---

11 I was being very brave doing all this revolutionary organising because it was happening in Liberal heartland. My seaside hometown of Warrnambool sits in Gunditjmara/ Dhauwurd Wurrung country in southwestern Victoria, within the Federal electorate of Wannon: a seat that's been held by the Liberal Party since a young Malcolm Fraser won it from Labor in 1955. Fraser handed the seat over to David Hawker in 1983, who would go on to sit in it for 27 years, become the Speaker of the House of Representatives and occasionally send me congratulatory letters when I did well in public speaking competitions.

Conservative though it may be, Warrnambool makes for a very pretty, friendly and safe corner of the world, replete with nice people, beaches, roundabouts, horses, Norfolk pines and folk music. More recently, there's also been quite a bit of crystal meth.

the results come through on my phone, trying to comprehend how the impossible had come to pass – the big wet idiot from *The Apprentice* was going to have access to nukes!!! – and quietly shitting myself about where all this was headed.

I began to question everything. Until then, I'd thought I was a reasonably well-informed, politically conscious citizen, but clearly I had absolutely no idea what the fuck was going on around here, and I needed to start asking some new, bigger questions about the forces that shape our world, why our country 'works' the way it does, and what I really believe. Over the past six years or so, I've been trying to interrogate and explore these ideas in my comedy and on my political interview podcast *Like I'm A Six-Year-Old*, which has seen me converse with everyone from Christian fundamentalists to communists to Sam Newman. I've read books and listened to other podcasts and had drunken conversations and become confused and changed my mind and developed my hot takes (and had some more ketamine), and I've muddled my way along a somewhat haphazard political education to become the public intellectual you know ~~and love~~ today.

GEN LEFT

Most Australian Millennials came of age in the era of John Howard, whose Coalition government won the vote of 18- to 34-year-olds in 2004. **But today the kiddies are overwhelmingly voting Left.** According to the Australian National University's Election Study, at the 2019 federal election, almost two-thirds of 18- to 34-year-olds voted for either Labor (37%) or the Greens (28%).

(By contrast, 59% of Australians aged 65 and over voted for the Coalition. Just 2% of the over-65s voted for the Greens, and they were my mum and dad, Julian Burnside and The Ghost of Malcolm Fraser.)

In 2022, voters under 45 made up 43% of the electorate and managed to kick the Tories out. The six seats with the highest proportion of voters under 30 all went to either Labor or the Greens.

We can see similar generational political trends around the world. Conservative lizards Ronald Reagan and Margaret Thatcher both won the youth vote during their times in office in the 1980s, but more recently American and British voters under 40 have overwhelmingly lent their support to self-described democratic socialists Bernie Sanders and Jeremy Corbyn. Millions of my fellow Millennials have been asking the same questions that I have, and are desperately hoping for something **radically different** – something that rejects the grinding incrementalism and political 'common sense' that we're expected to swallow.

SO I DID A BOOK

I was already on my journey towards enlightenment, then the pandemic happened, and things were crazier than ever, and I suddenly had a shitload of free time on my hands, so I decided to write everything down to try to make some sense of things and to work through my anger issues.

This is an accounting of what our country and our world has become in the forty years since Australian Millennials first arrived. Drawing on books, podcast interviews, academic research papers, some funny tweets I remember, and my gut, I want to explain how my generation has been comprehensively screwed over when it comes to the fundamentals of a good life: **work, having somewhere to live, learning stuff, collectively owning stuff, economic democracy** and **the natural world.**

I've tried to write the book that I wish someone had handed me long ago: something that cuts through the bullshit, explains the basics, connects the dots, and can shed some light on why the world feels so weird and bad, and precisely who – or what – is responsible.[12]

---

12 I've done lots of proper research for this book and done fact-checking and things, but obviously if any of it doesn't make sense or is straight up wrong, that's just me being a funny comedian.

   If you have any issues with any of the following content whatsoever, please don't hesitate to send me your questions and concerns via my email address, **tony.abbott@bigpond.com.au**

This will not be one of those boring books, because there's going to be lots of swearing and pictures like this

and amongst all the political economic theory shit, I'll be peppering in some self-indulgent reflections on my personal experience of being alive for the past 33 years. (Obviously, as a homosexual Millennial comedian, I am obsessed with me, and I assume you are too.)

I'll even do a nice bit at the end about why all this shouldn't make you want to kill yourself. Promise.

So – **let us begin.** As I see it, if we're to have any hope of building a better, non-*Soylent Green* future – for Millennials and Boomers and everyone else – we must first understand how things came to be so broken in the first place.

Logue (?)

The Millennial Life & Its Discontents

1

WERK

'There are no more unions or bosses.
There are just Australians now.'
— Scott Morrison, April 2020

'We cannot have the militant end of the union movement
effectively engaging in a campaign of extortion against the
Australian people . . . This is just extraordinary, appalling
behaviour . . . That is just straight-out extortion. That is
reprehensible . . . It's not on.'
— Scott Morrison, September 2020

Like most of the people in the generations that have come before us, **Millennials have to work.** We're all expected to get a job and be productive members of society, or maybe a comedian.

It starts early. From the moment we're conceived, people start thinking about how we'll be put to work. Expecting parents will discuss what career path their foetus might grow up to pursue, or just presume their kids will one day take over the family business. As soon as we can walk and talk, they ask us 'So what do you want to be when you grow up?', and when we answer them honestly, they tell us that it might be 'unrealistic' to expect a stable career as a full-time Dinosaur Space Pirate (in *this* economy?), so perhaps we should consider retail.

As soon as we've made it through Year 9, we're expected to start punching the clock, and then we're expected to keep that going and orient our entire adult existence around what we do for a living for eight hours a day, five days a week, for as long as we possibly can.[1]

My working life began at eleven. I really wanted a dog, but my parents had refused to get us one, so I decided to become one of Australia's beloved entrepreneurs and start my own dog-walking 'business', allowing me to monetise my passion for hanging out with dogs. (In the corporate world, this is known as **synergy**.) I designed a business card advertising my services in Microsoft Word (featuring some dog-based Clipart and some WordArt screaming 'Call Tom Ballard – *The Lord of the Leash!*') and dropped one of them into every letterbox in the neighbourhood. Then I sat back and waited for the pooches and profits to start rolling in.

I quickly discovered that local consumer confidence was weak. I only heard back from one potential client: Mrs Godfrey, a pensioner who lived around the corner with her German Shepherd, Thumper, who was big enough to eat me without chewing. In an employment arrangement that surely broke multiple child labour laws, I went on to walk Thumper two to three times a week for the next seven years on a wage

---

1   As you read this, the Australian pension age is slowly being raised to 67 by 2023. By the time the oldest Millennials reach that age in 2048, it will probably have been raised to 84, or the welfare state will have been so degraded that it won't even provide a pension anymore, or the very concept of 'money' will be completely irrelevant because we'll be back to the bartering system, and all the Centrelinks will have been seized and turned into barracks and mass graves as humanity wages a bloody civil conflict for its very survival in the Resource Wars.

   Of course, you might not even make it to retirement, as you may be one of the estimated 2.7 million people who die in workplace accidents globally every year. Good luck!

of $1 per walk (no super), with the understanding that I would bring my own plastic bag to pick up his massive turds.

It wasn't all bad. I was hanging out with a dog, after all, and I was paid cash in hand and I got to enjoy some exercise and fresh air.[2] But it was still *work*, and it taught me that work can be a stupid, annoying obligation that ruins your day, and I vowed to avoid having to do as much of it as possible for the rest of my life.

So far, so good. As a teenager I was paid handsomely to dress up as a sea captain with an 'English' accent in the local council's sound and light show *Shipwrecked!*, and all I had to do was recite a short script to bored tourists and play my Nintendo DS while they watched the show.

All aboard

---

2   When it wasn't smelling of dog turds.

After high school I moved to Melbourne and worked for a few months in a call centre for the Movember Foundation, which was a fun and easy job except for the fact that it came with a lot of pressure to 'Grow The Mo' in Movember. I cannot do this, and after four weeks of trying it just looked like a moustache had died and decided to haunt my upper lip. At the end of the month, we were encouraged to wear a costume that best captured the 'spirit' of our Mos, and everyone told me that I had to go dressed as an old lady with Grandma whiskers.

Even in a full-colour, high-res version of this photo,
the moustache cannot be seen

Apart from that, since the age of 19, I've worked almost exclusively as a professional (?) stand-up comedian and as a broadcaster at the ABC, where employees are paid mountains of taxpayer money to just sit around all day and be as unproductive and elitist and gay as possible. My entire 'job' is to think up things and make people laugh (usually when they're drunk), and I'm able to make a comfortable living having fun and sleeping in. My hands remain soft and delicate, and I generally find people with actual skills intimidating and hard to relate to.

Somehow, I've managed to get away with this. But I'm one of the lucky ones.

WORK SUCKS / I KNOW

I may have avoided having a shitty job myself, but I have a sense of just how shitty modern work can be, because I have eyes and ears. I see bathroom attendants getting racially abused in nightclubs. I see public school teachers drowning in correction. I've seen a tip jar on the counter of a 7-Eleven.

I also watch the news, and have followed the regular horror stories that come out of the world of real work, like the one from 2017 about a Coles manager in Perth who asked staff to work extra hours in return for free carbs.

'As you can see we have an enormous amount of stock out the back in the stockroom,' he wrote in a notice to the staff. 'I am asking team members to give me 4hrs free labour . . . I plan to kick off the evening at 5:30pm and work through to 9:30pm. Pizza will be plentiful at 9:30pm.'[3]

---

3 And that's just the exploitation we can see locally. Every now and again we hear some news story about a person finding a note inside their handbag or a photo on their new phone that's come from a desperate worker in some kind of labour camp on the other side of the world where people are forced to work for 20 hours a day making $11 a year with no free pizza whatsoever, and we all have a moment to reckon with the bloodstained reality of our consumption habits in the global north and their consequences for a persecuted underclass that we'll never meet or see, and then we decide we're not going to think about that anymore and carry on with our day.

For the most part, **work sucks**. Obviously, it needs to exist *in some form*; people need to do lots of things and produce heaps of stuff in order for society to function. But you'd hope that the economic system designed to facilitate all that would ensure that it provides the people doing the work with the means to live a decent life – ideally, in the form of secure, well-paid, and fulfilling jobs.

That's not so. Instead, work has been a real pain in the hole for billions of human beings for ages; especially for the human beings who were never paid for their work and were considered the property of some other human beings. Bosses aren't legally allowed to do that kind of thing anymore (PC gone mad), and it's cool that we get overtime and Casual Fridays now, but employment still sucks in numerous ways for lots of people, every single day. In its 2022 *State of the Global Workplace* report, the polling company Gallup found that 79% of the world's one billion full-time workers aren't 'engaged' at work. That's almost four out of five workers who are either completely checked out in the workplace, or who actively hate their job because it's pointless or stressful or soul-crushingly boring or it involves having to work with *Craig*.[4]

Work certainly sucked for our parents' generation, too, but over the past forty years, it's become noticeably suckier. Lots of Baby Boomers enjoyed secure, well-paying jobs with a bunch of benefits for life, while young people today are told to prepare for 17 jobs across five different careers, whether we want that or not. As heaps of Boomers head off into comfortable retirement, Australian Millennials are now dealing with a labour market in which job security has evaporated and is quickly being replaced by what the Australian

---

4   The remaining 21% said they were 'highly involved in and enthusiastic about their work and workplace', but I'm assuming that's because they had to fill out the survey in front of their boss.

Council of Trade Unions (ACTU) calls **insecure work**: employment that '**provides workers with little social and economic security, and little control over their working lives**'. This is a global trend, but Australia is a world leader: we now have the third-highest rate of insecure work in the OECD.[5] Less than half of all working Australians are now in permanent, full-time jobs, and insecure workers make up about 44% of the workforce, trying desperately to navigate various casual/part-time/gig-economy/sub-sub-sub-contracted/seasonal/outsourced arrangements and experiencing brand new and exciting forms of ~~exploitation~~ flexibility for the 21st century.

Millennials get this, because we are **Generation Casual**. Casual workers made up 13% of the Australian workforce in 1982; today they account for about 25%, and they're most prevalent in industries with younger employees, like education, hospitality and retail. Being 'casual' sounds super fun and chill, but it's really not; casual workers can be fired at any time for no reason, and they have no basic holiday or sick leave. In theory, they're compensated for this with 'casual loadings' – a pay rate of up to 25% more than permanent workers. In reality, in highly casualised industries – like hospitality, where nearly 80% of the workforce is in casual work – the loading works out to be just 5%. According to the ABS, one-third of casuals say they don't receive their loadings at all.

Thanks to the widespread conversion of full-time work into these casual, part-time, only-when-needed, just-in-time,

---

5   That's the **Organisation for Economic Co-operation and Development**, made up of 37 developed (i.e. rich) countries with market economies and high standards of living. The OECD regularly publishes credible and interesting economic data that can help us see how we're doing in comparison with other similar countries.

    All the OECD countries are functioning democracies, except for the US, where elections are regularly rigged and stolen by the Deep State, dead people, Russians and Hollywood sickos.

no-idle-waiting-around jobs, fewer people are able to find as many hours of work per week as they'd like. The Foundation for Young Australians tells us this phenomenon, known as **underemployment,** has exploded by 270% since 1985. Once again, that falls on us: well over half of those who are under-employed are Millennials.[6]

More 'flexible' work arrangements aren't necessarily a bad thing, of course. In theory, they can empower working people and help deliver better work/life balance. **But that's not what we're talking about here.** Employers don't opt for these kinds of arrangements out of the goodness of their hearts; over-whelmingly, insecure work is designed to help bosses boost profits by reducing labour costs, minimising risk and keeping workers disorganised, even if this means those workers who need to support their families and plan their lives get screwed. In this glorious new gig economy, food delivery drivers, for example, are considered 'independent contractors' rather than employees, and receive no sick leave, superannuation, penalty rates or insurance (so flexible!). They have to supply their own cars and bikes, and they can work for more than 40 hours a week and still earn less than the minimum wage, as they put their lives on the line to pedal through the pouring rain to bring us a chocolate mousse from Nando's at 9.43 pm on a Tuesday.

While Millennials' job security may be disappearing, **at least the pay is shit.** For more than 12 years, as workers' productivity has continued to rise and corporate profits

---

6　On the other end of the spectrum, many Australians are working *way too much.* According to the OECD, 13% of Australian employees work more than 50 hours a week, compared to just 4% in Germany. In fact, the average German employee works 386 fewer hours a year than the average Australian worker, and yet Germans enjoy a higher median household income than we do.

　　No doubt those blasted Krauts use all that spare time to sit around reading Australian employment statistics, revelling in the *schadenfreude.*

have only gotten healthier, household incomes have flat-lined.[7] According to Melbourne University's Household, Income and Labour Dynamics in Australia (HILDA) survey, **the median Australian household income was lower in 2018 than it was in 2009,** while the cost of everything has been going up. Workers over the age of 35 have seen their wages increase a smidge since the 2008 Global Financial Crisis, but for the young, wages have actually fallen year on year. The decade leading up to the COVID crisis was defined by the lowest wage growth on record, and now the Reserve Bank of Australia (RBA) tells us it's unlikely workers will be seeing a meaningful pay rise until the very end of 2023.

So Millennial workers are insecure, over/underworked and underpaid. Even though this sucks, we tend to put up with it, **because as far as we know, we have no other choice.** Due to our human needs for food/shelter/basic treats etc., having no job and no money tends to be even shittier than having a

---

7   **Productivity** refers to how much **output** (goods and services) is produced with a given set of **inputs** (mainly **labour** [that's you!] and **capital** [cash, buildings, machinery, vehicles, computers, etc.]).

Productivity *increases* when you produce more output with the same amount of inputs (e.g. you get a Macca's employee to make more Big Macs per hour), or when you produce the same amount of output with fewer inputs (e.g. you replace all the super-market check-out staff with self-check-out machines, which involves substantial capital investment upfront but will save you money in the long run because you don't have to pay the workers' wages and you can just get all your customers to scan and bag all their items themselves, even though we don't always do it correctly because it's not actually our fucking job so inevitably that fucking 'UNEXPECTED ITEM IN THE BAGGING AREA' message goes off every two minutes which means we have to stand there next to the machine that's flashing red and we feel like idiots as we wait for one of the few remaining human beings left working at the supermarket to come over and check that we brought our own bags and that we're not being dirty criminals and they fix it but then it happens again and the staff member has to come over again and it's so fucking frustrating and you feel this surge of anger directed at the staff member even though it's not their fault at all, because they're just trying to make a living and really they're even *more* of a victim of the situation because they're getting paid minimum wage to help customers troubleshoot the machines that have replaced workers just like them anyway that's why I don't feel bad about stealing stuff from supermarkets.)

The general idea is that productivity increases will lead to bigger profits, which will then lead to higher wages for workers. This is a very nice theory, **but labour productivity growth has outstripped wage growth for the past twenty years.** Australians are now working harder for the same (or even less) money.

shit job, so we carry on having to do the shit jobs so we can get the money to meet our needs, and we just try to put up with the shittiness of the job and hope it doesn't get much shittier.

In contrast, when work sucked particularly badly for Baby Boomers, they had some options to make it suck less. They relied on these things called **'trade unions'** (sp?) and sometimes they performed magical ceremonies called 'strikes' where they didn't go to work even though it wasn't a long weekend or anything and they didn't get fired for it – in fact, **things actually got better.**

Most young people today don't join a union, because most of us don't really know what they are, what they do, or what they could mean. We haven't seen them play a meaningful role in our lives, nor are we taught about how important they've been in shaping our world today. Quite honestly, until I bothered to find out more about this in my late twenties, I reckon almost my entire understanding of unionism came from the *Simpsons* episode 'Last Exit to Springfield', in which Homer leads a strike at the nuclear power plant to save the union-won dental plan.[8]

It was very funny, but it was also a cartoon. What did any of that stuff – strikes, unions, boss/worker conflict – have to do with me?

WELCOME TO CLASS

The story of why we have to work, why our jobs dominate our lives and how it's all come to suck so hard for Millennials is rooted in the significant matter of <u>class</u>.

When I was growing up, I rarely heard people talking about social classes in a meaningful way. I slowly got my head around the fact that the world has rich people and poor people in it, but my family wasn't either of those things (in the Australian

---

8   *'Lisa needs braces!'*

context anyway), so I figured we were somewhere in between. My parents were university-educated public sector workers who read a lot of books, we lived in a nice house and we had two cars, so that felt solidly 'middle' class, as far as I could tell.[9]

But then I'd hear stuff about the '*upper* middle class' and '*lower* middle class' and the 'working class' (my parents still went to work?) and 'bogans' (who were supposed to be poor, but then there were 'cashed-up bogans', who had heaps of money). Then I'd hear that the whole idea of class was outdated, and we were now living in a classless society, but then Shannon Noll sang 'Working Class Man' on *Australian Idol* and apparently working class men were still a thing and their blood was made of denim, and then later I'd hear terms like 'Howard's battlers', blue/white collar workers, the 'underclass' and *bourgie*.[10] It all seemed very confusing and vague, and quite removed from the reality of day-to-day life.

---

9   In the early 2000s, my brother and I became obsessed with Ben Folds, and when I heard the line from his breakthrough solo pop hit 'Rockin' the Suburbs' about not knowing what it's like to be male, middle class and white, I thought, 'But I *do* know what it's like, Ben! I'm all those things! I feel seen!'

I would later learn that the song is a satirical attack on self-obsessed and privileged white male celebrities, and therefore wasn't relevant to me at all.

10 This is slang for the sociological term *bourgeoisie* (pron. 'buorzh-waa-zee'), which translates literally to 'town-dweller'. The term was used in medieval France to refer to the craftsmen, artisans and merchants who lived inside the walls of market towns and cities. They weren't hanging out in the fancy castles with the nobility, but they weren't shit-eating peasants eking out a living in the fields, either.

When the Industrial Revolution kicked off in the late 1700s and changed everything forever with mechanised factory production and steam, the *bourgeoisie* began to own those factories and become wealthier, and the class grew and changed in nature. A certain German philosopher and philanderer named **Karl Marx** wrote about them a lot in the 1800s, and today, the term is broadly used to refer to the **economic ruling class** of a society. It has some sub-categories, from *the haute bourgeoisie* (the aristocracy, like the Rineharts, Packers, Forrests, Murdochs, the Bluths) down to the *petite bourgeoisie* (small business owners, landlords, doctors, lawyers, judges, bankers, Harold Gribble from *Round the Twist*). But generally speaking, when you're talking about the bourgeoisie, you're talking about the people at the top, with serious wealth and power.

In everyday life you're more likely to hear *bourgie* used to describe things that are a little bit fancy or la-di-dah, like almond milk, hosting dinner parties, reading *The New Yorker*, sending your kids to private school or driving your Tesla to a winery for brunch and a conversation about the property market. Members of the bourgeoisie certainly do enjoy doing these things, but that's far less important than the shit they get up to when they're doing the whole 'ruling' thing.

Most Australians today will self-identify as either 'middle' or 'working' class. We tend to base it on general vibes. A person's class is thought to be determined on things like their job, their education, how much money they earn/have, and what their lifestyle looks like, including all their cultural pecca-dilloes: rugby league (working class), tennis (middle class), opera (upper class), the ABC (middle and upper class), Channel Nine (working/lower-middle class), horse racing (upper class in the corporate boxes, middle class in the stands, working class watching it on TV at the TAB), etc.

But viewing class solely in terms of income brackets or aesthetics doesn't really tell us much about where class comes from, or how it works, or why we have it, or what different classes have to do with each other. It also gives us the strong (and false) impression that the social hierarchy of class just *is*; it's the natural order of things, and it cannot change.

The truth is **we live in class society today because of the political economic system under which we live.**[11] Under

---

11 That would be **CAPITALISM™** – the main villain of this book.

You'd be forgiven for thinking that 'capitalism' simply refers to the natural exis-tence of markets and trade or just The Economy, because that's often how it's talked about and sold to us. But humans have been trading and using markets for thousands of years, whereas capitalism has only been around for the past three or four centuries. (Before that, Europe was enjoying the fun of **feudalism**, in which peasant serfs were required to give their labour, produce and their love to the land-owning nobility that lorded over them in return for the privilege of being allowed to stay alive.)

Capitalism refers to a specific **mode of commodity production** ('commodity' meaning 'stuff', meaning anything that is bought or sold: food, cars, houses, keychains, chairs, iPhones, iron ore, software, hardware, art, furniture, socks etc., as well as services like education, healthcare, financial services, hilarious comedy, sex work, etc.). Under this system, the **means** of producing those commodities are considered **private property**, and are controlled by private owners, in the interests of making **profit** (rather than in the interests of, say, meeting human needs).

Ol' Capitalism is undoubtedly shit-hot at making stuff at a mass scale and creating enormous wealth. It just also has an annoying habit of concentrating the bulk of that wealth in the hands of a tiny few at the top, and fucking everyone else over. Capitalism also has a tendency to **exploit** the people who do most of the work (more on this soon); it loves to turn absolutely **everything** into a commodity (including people, their labour, animals, nature, your soul); it demands private property rights are enforced to create **artificial scarcity** (so people in our society starve, not because there's a lack of food, but because of their lack of money); it relies on relentless **competition** between everyone at all times, even when that competition is very stupid and damaging; and it demands **infinite growth** (which is tricky, seeing as we live on a planet with finite resources), otherwise it will explode.

capitalism, we're all busy producing goods or providing services, but different classes of people relate to that process of production in different ways. Lots of people might work at the factory, but someone else actually owns it. I think it's most useful, then, to think about class in terms of a relationship – specifically, your relationship to the social economic production of stuff and the creation of wealth.

THE 3 MAIN CLASSES YOU NEED TO KNOW ABOUT

#1 – THE PEOPLE WHO OWN STUFF

(Photo: iStock.com/Tom Merton)

If you're reading this book in the Chairman's Lounge while you're waiting for your private space jet to take you to visit one of your factories, then: fuck you.

Also – chances are you're in the class that sits right at the top of things. If you own the major stuff that's used to produce other stuff (factories, buildings, mines, machines, infrastructure, land, shops, corporations, commercial property, intellectual property, sports teams, tech platforms, newspapers, TV networks, etc.), that means you own some serious **capital**, and you've secured yourself a position in the capitalist / ruling / corporate / *haute bourgeoisie* class.

This is called **owning the means of production**, and for you, it's pretty great. You ultimately call the shots when it comes to the fates of the people who work for you and where all the profits go (Another warehouse? Another racehorse? Sex island?).

You're a Titan and a Captain of Industry. You hold massive power and influence over the wider economy and the public sphere, which you can use to buy and own more stuff. The more capital you own, the greater your political clout, and the less you have to worry about little things like public opinion, the common good, the law, or the truth.

#2 – THE PEOPLE WHO RUN THINGS

(Photo: iStock.com/pixelfit)

Hanging out below the overlords is the '**Professional-Managerial Class**' ('PMCs'[12]). They are here to help you achieve your optimal work/life fulfillment growth strategy KPIs.

They are the *petite bourgeoisie* – the little capitalists, or 'middle' class – tasked with keeping the wheels spinning and the profits growing, and who like to get drunk and touch you at the office Christmas party. They're the managers, CEOs, specialists, administrators, consultants, private school principals, high-level bureaucrats, team leaders, yuppies and the weirdos in HR. Basically, Neil Godwin from *The Office* (UK), or anyone who's ever read *The 7 Habits of Highly Effective People*.

The PMC can also be defined more widely to include the professionals who 'manage' the country (the political class, with its professional politicians, party apparatchiks, media advisors, staffers, economists and think tank wankers) or who 'manage' the culture (the media class, with all its shiny celebrities and

---

12 A term coined by social scientists John and Barbara Ehrenreich in 1977.

entertainers [hello!], advertising executives, the academic 'intelligentsia' and the commentariat: the columnists and pundits and batshit crazy shock jocks on Sky News yelling at you about how change is bad and Greta Thunberg is a Chinese asset and school drink taps should be filled with hydroxychloroquine).

Coincidentally, the PMC's wonderful professional management of things tends to serve the interests of the capitalist class (the PMCs' bosses), and not so much the interests of . . .

#3 – EVERYBODY ELSE

(Photo: iStock.com/Goodboy Picture Company)

If you don't own the big stuff that makes stuff, and you don't help to oversee the process that makes stuff, chances are you have no choice but to actually make the stuff. **All you have to sell in the market is your time and your labour power**, and you sure hope the PMCs and the capitalist class are looking to buy. If they're not, you won't get a wage, and you might not be able to feed and clothe yourself and help your landlord pay off their mortgage.

You do your work, you (hopefully) get paid, and the people who pay you get to profit from the work you do. You are part of the *proletariat* (or a 'prole'), you are a wage slave, a **worker**, and **you are in the working class**.

Some people in 'classless' Australia might be shook to view themselves in these kinds of class terms, particularly the minimum-wage Subway employee who considers herself middle class because she once went on a snow trip, or the millionaire property developer who thinks he's still a working-class battler because he grew up in a rough neighbourhood. And yes, there are plenty of messy exceptions; as a freelancing comedian, I'm some kind of freaky hybrid of working class and PMC. I still have to work in order to live and I'm regularly employed by other people who own things, but I also technically run my own 'business' (me, talking), I produce and manage words, ideas and content for cultural entertainment (very media class-y), and worst of all, I have a verified Twitter account, which makes me a Blue Check member of the Twitterati – *very* PMC.[13]

But generally, this class lens is far more instructive than the typical 'working/middle/upper' distinctions we're familiar with. As the American economics professor and author of *The Working Class Majority,* Michael Zweig, has put it:

> *By looking only at income or lifestyle, we see the* **results** *of class, but not the* **origins** *of class. We see how we are different in our possessions, but not how we are related and connected, and made different, in the process of making what we possess.*

With this in mind, just for a moment, put aside how much you earn, your job description, your thoughts on *Married at First Sight* and whether you drink Prosecco or XXXX, and consider how you might fit into the framework: in your job and your life, **how much control do you have over the way stuff is produced?**

---

13 This does *not* mean I deserve to be punished in The Revolution, though, because I'm quite nice, and I'm actually a class traitor who is working to bring the system down from the inside.

I'm guessing the answer is 'Not much, really' and you're in **class #3**. This might come as a surprise if, like me, you've been under the impression that 'working-class people' do nothing but manual labour, wear nothing but high-vis and listen to nothing but Rose Tattoo. This was never really true, but it's definitely not true today. Since the 1960s, Australia's manufacturing sector and blue-collar jobs generally have been in steady decline, and our country's shift to an overwhelmingly services-based economy has massively transformed the composition of the Australian working class. The government's National Skills Commission tells us that the industry which employs the most Australians today is 'Health Care and Social Assistance' (registered nurses, aged and disability carers, kitchenhands and cleaners in health facilities, etc.), which accounts for 14% of all workers. It's followed by the 'Retail Trade' at 10%. The people employed in those jobs might have collars that are white or pink or rainbow or whatever, but they are absolutely *workers*. Yes, the working class certainly includes labourers, miners, factory workers, warehouse staff and boilermakers, etc., but it's also made up of nurses, teachers, shop assistants, call centre workers, taxi drivers, bank tellers, cinema staff, paramedics, posties, baristas, cleaners, artists and pretty much anyone else who can't fire anyone and is playing by somebody else's rules in order to make a living.[14]

---

14 One could argue that even highly skilled professions like airline pilots or head chefs should be considered workers, because ultimately, they have to answer to owners and management. Increasingly, some folks in the PMC (such as those in academia, health professions, human services and the tech world) are finding themselves getting 'proletarianised' – they're still well-educated and tend to earn more than typical workers, but their jobs are being casualised, neutered, outsourced and automated, and they are now 'downwardly mobile', on their way to joining the rest of the dirty working scum down the bottom.

If you then add in all the other folks who have little control over the means of production – like most retirees (people who *were* workers) and the unemployed (people who are still expected *to be* workers, even if they don't currently have any work) – you'll see that 'the working class' is a shitload of people. In fact, it's *most* people. Zweig and labour journalist Kim Moody have (conservatively) estimated that the US workforce is around 63% working class, 35% PMC and 2% corporate/ruling elites, and estimates for Australia are similar.

So really, it's impossible to say what The Working Class looks or sounds like, because it's the biggest and most diverse class there is. The further you go up the ladder of wealth and power in Australia, the whiter and blokier it becomes, while the working class is white, Black, Blak, brown and every other possible variation. It stretches from teenagers right up to centenarians, and includes all the genders and faiths you care to name. Working class people live in big cities (even in the inner-cities, and some are renting even in the richest suburbs), in regional centres and in the outback. Plenty of us didn't finish high school, plenty have been to university, heaps of us vote conservative, most of us aren't in a union, almost none of us are members of a political party – and we're *all* getting screwed over by the classes above us.

THE STRUGGLE IS REAL

Being able to recognise the class make-up of our society and the relationship between those classes is key to understanding why work sucks so much. Although bosses love to present the workplace as one big happy 'team' or 'family', **different social classes hold diametrically opposed interests:** your boss wants to pay you the least amount of money she can get away with to maximise her returns, while you want to be paid as much money for your labour as possible so that you're able to live a decent life.[15]

Plus, when bosses buy your labour power through wages, they pretty much own you for the duration of the working day, and control everything. They're driven to squeeze as much productivity and loyalty out of their little worker ants as possible, even if that means doing creepy things like timing your toilet breaks, restricting which websites you can visit on company time or telling you what you can and can't wear on your own body.

(Weirdly, all the people who love to talk about the wonders of *freedom* and *democracy* in this country are often silent about the stark lack of freedom and democracy in the arena in which people spend most of their time: the capitalist workplace, where the unelected boss is sovereign, and sets the terms on which everyone else has to live.)

Thanks to capitalism, most big things in our society and recent history pretty much boil down to **Capital vs. Labour.** And frankly, capital has been getting away with as much shitty behaviour and exploitation as it can for as long as capitalism's been around, whether that's meant doing slavery, paying adorable children in gruel to work at your textile factory, or creating Human Resources. This exploitation was brought to Australia via colonialism, when the British invaded, stole and colonised the place with the 'help' of free convict labour and enslaved First Nations people and imported indentured workers, and working people around here have been getting a raw deal ever since.

The only way that workers have been able to make this

---

15 To get a sense of how much we're getting taken for a ride: in 2019, the ABS reported that across all the major industries in Australia, bosses spent an average of $60k in labour costs per worker, and made an average profit of $39k for their trouble.
   So bosses get an average 65% *return on investment* for employing the working class. And yet, if workers dare to ask for a bigger slice of the pie they're helping to bake, they're told that they're being greedy, and they're lucky to have any pie in the first place.

exploitation suck any less in the past is by engaging in **class conflict** through **class struggle:** by fighting back, *as a class*, against these economic tyrants. Workers have had to do the same thing, time and again: recognise their collective interests, get organised, and use the one weapon at their disposal to get a better deal: **the power of withdrawing their labour.** If enough workers go on strike and cost the bosses enough time and money, they can start to fight back against their employers' domination over the workplace, and win some more control over their working lives.

Traditionally, we've been quite good at this. Since the early 1800s, Australian workers have organised into societies and trade unions, and downed their tools to win cool things like better pay, voting rights and the eight-hour workday.[16] Nineteenth-century ruling elites hated handing out such concessions, of course, and wanted to make it very clear that workers were their little bitches who would be spanked if they stepped out of line. They moved to suppress workers' power: trade union membership was criminalised, union leaders were imprisoned and strikes across the colonies were violently crushed by police and soldiers.

After striking shearers, wharfies and miners had their arses handed to them by their bosses in the 1890s, the labour

---

16 Before the eight-hour workday was won by striking stonemasons in the 1850s, most workers were pulling 10- to 14-hour days, six days a week, with no sick leave or holiday pay, and lived under the constant threat of being fired at any time for any reason. Thankfully the masons had the courage to do something about this nonsense, even though it meant that ruling-class media outlets like the *Melbourne Herald* would attack them as 'stupid mischievous blockhead[s]' who were engaging in 'childish and useless perambulations'.

There is a cool monument commemorating this working-class victory opposite the Victorian Trades Hall in Melbourne; a tall granite column, with a bronze globe on top and an emblem reading '888'. The monument was originally located outside the state parliament building on Spring Street, but it was relocated in 1923, apparently because its presence 'offended' right-wing members of the legislature.

It is hard to imagine a more pathetically cunty act than this, but I'm sure today's conservatives are busy cooking something up that will give it a run for its money.

movement decided to try a new strategy to improve things: winning government. (As one unionist in Rockhampton put it, 'Throw your old guns aside, my boys; the ballot is the thing.') The defeated workers helped to form the **Australian Labor Party** – a mighty political force that would go on to achieve many more defeats in the future. The ALP managed to form the first national labour government in the world, and established Australia's industrial relations system of **compulsory conciliation and arbitration**, in which wage-setting and industrial disputes were settled before 'independent umpires' sitting on a national tribunal. Unfortunately, this meant that going on strike and any other **direct industrial action** was now considered very naughty, and were punished with massive fines. Regardless, the ALP celebrated the idea of relocating the workers' struggle from the workplace and the streets to the courts, and the system would stick around for the next eight decades.

Sometimes these courts came up with good stuff for workers, like a system of awards that protected conditions and the creation of a national minimum wage. But broadly, the tribunals were filled with justices who hailed from and were sympathetic to the ruling classes, and were happy to cut workers' wages and clamp down on their right to strike.[17] Some militant workers and unions got fed up with this, refused to listen to the stuffy judges and opted for direct action instead. Throughout World War I, the Roaring Twenties and the Great Depression, there were hundreds of 'unlawful' strikes for better pay and conditions in the cities, in the coal mines, on the railways and on the waterfront. In return, the labour movement regularly got pwned: it was hit with even

---

17 In 1931, during the worst of the Great Depression, the Arbitration Court decided to cut the basic wage by 10%, claiming that the fall in wages would lead to an increase in profits and more jobs. The following year, unemployment would hit a record high of 32%, and everyone laughed at the judges and their Epic Fail.

more fines, draconian union-busting laws, and numerous police batons to the face.

THE BOOM

So the ruling elites mainly had the upper hand for a good century and a half, and fair play to them. But in the wake of World War II – just as our parents' generation was arriving into the world – things would change dramatically.

During the war, millions of workers had been collectively mobilised at home to help the war effort, and now people figured that all that collective control shouldn't go to waste during peacetime, because that's what Hitler would have wanted. Under Labor Prime Minister John Curtin, his successor Ben Chifley, and even under the founder of the Liberal Party, Robert Menzies – who won the Prime Ministership in 1949 and wouldn't rack off for another 17 years – Australia pursued an economic policy of **full employment.** The government maintained ownership of large sections of economic production and spent enough on goods and services to ensure that everyone who wanted a job could get one.[18] The Curtin and Chifley governments basically constructed the **modern Australian welfare state** (featuring pensions, benefits and a government-run Commonwealth Employment Service), and funded major public works programs and the building of tens of thousands of houses for returned soldiers. There was heaps for workers to do, and the results speak for themselves:

---

18 Well, *pretty much* everyone. Even an economy in full employment will have some **frictional unemployment**: about 2% of the workforce who might be temporarily out of work as they voluntarily move between jobs. Ideally, that period of unemployment should be as brief (and painless) as possible.

As we'll soon see, this idea of 'full employment' has since been sent to live on a farm, with some pretty dire results.

before the war, the unemployment rate had averaged about 10%, but by 1948 it dropped below 1%.[19]

All that coupled with a mass immigration program and rising prices for our major export, wool, blossomed into what Reserve Bank Governor Glenn Stevens would later describe as a '**golden age for the Australian economy**'. During the thirty years after the war, unemployment averaged well under 2%, prices remained steady, and the economy was growing by more than 4.5% every year. (Australian Millennials have never experienced an economy or a labour market anything like this, even during the mining boom of the early 2000s.) Our grandparents celebrated this Long Boom by having lots of passionate and sweaty sex, and there was a Boom of Babies who grew up to become our beloved **Baby Boomer** parents.[20]

Throughout the Booming, the Australian working class continued to organise and grow its **class consciousness**. Well over half of the Australian workforce was unionised in the 50s and 60s, and in sectors like manufacturing (which accounted for almost a third of all jobs at the time) density was even higher. By the 70s, most workplaces were 'closed shops' – if you wanted to work there, you had to join the union, Sunshine – and workers with both blue and white

---

19 Both Labor and Liberal governments of this era were following the theories of a rockstar British economist named **John Maynard Keynes**. Before the 1940s, prevailing economic thought had been dominated by **neoclassical economics**, which was all about free markets and limited government and balanced budgets, and had visited misery on working people and the poor during the Depression. Keynes' **demand-side economics** (AKA **Keynesianism**) theorised that economic activity is actually driven by aggregate demand for goods and services, and so during an economic downturn, governments should spend into the economy to boost demand, stimulate growth and get the country to full employment – even if that meant running a budget deficit, and going into debt. In the post-war decades across much of the Western world, this Keynesian consensus was all the rage.

Side note: Keynes was a bisexual atheist with a sick moustache who fucked around quite a lot, hung out with the likes of T. S. Eliot and Virginia Woolf and was very enthusiastic about eugenics. Quite the character.

20 To give you an idea of just how big this Boom was: in 1966, Baby Boomers made up almost 40% of the Australian population.

collars began to seriously swing their collective dicks around to get a slice of the country's prosperity. Tens of millions of workdays were 'lost' to industrial disputes as militant unions went on strike and engaged in **pattern bargaining**; that is, pursuing the same claims for better wages and conditions in multiple workplaces across the one industry.

As always, the ruling classes considered such strikes to be The Devil, particularly any strikes organised by radical communists, because now the Cold War was happening and everyone had to be fucking hysterical about that sort of thing.[21] Both Liberal and Labor governments used the military to break up strikes in the coal mines and on the waterfront, while the arbitration system imposed crippling fines on unions and their members.

But workers still won, **because it's going on strike what gets the goods**. Between the mid-1960s and the late 70s, average weekly earnings in Australia increased by more than 30%, and the gains were spread to other workers thanks to pattern bargaining and the centralised arbitration and wage fixing system. Thanks to militant union action and strikes, working people won heaps of things that we take for granted today, like gender pay equality, four weeks' annual leave, maternity leave, workers' compensation, the banning of the use of asbestos and a little thing called the motherfucking weekend.[22]

---

21 Think back to what the national mood was like around 2002, replace 'Muslims' with 'commies', and you'll get the vibe.

22 When the 40-hour, five-day working week was introduced in 1948, the capitalist class was outraged at such radical insanity.

'Australia is committed to an unnecessary and dangerous experiment in the midst of an inflationary period,' said Mr C. N. McKay, the president of the Chamber of Manufactures, 'and it is to be hoped that the burden will not fall too heavily upon those whom it was intended to benefit.'

This happens any time workers manage a win: bosses will freak out and claim it'll all lead to economic ruin, then that doesn't happen, and the next time the bosses shit the bed all over again. Truly, they are the industrial equivalent of overacting soccer players, clutching their shins in pain after being viciously attacked by a light breeze.

And it wasn't just about work and money, either. Today, working people are often presumed to be as reactionary as the Murdoch commentators that patronise them, but in fact it was empowered workers' movements in the post-war years that were at the forefront of progressive change. Militant trade unions withdrew their labour on moral grounds and boycotted everything from shipping arms to Dutch-occupied Indonesia to the Apartheid South African Springboks' 1971 Australian tour. In 1966, Vincent Lingiari led the Gurindji workforce off the Wave Hill cattle station in the Northern Territory, beginning a seven-year strike demanding the return of their homelands around Daguragu.[23] Masses of workers went on massive strikes against the Vietnam War and cuts to universal healthcare, and in support of social justice and the environment. In the early 70s, branches of the militant Builders Labourers Federation (BLF) in Melbourne and Sydney refused to work on construction projects that were environmentally or culturally destructive, or would screw over working-class communities by destroying low-cost housing, or were just fucking ugly. This **Green Bans Movement** saved Melbourne's Victoria Markets, Sydney's Royal Botanic Gardens and many other green public spaces from godawful, profit-driven developments.[24]

This was all pure, uncut, glorious, progressive **working-class struggle and solidarity**, and it ruled. This was working people recognising the *social responsibility* of their labour, and the political power they could wield when they chose to withdraw it in the fight for a better world.

---

23 The Wave Hill Walk-Off and subsequent Gurindji strike led to a small portion of land being returned to the Gurindji and the passing of Australia's first land rights legislation. It also inspired the Paul Kelly and Kev Carmody song 'From Little Things Big Things Grow', which is almost the best Australian song ever written, second only to Scandal'Us' 2001 ARIA Singles Chart-topping hit, 'Me, Myself & I'.

24 When Macquarie University expelled a student from his accommodation for the crime of being openly gay, labourers declared a **pink ban** and refused to finish works on the uni grounds until he was reinstated. YASS, kweeeen!

Heck, going on strike was so cool in the 70s, **even my dad was doing it**. For years, Neil Ballard served as the branch secretary of the Technical Teachers' Association of Victoria (TTAV) at White Hills Technical School in Bendigo, where around 80% of the staff were in the union. He helped organise TTAV strikes against overcrowding – at one point, some classes were forced to take place in the agricultural storeroom – and to protest the Education Department's slashing of teaching jobs. In 1979, three teachers were forcibly transferred from Footscray Technical School, prompting a state-wide sympathy strike that lasted for weeks.

'There have been many pious and passionate statements that all this interruption to tuition is *for the good of the children* – despite the point that this cannot be so, particularly for the children now being deprived,' wrote some arsehole at the *Bendigo Advertiser* in an editorial at the time.

'What it does seem to be about is power, and who will run education. It will be the Department, empowered by the elected government; not any group which fancies it knows what is best for the proletariat.'

My papa would not stand for such sneering. He responded with the full force of a politely worded letter to the editor the following day:

As a result of the Education Department's policy of reducing the numbers of teachers in schools, at White Hills Technical School most of the remedial maths program has been cancelled, and some remedial reading classes have been dropped.

Does the Bendigo Advertiser *really believe that action aimed at preventing this sort of thing happening in schools throughout Victoria is 'not for the good of the children'?*

HELL yeah, Dad! Fuck him up!

THE BUST

Unfortunately for you and me, this era of prosperity and worker power would disintegrate in the 70s and 80s. A crisis emerged, and things went badly awry – just in time for Millennials to arrive and inherit the shitshow.

The crisis was rooted in the complicated matter of **inflation**.[25] In the post-war years, the Keynesian consensus believed that there was a trade-off between the level of employment and inflation: full employment meant that workers had more bargaining power (because labour was scarce), which meant higher wages, and therefore greater demand and higher costs, so inflation increased. When more people were out of a job, the balance shifted: workers had less leverage (because there was more competition for jobs), which would suppress wages, and people would have less money to spend, which would lower demand, and inflation would tick down.

Low unemployment = higher inflation and *vice versa,* the theory went, and during the post-war years, these forces were held in balance: unemployment remained consistently low, but because the economy was Booming, inflation was perfectly manageable. Things got a little more expensive, but keeping everybody in a job and growing the economy was considered worth it.

---

25 **Inflation measures the rate at which prices rise over time.** If annual inflation is at 5%, something that cost you $100 last year would cost you $105 now. We generally measure the level of inflation in the economy by the **Consumer Price Index (CPI)**, which tracks the price rises of selected goods – otherwise known as 'the cost of living'.

  Prices tend to inflate when demand outstrips supply. In 2011, for example, when Cyclone Yasi hit Queensland, multiple banana plantations were destroyed; supply was suddenly restricted, demand remained steady, and bananas jumped to $15 per kilo. During the COVID pandemic, the supply of facemasks, hand sanitiser and Rapid Antigen Tests often couldn't keep up with the demand shock, so prices spiked.

  Prices can also be dramatically inflated when businesses pass on new costs to consumers, or just shamelessly try to boost their profit margins by jacking up prices when they can get away with it. The most consistent and egregious form of inflated prices can be found at every airport, where toasted sandwiches cost $11, even though they're just normal toasted sandwiches.

'Well that's all fine during the Long Boom after the Second World War, but then it all goes to shit,' political economist Dr Elizabeth Humphrys tells me. Humphrys has written extensively about Australian trade unions and social movements, and I've even read one of her books about this period in labour history and I understood most of it.

'In the early 1970s, unemployment and inflation, for the first time in history, start going up at the same time. And that's the dilemma.'

This dilemma would come to be known as **stagflation**: an unprecedented combination of stagnant economic growth, featuring rising unemployment *and* rising prices. In Australia, the average rate of inflation rose from about 4% in 1965 to almost 18% in the mid-1970s, while unemployment hit 5% for the first time in thirty years.

This wasn't a uniquely Australian problem. Stagflation was happening across much of the Western world, which had become increasingly interconnected through a global system of finance and trade. The Australian economy was particularly exposed to global instabilities, like the very expensive Vietnam War that was going on, Richard Nixon's decision to suspend the 'Bretton Woods' international monetary management system' and move the US dollar off the gold standard, and the **1973 oil shock**, when the Organization of Arab Petroleum Exporting Countries (OAPEC) placed an oil embargo on a bunch of countries over their support for Israel. The shock caused the price of oil to surge by nearly 400%, which made pretty much everything more expensive, and triggered a global recession.

So there was a fair bit going on.

Still, Australia's political, business and even trade-union elites soon decided that the real issue here was **the working class making too much bank.** By the mid-70s, thanks to the union movement's size and militancy, the share of national income going to labour (as opposed to capital) reached an all-time high of 63%. At this point even the Labor Prime Minister **Gough Whitlam** and the ACTU President **Bob Hawke** (who was also the President of the ALP) agreed that this was very bad, actually, and **the only way to tackle stagflation was to stop the squeeze on profits and put a lid on wages.**

Whitlam was Dismissed by the Governor-General Sir John Kerr before he could do very much about this, in 1975.[26] His Liberal successor Malcolm Fraser then had a crack – jacking up interest rates, cutting government spending, freezing workers' wages through the arbitration courts, and going to war with the unions. He passed legislation to undermine closed shop agreements and outlaw **secondary boycotts** (like Green Bans, or going on strike in solidarity with other striking workers), established the Industrial Relations Bureau (an anti-union police force) and, just to be dramatic, used the RAAF as strikebreakers during the 1981 Qantas dispute. Stagflation had discredited Keynesianism and put an end to full employment policy under Whitlam, and now the Fraser government argued that in order to control wages, we had to shoot for a **'natural rate' of unemployment:** a rate which you couldn't possibly go below, because that would stoke inflation, and that would be as unnatural as bestiality or Simon Cowell's face.[27]

It was all very bad and slimy stuff, and it didn't even work. The unions were still too powerful, and Fraser couldn't

---

26 This Dismissal was unquestionably a plot orchestrated by the CIA. Don't @ me.

27 This idea was first theorised by the American economist **Milton Friedman,** who was smart enough to predict stagflation, but dumb enough to conclude that it meant that government spending was bad and free markets could fix almost everything. Friedman rejected Keynesianism's focus on demand-driven policies and came up with **monetarism,** which is concerned with the supply of money in an economy and the stabilisation of inflation, and not much else.

Malcolm Fraser and the Australian 'New Right' were highly influenced by Friedman's ideas, especially after Friedman's 1975 Australian speaking tour, which I'm sure was an electric affair, filled with coke parties in the RBA boardroom and neoclassical economics groupies flashing their tits.

get them onside or successfully defeat them in combat. By Fraser's second term in the early 80s, stagflation was still a problem; the labour share was still above 60%, the country was copping more recessions and both inflation and unemployment were in the double digits. Australia was still in the poo.

COMING TOGETHER (TO GET RIPPED OFF)

In this time of crisis, the ALP would arrive with some fresh new thinking that would fundamentally shift the power dynamics between Australian workers and bosses forever more, and would play a huge role in determining just how much work sucks for us now.[28]

Labor's pitch to rescue the country was titled the *Statement of Accord by the Australian Labor Party and the Australian Council of Trade Unions Regarding Economic Policy*, which wasn't very catchy. But this **Prices and Incomes Accord** was an historic, formalised agreement that offered the union movement a compromise: if they agreed to restrict their wage claims to the level of inflation and cool it with all the strikes and everything, a Labor government would make it worth their while. Workers would be rewarded with the end of stagflation and an expanded **social wage**: greater public funding of the healthcare system, improved pensions and unemployment benefits, tax cuts and (eventually) a retirement savings scheme. The plan was to get the country back to full employment *eventually*, but

---

28 Under the leaderships of Bob Hawke and Paul Keating, Labor would hold office for 13 years.

For as long as I can remember, I've been given the impression from people in my life, the media class and of course the ALP itself that these five terms of government were the absolute bees' knees. The Hawke-Keating era was a time of glorious political leadership and bold reforms that were necessary and correct, and oh weren't they good and why can't things be like that again now please?

In the coming chapters, we'll see why much of this hagiography can get in the bin.

for now workers would have to sacrifice wage increases and refrain from industrial action in The National Interest.

Some radical unions were sceptical, but the majority of the generally exhausted labour movement opted for the ALP's consensus approach. By 1983, Hawke had entered parliament, and he quickly become the new Labor leader, campaigned in that year's election on enacting the Accord and on the promise of *Bringing Australia Together*, and Labor flogged the Liberals in a landslide.

Now sure, in some respects, the Accord – this grand bargain between the state, labour and the wishes of capital – 'worked'. Profits were restored to the private sector, stagflation kinda-sorta trended down over the 80s, and the social wage was certainly expanded with the creation of Medicare and the compulsory superannuation system.[29] After the chaotic, big-spending days of Whitlam, Labor had proved they were now Responsible Economic Managers, and thanks in no small part to the Accord and its reforms, they won five elections in a row.

But it came at a cost.

'The agreement was: we're going to hold down wages so that everybody's living standards will pretty much remain the same, and wages will keep pace with inflation,' Elizabeth Humphrys explains to me. 'And that's one thing; you can have a view on whether that's reasonable.

'But that's not what happened.'

What happened is that **workers got boned**. The unions signed up to the project of suppressing workers' wages, which is kind of the opposite of what they're supposed to do, and during the first seven years of the Hawke government, the average Australian worker's **real wages dropped by around 5%**.[30] At the same time in the US and the UK, even as

---

29 *Kind* of – more on this later.

30 **Real wages** are wages that are adjusted for inflation, as opposed to **nominal wages**, which are not.

conservative demons Ronald Reagan and Margaret Thatcher waged all-out war on the union movement, average real wages *rose* by more than 10%. British and American unions knew who their enemy was and fought back; for workers in Australia, living under a Labor government, the call was coming from inside the house.

'For me, wages are like a barometer for class power,' says Humphrys. 'And in the end, you can't substitute for class power.

'It took the Labor Party in that moment to do the hardest thing possible, which was to actually **send workers' power backwards**.'

This is the crucial point. Some will argue that the good of the Hawke/Keating/Accord years outweigh the bad, and others will claim there was simply no alternative, but the bottom line is this: **the Australian labour movement emerged from this period weaker and more disorganised than before.** Union membership had already started shrinking as manufacturing and closed shops disappeared, but the decline accelerated under Labor; density went from 50% of the workforce in 1983 to less than a third by 1996. Dozens of unions were amalgamated, radical unions like the BLF were deregistered and the number of days lost to strike action collapsed. The ACTU and the Labor government actively suppressed industrial action and disciplined unions who went on strike, all in the name of preserving the Accord and the precious '**industrial peace**'. Actual workplace struggle and militancy was now frowned upon. Workers' bargaining power tumbled, the labour market was deregulated, and the scourge of insecure work started to emerge: during the 1980s, casual work exploded by almost 90%.

Perhaps the shittiest reform of all came in 1993. The Keating government and the ACTU worked in cahoots with employer groups to replace pattern bargaining and wage indexation with **enterprise bargaining**, in which collective agreements were negotiated between the workers and bosses of a particular business. Any gains would no longer flow on to other workers in the same industry. Plus, while Keating enshrined the right to strike in legislation for the first time, it was still ridiculously limited; striking was only allowed a) during the bargaining period in between workplace agreements (and at no other times) and b) when preceded by 72 hours' written notice of the intention to strike.

This is what the working class was reduced to: being compelled to write a little letter to your boss asking them to pwease let you have a whittle stwike, if dat's okay with Daddy.

'Decent rights for workers went out the window when enterprise bargaining came in,' former Labor senator Doug Cameron told me on my podcast in February 2021. 'Instead of looking up and looking around as to what's happening, all you'd be doing is looking at your toes.'

Cameron immigrated to Australia from Scotland in the 1970s and joined the Amalgamated Metal Workers and Shipwrights Union when he worked at the Liddell power station in NSW. He saw first-hand what could be achieved when unions had real power.

'Even if you were in a weak shop, you knew you were part of a strong organisation that would have a strategy for improving your wages and conditions. We'd fight that out in the strong workshops and then spread that across the industry.

'We would not have superannuation, we would not have better annual leave, we would not have a shorter week if it was all enterprise bargaining, and you were doing it workshop by workshop.'[31]

---

31 Cameron is something of a rebel, which I quite like. When Whitlam was dismissed (by the CIA) in '75, Hawke as ACTU President (and also secretly an informer for the US government and the CIA, look it up this is actually true) specifically told unionists to 'cool it', and resisted calls for a general strike.

  But Cameron told me he thought the whole thing was 'outrageous' and he and his fellow workers walked off the job immediately.

  'The view from my workshop was: **Go to hell, Bob Hawke.**'

For Elizabeth Humphrys, the ALP's decision to tackle stagflation by hobbling working class power illustrates a bigger point about our economic system.

'Capitalism is a system with in-built crises, and those tendencies can't be gotten around,' she tells me. 'During those crises, government's main interest is in keeping capitalism as stable as possible, even if that's not in the best interests of workers.

'Capitalism prioritises private investment, so at a time of crisis, you can't just point to people making massive profits and say, "Oh well, you'll just have to reduce your profits" – that's just not how capitalism works.'

THE DECLINE

So that's the lay of the land when the first Millennials start entering the workforce in the mid-90s: the working class has been hoodwinked and kneecapped by its own side of politics, and John Howard hasn't even happened yet. My generation has been watching our industrial muscle dwindle ever since.

Howard used his time in office to wage an all-out assault on the union movement.[32] He banned any kind of compulsory unionism, and ensured that union-won benefits had to be extended to all workers, whether they were members of their union or not. (This drastically reduced the incentive for non-unionised workers to sign up; if you're going to get all the stuff the union wins anyway, why bother paying your dues?) The Howard government also helped

---

32 Howard's rabidly anti-union, pro-business Coalition government rejected the whole 'class' thing entirely. On the Liberal view, there aren't 'bosses' and 'workers' and a power imbalance between the two; there are just *individuals*, buying and selling labour in the free market like any other commodity. If you don't like your job, you should be *free* to leave and find another one (easy!), and individuals should be *free* to negotiate their employment contract with multinational corporations, who should in turn be *free* to pay workers in acorns and band-aids.

employer groups smash the Maritime Union of Australia, launched a royal commission into construction unions, set up a union-busting watchdog and delivered the legislative turd of **WorkChoices**: a complete overhaul of the industrial relations system that junked unfair dismissal laws, restricted union activity and allowed bosses to shoot an employee out of a cannon if they'd ever had a dream about reading an article about going on strike.

This would eventually prove to be an excessive amount of class warfare, even for Howard. The ACTU staged its massive *Your Rights at Work* campaign against the *WorkChoices* reforms, Labor promised to overturn them and Kevin Rudd won the 2007 election in a Ruddslide. Howard even lost his own blue-ribbon seat of Bennelong, which is one of the few good things to happen in Australian politics, ever.

Annoyingly, Labor's victory didn't exactly usher in a workers' paradise. Rudd's *Fair Work Act (2009)* scrapped WorkChoices' unfair dismissal laws and introduced a 'Better Off Overall Test' to protect conditions, but it kept much of the union-busting architecture in place.

As a result, thanks to Labor, non-union members still get any improved wages and conditions that are negotiated by unions; pattern bargaining is illegal; and the right to strike is still subject to draconian limitations. In The Land Of The Fair Go today, you and I can't legally go on strike unless:

- ☑ 'good faith' bargaining between unions and employers has failed
- ☑ a majority of union members have voted in favour of strike action in a secret ballot (conducted by mail)
- ☑ we've informed our bosses of precisely what the strike will involve and how long it will go for
- ☑ we give our superiors at least three days' notice before the strike begins

☑ Saturn is in retrograde

and

☑ we can answer a Troll's riddles three.

Sympathy and political strikes are unlawful, including strikes against the unjust laws which limit your ability to go on strike. Any strike that doesn't abide by those rules doesn't constitute 'protected action', and can result in you and your union copping million-dollar fines. It's all extremely Fair.

Labor created the Fair Work Commission (FWC) to oversee this regime, and the subsequent Coalition government stacked it with as many employer-friendly ghouls as possible, including the former Liberal MP and enthusiastic WorkChoices supporter Sophie Mirabella.[33] In recent years the 'independent' Commission has handed down decisions to cut Sunday and public holiday penalty rates, approved workplace agreements that would see workers getting paid below legal minimums, and used its (ridiculous) power to terminate industrial action that it believes might cause 'significant economic harm' to a boss or the Australian economy. In 2018, the Rail, Tram and Bus Union in NSW had their application to engage in a 24-hour rail strike pre-emptively suspended by the Commission on the grounds that it would cause too much economic disruption for Sydneysiders, i.e. it would do precisely what a strike is supposed to do, and **exercise workers' power.**

It's really gotten quite silly. These days, Australia's attitude towards unionism seems to be closer to that of the batshit Tories who moved the 888 monument than it is to the people who had it erected. Now, the Fair Work Ombudsman thinks

---

33 Mirabella has no experience in employment law or industrial relations, but she does have extensive experience in asking important questions in Parliament, like the time in 2002 she asked then-Minister for Employment and Workplace Relations Tony Abbott, 'Would the Minister inform the House how ultramilitant unions damage investment and destroy jobs . . .?'

that displaying a large inflatable rat called 'Scabby' on a picket line is an act of 'unlawful abuse', and it's been perfectly legal for bodies like the Australian Building and Construction Commission to ban construction workers from displaying the Eureka flag or union slogans on their hardhats, toolboxes or mobile phones.

No matter how successful the ruling class has been in strangling organised labour over the years, it's never enough. They won't even let us enjoy our inflatable rodents, or put cool stickers on our pencil cases.

GET A JOB

Moreover, if you're unable to find yourself one of the union-free, insecure, sucky jobs that exist today, then don't worry – **you'll still get a chance to be treated like trash.**

Under capitalism, human worth is measured by one's ability to produce things and create wealth, so being an adult *outside* of the production process tends to make you something of a pariah. Over the years, this has been reflected in laws like King George's classic *Vagrancy Act* of 1744 (which made not having a job a crime), and in the proactive policy solutions of people like Senator Pauline Hanson, who told *The Today Show* in 2019:

> *All those people out there, 'Work for the Dole' doing absolutely nothing . . . put down the iPads, get out there, collect the cane toads, take them to your local council, put them in the freezer, get rid of them and clean up our environment!*

When they're not getting shunned, demonised, drug-tested, hounded by *A Current Affair*, sterilised or enlisted in some kind of horrific Dole Toad Death Squad, Australia's unemployed are forced to navigate the punitive hellworld of Centrelink. Here they're faced with onerous and stingy means-testing, payments suspensions, and brutal debt-recovery schemes to make sure they haven't been 'overpaid' in the course of receiving one of the lowest unemployment benefits in the OECD. After being briefly lifted above the poverty line in 2020, the Morrison government dropped the JobSeeker base rate to just $43 a day, because fuck 'em. It *has* to be that low, we're told, otherwise people won't have enough *incentive* (/desperation) to go work at their nearest exploitation factory, and after all, **'the best form of welfare is a job'.**[34]

Our country has never been hugely sympathetic to the unemployed, but at least during the post-war boom, there was a general understanding that unemployment wasn't their fault. It was considered the government's responsibility to find work for people, and **unemployment was a policy failure.**[35] Means-tested unemployment benefits were introduced by the Curtin government in 1945 to provide workers a basic safety-net, and for decades the government-run Commonwealth Employment Service (CES) actively monitored the full employment labour market and found work for those in need.

But the turbulent 70s began to undo this, too. Around the same time that the country abandoned the objective of full employment, the stigmatisation of the unemployed ramped up. The term 'dole bludger' began to be deployed by politicians both red and blue: after all, at a time of rising

---

34 It isn't. The best form of welfare would include free food, free wi-fi, Gold Class cinema tickets and blowjob robots. Way better.

35 In 1939, a headline in Sydney newspaper *Smith's Weekly* screamed, '200,000 AUSTRALIANS ON STARVATION DIET'.

 'Organised starvation of the poor by Australian governments promises to leave on the political records of this generation the darkest stain in the Commonwealth's history,' the story began. And later: '[Politicians] must be forced to remember that the first responsibility of any government is to ensure that the people are properly fed.'

unemployment and economic crisis, it's handy to take some of the heat off your government by punching *down*. 'Welfare' became a dirty word. The Hawke/Keating governments began to tighten the screws on welfare eligibility, and dished out penalties for noncompliance with pointless 'mutual obligation' requirements. You didn't simply have a right to not starve, *this was a two-way street.* The Howard government completely privatised the CES in the late 90s, and the responsibility for finding people work was handed over to privately-run employment service providers; companies which tend to be far more invested in making massive profits from the unemployment 'industry' than they are in finding people meaningful, secure work.

Today, our society has entirely shifted the blame for unemployment onto the unemployed. This is a particularly cruel move since, as we've seen, **our system now *requires* a certain percentage of people to be jobless,** to keep wages and inflation in check. For decades, we've been living in a topsy-turvy world in which 'full employment' actually means 'keeping unemployment at the "natural rate" of around 5%' – which involves more than 600,000 people being out of work.[36] There are literally fewer jobs than people *by design.* Unemployment is a *feature* of our market economy, not a bug.

Indeed, ordinary workers have as much control over the number of jobs that exist as they do over the weather or the arrival of a global pandemic, and yet people without jobs are still blamed for not having jobs. They're just bludgers who refuse to work because they're *lazy,* clearly, and it's just

---

36 The actual 'natural rate' of unemployment is something of a mystery. It's supposed to shift up and down, depending on the state of the economy, but it's not technically 'observable'. It's more of a *vibe,* man, calculated by Treasury and economists at the RBA consulting Ouija boards and picking through entrails and spreadsheets.

Unfortunately, their guesstimates have very regularly been way off. In May 2021, both the RBA and the Coalition government admitted that what they thought was 'full employment' was not actually 'full' at all, and unemployment had been much higher than it 'needed to be' for years, which is something of a major oopsy.

a *coincidence* that there are sudden outbreaks of laziness during economic crises and that laziness seems to be weirdly higher in poorer, regional communities, amongst First Nations peoples and people with disabilities.

We could probably stop and think a bit more deeply about this apparent 'laziness', but frankly, we can't be arsed.

THERE IS (STILL) POWER IN A UNION

Take the decades-long attack on the trade union movement, chuck in some deliberate unemployment and add a corporate media that's happy to demonise any 'thug' union leader with a tattoo, and you'll get to where we've ended up: **a world in which workers' bargaining and political power has been decimated.** Millennials were born into a society in which almost half of all workers were members of their union; today, union density has dwindled to less than 14% of the workforce.[37] All forms of collective bargaining have been declining – less than 15% of all Australian employees are covered by an enterprise agreement – and we live under some of the harshest restrictions on the right to strike anywhere in the developed world.

In fact, workers' bargaining power has been so thoroughly suppressed, the whole theoretical relationship between low unemployment and wages growth has now completely broken down; 2022 has seen the country experience the lowest level of unemployment in almost fifty years, and yet there's still no major upwards pressure on people's pay packets, because there's so little collective worker strength to provide it.

This decimation has allowed capital's unrelenting push to drive down labour costs and maximise profits to win out. Australian workers' share of income has been in steady

---

37 For young people, it's even lower: somewhere between just 5 and 9% of Australians under the age of 25 are union members.

decline since that peak in the mid-70s. **In 2020, it fell below 50% for the first time in sixty years.** Wages are stagnant, we don't know how to ask for a pay rise, the minimum wage has been slashed in relation to the median wage, a record number of people are working multiple jobs, and the economy is plagued with insecure work and the '**working poor**'; the Australian Council of Social Service (ACOSS) estimates 38% of Australians living below the poverty line are in some kind of work. People feel atomised and alienated at work, there's a new wage theft story every other week, migrant fruit pickers are paid with loose change, Amazon employees are peeing into bottles to meet delivery targets, and The Wiggles are doing ads for UberEats.[38]

'Where we are now is terrible,' decried Doug Cameron. 'It's no wonder that many young people don't see the struggles that we've had in the past to get where we are. And with the gig economy, it's going to get even worse.'

Australian workers have been losing the class war for quite some time, and Millennial workers have been left to cop the consequences. Baby Boomers knew a world with strong and active trade unions that could shape working people's lives for the better, but for most people my age, they're just not a *thing*.

'I teach a social and political course to 18- to 23-year-olds that's about social change,' says Elizabeth Humphrys, 'and it's not unusual for me to ask a class of thirty students in a Future of Work unit I teach, "Who is a member of their union?", and it will be zero or one person who will put up their hand.'

This fading of class consciousness – the great *forgetting* of worker power – is a fucking travesty. It means Millennial and Zoomer workers will inevitably miss out even more.

---

38 We also have an Australian 'Labor' Party who appears to be in complete denial that there's any conflict between capital and labo(u)r at all. At a business fundraiser ahead of the 2022 election, Anthony Albanese declared that the 'pro-business' ALP believed that 'when business does well, workers do well, and vice versa', which sounds like a delightful fantasy world that I'd like to visit sometime.

As diminished as the labour movement has become, **it still pays to be union;** in 2020, Australian union members earned an average of 32% more per week than non-union members, and across the country, workers were kept COVID-safe and won paid pandemic leave thanks to radical collectives like the Retail and Fast Food Workers Union (RAFFWU) and the United Workers Union. The benefits of a strong, organised working class are clear to see globally, too; in Denmark, where more than 60% of the workforce is unionised and collective agreements and pattern bargaining are common, even McDonald's workers get a living wage, six weeks' annual leave, a year's paid maternity leave and a pension plan.[39]

But, in unionphobic Australia, most of us just have to accept work for what it is, and the various ways in which it sucks. We lack the power to make it suck substantially less, and we certainly lack the collective power to have a strong voice in what the future of work could look like; I'm thinking a four-day work week, democratic workplaces (imagine if you got to elect your boss?) and a full employment economy might be nice.

But whatever we're hoping to get as workers, the ruling class is not going to give it up willingly. They never have.

'Industrial action is the only way that workers have ever been able to secure outcomes,' RAFFWU Secretary Josh Cullinan explained on my podcast in June 2021. 'The only reason we have kids out of coal mines and health and safety legislation and decent wages and other things is through workers withdrawing their labour.'

---

39 Research out of the Deakin University Business School in 2019 found that despite the business propaganda to the contrary, **trade unions don't hurt a business' productivity.** In fact, unionised workplaces with better conditions are almost always far less shitty places to work at, and thus produce happier and more productive employees.

The same research found that unionisation **is** associated with lower profits, because unions generally do their jobs and secure higher wages and benefits for their members – which helps to explain why the ruling class fucking hates them.

A lot has changed for the Australian working class since our parents' generation were punching the clock. But it seems to me that if we Millennials hope to win a better deal for ourselves and each other in the workplace, we're still going to need the same thing that workers have always needed: **a big fat load of class struggle, and an endless supply of solidarity.**

2

Give Me A Home
Among The Gum Trees

'Australians are among the best housed people
in the world and they are perhaps the most
equally housed.'

– academic David Donnison,
The Government of Housing, 1967

'Hey Tom, did you know that there are about 25 million people in
Australia and a little over 18,000 of us have 6 or more properties?
That's only 0.01% of our population.
We want to help YOU become a part of that number!'

– promo email from binvested.com.au, 2021

My dad bought his first house in Bendigo in 1976. He was
a public school teacher in his mid-twenties, and it cost him
$15,500 (about $102,400 today). He then had to spend an
extra $10k to 'make it habitable'.

'I thought, "Oh well, I might as well get this cheap house
on a big block",' he tells me. 'It had a certain amount of
rustic charm.'

I ask if buying it felt like a big deal at the time.

'I guess I just didn't think much about it,' he replied. 'The house was so cheap, so why pay rent?'

Dad rented the other bedrooms to his teacher friends, charging them $25 a week (about $160 today). Eventually he met my mum, who was also a teacher, and she moved in to live there, rent-free. The two were soon married (gross), they changed jobs and relocated to a rental in the tiny town of Koroit, as they continued renting out the place in Bendigo. They had my brother Gavin (gross), then bought a house in Koroit, and then in 1988 sold both the Bendigo and Koroit places to help them buy a house in Warrnambool for a whopping $103k.

'I *never* thought I'd ever pay a hundred thousand dollars for a house!' says Dad.

'In those days you did think that if you couldn't afford to buy it, you just wouldn't do it,' says Mum. Dad agrees: 'We wouldn't have thought of taking out a housing loan for hundreds of thousands of dollars, like people do today.'

I spent the first few years of my life in that hundred-grand house. After a brief stint living in Ballarat, we ended up back in Warrnambool in what would become my home for the next decade, before I moved to Melbourne to make all my dreams come true. My mum bought the half-acre property for $145k in 1998 (about $256k in today's money) with a small mortgage that was paid off quickly. Over the years it's been spruced up thanks to some substantial renovations, and by now it's at least doubled in value.

Owning your own home was just 'what everyone expected to be able to do one day,' recalls Mum. 'It wasn't thought to be unrealistic. If you had a job and you worked hard and saved, you could get a house.'

'We've never really had to scrimp and save to pay off the mortgage or anything like that,' says Dad. 'Not like you're going to, Tommy!'

Then they both laugh in my face.

THE AUSTRALIAN NIGHTMARE

Homes are great. They're where humans tend to live. They're where we eat, sleep, raise our families, hang out and masturbate. Secure housing is a basic requirement for anybody who's hoping to live a decent life and be happy, because **shelter is a fundamental human need**.

After all, if you *don't* have it, you're pretty fucked.

No wonder, then, that the idea of home ownership has been so popular for so long. Ever since the post-war boom, Australian economic life has been centred around the idea that you can achieve the **Great Australian Dream** of owning a place of your own.[1] That's just what adults are supposed to do: get a job, work hard, save up a deposit, buy your own place, start a family, then watch Channel Seven until you die.

We're still very fond of this ideal today. A 2017 survey from the Australian National University found that 75% of Australians still believe that home ownership is a big part of 'the Australian way of life'. This included over 60% of Australian Millennials, who – despite what you may have heard – still reckon that renting forever sucks and being able to enjoy a secure home would be not only 'dope', but also 'Based' and 'on fleek'.

The problem is that **this Australian Dream is now dead**. Or at least, it's been severely bashed and stabbed, and is now on life support. For almost three decades, our country has been in the grips of an ever-worsening, batshit housing affordability crisis that threatens to lock entire generations out of the basic material security that comes with home ownership. It's taking a big ol' dump on any notion of an egalitarian 'Australian way of life', and it's driving us all insane.

---

1   Preferably a detached house on a quarter acre suburban block, complete with a garden, a Hills hoist, a barbie, 2.5 kids and a low-level-but-constant sense of suspicion and resentment towards one's neighbours.

My parents in their 30s:

Let's buy
a house

Me in my 30s:

I guess I
can't afford
to have teeth

(Source: https://www.reddit.com/r/me_irl/comments/nwuj09/me_irl/)

Australia's $10 trillion housing market is monumentally cooked. While we Millennials were busy learning how to tie our shoes, watching *Feral TV* and growing our pubes, house prices have been soaring out of our reach. The median Australian dwelling – that's everything that people live in, from houses to apartments to burrows, cubby houses, bunkers, long-term tents, etc. – is now around $730k, while **the median house price across our capital cities is more than $1 million.** The year my dad bought his first house, the median house price in Sydney was $36,800 (or $243k today); in June 2022, it hit $1.59 million.

These skyrocketing prices wouldn't be *quite* so bad if people's wages had been able to keep up, but they totally haven't. As we've seen, since the 70s, the ruling class has managed to smash workers' power and deregulate the labour market to keep wages nice and low; at the same time, house prices have been absolutely popping off. National median house prices have increased from around three- or four-times median household incomes in the 70s **to almost nine times median incomes today**. The price of a typical house in Sydney has multiplied by 17 times over the past forty years – that's three times faster than wages.[2]

(Source: https://imgflip.com/memegenerator/246949658/Big-dog-small-dog)

The higher the sticker price, the chunkier the deposit you have to scrape together in order to convince a bank to give you a home loan so you can spend the next thirty years in debt peonage paying it off. The typical house deposit in Australia is now more than $105k – an amount that's nigh on impossible to save up for by yourself. In the early 80s, almost half of all homebuyers aged 25 to 34 were single income households, but by 2016 these lonely virgins made up just 13% of purchasers in the same age bracket. These days you really need two incomes to get on the ladder, at *least*;

---

2   It's even more cooked in beautiful Tasmania. Tassie wages are the lowest in the country, but local house prices are still exploding because everyone's discovered how nice it is down there and MONA-loving wanker mainlanders are buying up properties as investments or as holiday homes or to turn them into overpriced quiche/wine/yoga delis. In the five years to 2021, Hobart prices have surged by 60%, as real wages have been going backwards. This is why, relative to incomes, the Hobart housing market is considered even more unaffordable than Sydney's.

if you haven't already, I seriously suggest becoming pansexual and pooling your savings with your lovers in your polycule to truly maximise your purchasing power.[3]

Saving all that money (and finding love!!!) takes a long time, and the more money you have to save, the longer it takes. In the early 90s, it took around six years to save a 20% deposit for a typical dwelling for an average household – **now it'll take you well over a decade.** The median age of Australian first homebuyers has risen from around the mid-twenties in 1981 to the mid-thirties today. More people in their late twenties are living at home now than ever before, and in recent years the number of people buying their first home in their forties and fifties has increased by more than 50%.

So this sweet combo of flat wages and ballooning house prices is forcing many people to wait longer than ever to enter the housing market, and pricing others out completely. Consequently, **home ownership is now dwindling across the board.** While the Australian home ownership rate was stable at around 70% of the population from the 1960s until the turn of the century, it's since fallen to 66%, and if trends continue, it's projected to fall to 60% by 2030.[4]

Things have gotten particularly worse for the young and the poor. Almost 70% of Baby Boomers like my parents had

---

3   In 2017, one survey found that 44% of aspiring British homeowners said they wouldn't have stayed with their partner if property purchasing hadn't been part of the equation, so that seems solid.

  In the same survey, 11% of respondents said they would stay in an unhappy relationship if it allowed them to buy their own property. Not just a 'casual' or a 'mediocre' relationship, mind you – *an unhappy one*. Reading that statistic, one can't help but imagine two young people trapped in a truly bleak and miserable romance, thankful they're no longer suffering in the purgatory of the rental market but still condemned to a lifetime of awkward tension, boring weekends and very occasional loveless sex just to keep up some vague illusion of happiness and security, neither of them able to cum unless the Bank of England lowers interest rates (i.e. the ideal British marriage).

4   Keep in mind that many of these people counted as 'homeowners' aren't really 'owners' at all: they **co-own** their home with some faceless demonic financial institution. Over the past twenty years, the proportion of **outright** home ownership for 25- to 54-year-olds has halved, while the proportion of people who still have mortgages in retirement has tripled.

become homeowners by the time they reached their early thirties; less than half of Millennials like me were able to do the same. Since the early 80s, home ownership for those aged 25 to 34 on the lowest incomes has crashed by a whopping 40%.

And, just to top all this off and make you feel extra special about our predicament: **Australia is a world leader in housing unaffordability.** Our rate of outright home ownership is 13% lower than the OECD average, and we're regularly listed up there with Hong Kong and New Zealand as one of the top locations on the planet for getting absolutely rinsed for the crime of needing somewhere to live. In March 2022, in a particularly gobsmacking and sickening piece of analysis, the ABC's finance guy Alan Kohler reported that **since 1980, real global house prices have risen by 68% – while prices in Australia have exploded by 568%.**

If you're a Millennial or Zoomer renter and you need a moment or two after reading that to bash your head against the wall in fury, please feel free to do so, but you probably won't get your bond back.

THIS IS FINE, ACTUALLY

Clearly, the housing situation in this country is unequivocally extremely fucked up and bad.

Unless, of course, you think it isn't.

'If housing in Sydney was unaffordable,' explained Liberal Treasurer Joe Hockey at a press conference in June 2015, 'no one would be buying it.'

This is **housing crisis denialism.** Despite the overwhelming and growing evidence all around us every day, plenty of moronic (and propertied) elites have been spending the past few decades telling us all that there's actually no problem here at all and we should all stop whinging – runaway house prices are fine, and nothing needs to really change. This cruel garbage has been spouted by the likes of Hockey, Tony Abbott ('As someone who, along with the bank, owns a house in Sydney, I do hope that our housing prices are increasing'), Josh Frydenberg ('Overall, it's a good thing for the economy when house prices go up as opposed to going down') and John Howard, who famously observed on ABC radio in 2003, 'I don't get people stopping me in the street and saying, "John you're outrageous, under your government the value of my house has increased".'[5]

It's not limited to conservatives, either. In 2016, Baby Boomer economist and Labor Party adviser Stephen 'The Kouk' Koukoulas wrote a piece for *Guardian Australia* entitled 'Millennials should stop moaning. They've got more degrees and low rates'.[6] The Kouk wrote that while Millennials' angst about their lot might be understandable, they 'would be wise to be a little more reflective whenever they snipe about how unfair life is'. Young people in 2016, he argued, enjoyed better levels of education and lower unemployment than previous generations, and most importantly, '[t]hose Gen Xers and the Baby Boomers who took the risk of buying a "cheap" house in the 70s and early 80s were confronted with interest rates that averaged 13% and peaked at 17% in the late 80s. If any Gen Y has ever put that sort of interest rate into their mortgage calculators, they might choke on their skinny soy lattes.'

Alternatively, some establishment mouthpieces like to suggest that if there *is* a problem with Australia's housing market, that problem isn't *structural* – **it's you**. Young people

---

5 Very few people *could* stop John Howard in the street, of course, because he was always fucking power walking. But, even if they could catch up to him, in 2003 they'd probably be less inclined to talk about house prices and more likely to say something like 'Hey could you please stop doing war crimes to Iraqis? You're outrageous!'

6 Koukoulas kindly came on *Tonightly* in 2018 to let me yell at him about the piece; he assured me that he didn't write the headline.

who want to buy a house these days, we're told, simply don't have the right attitude, budgeted lifestyles, or brunch.

'I have seen young people order smashed avocado with crumbled feta on five-grain toasted bread at $22 a pop and more,' wrote demographer Bernard Salt in a column for *The Australian* in 2016, just six months after Kouk's anti-moaning piece. 'I can afford to eat this for lunch because I am middle-aged and have raised my family. But how can young people afford to eat like this? Shouldn't they be economising by eating at home? How often are they eating out? Twenty-two dollars several times a week could go towards a deposit on a house.'

Salt has always said that he was taken out of context and the original column – titled 'Moralisers, we need you!' – was in fact *satirising* the kinds of conservative thoughts that run through Baby Boomers' brains when they frequent hipster cafes full of young people. Reading over the piece today, I'd say that's fair enough; his tongue is firmly in his Boomer cheek. But Salt's *actual* thoughts on the housing affordability crisis might not be miles away from those of his fictional Boomer 'character'. In 2007 he described Millennials to the *Sydney Morning Herald* as 'the Gimme generation saying "I have got my Gameboy and iPod – where's my house? I am entitled to it without putting in those boring years of saving".' When author Nicole Haddow spoke to him for her 2019 book *Smashed Avocado: How I Cracked the Property Market and You Can Too*, Salt reiterated the satirical nature of the piece, but also told her, 'I think that the house price issue has eased since October 2016 when this story broke. Sydney house prices and even Melbourne house prices have eased since that time, with possibly further to fall. Good news for Millennials.'[7]

---

7 Nope.

Whatever his original intentions, Salt's piece sparked viral Millennial outrage across all social media platforms and solidified the 'Millennials can't buy a house because they spend too much on brunch' meme in the popular consciousness. The story was picked up by multiple international outlets, including the BBC. 'Smashed avo' came runner-up for the 2016 Australian Phrase of the Year, and ME Bank even capitalised on the moment by offering a 'Smashed Av' home loan promotion. It soon got another run in 2017, when Millennial property mogul Tim Gurner told *60 Minutes* in an interview, 'When I was trying to buy my first home, I wasn't buying smashed avocado for $19 and four coffees at $4 each.'[8]

'You can't have it both ways,' the Kouk tells me when I contact him to pick his Boomer brain for this book. 'Either have your turmeric lattes and avo and rent, or have tap water, Nescafé Gold and Vegemite on toast and save for your house.'

If Australian Millennials had a dollar for every time we'd received this kind of quality advice about how we can buy a house, we could probably afford to buy a house. When we're not being scolded for what we're eating, we're being chastised for what we're drinking (*Sydney Morning Herald* headline: 'Your morning coffee adds 154 minutes to your mortgage'), or being ordered by Barnaby Joyce to simply move to the country ('If you've decided you've got the gumption in you and you want to move to Charleville [in regional Queensland] – you're going to have a very affordable house'), or receiving Joe Hockey's maverick property-buying tips: 'The starting point for a first homebuyer is to get a good job that pays good money . . . then you can go to the bank and you can borrow money.'

---

8 Over his career, Tim Gurner has amassed a $929 million fortune through his luxury property development business. I presume he now spends his time eating three square meals of smashed avocado a day, drowning himself in coffees and frequently going to the toilet.

Cheers, mate.[9]

Otherwise, we're being subjected to a deluge of gaslighting profile pieces about young property owners, whose experiences PROVE that getting into the property market IS possible if you just have the right grindset and hustle (and rich parents). A remarkable headline will grab your attention (domain.com.au: 'How I really did it: The young Melburnian who bought a townhouse on a single income'), then buried in the body of the article is the brutal truth ('Nicole started seriously looking for a property to buy in mid-2019. Rather than applying for a home loan herself, **it was decided her parents would buy the property on her behalf.**')

One of the all-time greats in this genre comes from 2015, when the *Herald Sun* profiled Stephanie Brennan, who owned six properties worth more $2.3 million at just 24 years old. According to the *Sun,* Brennan was proving that 'it's possible for young professionals to get on the housing ladder'. Wow! Cool!

Turns out all she had to do was be born to a wealthy family, be educated at one of Sydney's finest private schools, have $100k in savings by the time she was 22, get her mother to be a $60k guarantor for her first home so she didn't have to pay a deposit, and then inherit $50k from her grandparents which she used to buy a plot of land in Scotland that came with a title, literally making her a fucking Lady.

Lady Brennan deigned to share with *Sun* readers one of her top tips for aspiring homeowners: 'Always pay off one

---

9   Between 1998 and 2015, Joe Hockey claimed around $184k in travel expenses to stay in a house in Canberra that just so happened to be owned by his wife, Melissa Babbage. Babbage bought the property for $320k in '97, but by 2015 it was valued at around $2 million.

   So for 17 years, the Australian taxpayer was chipping in extra money to help a weapons-grade failure of a treasurer on about $365k a year pay rent to his wife to help her pay off her multimillion-dollar house.

   Now *that's* a good job that pays good money.

property as quickly as you can because then you will always have a place to live.'

Kill me.

IN NO WAY IS THIS FINE

All of this distraction and obfuscation must be thrown into a volcano. With all due respect to The Kouk, the 'but mah interest rates!!!' argument is hokum: Australian house prices have become so extraordinarily bonkers expensive now that by 2022, adjusting for inflation, the cost of servicing a new 80% mortgage in Sydney is just as burdensome as it was in 1990, when rates were at 17%. So not only do Millennial and Zoomer homebuyers have to get together much bigger deposits than our parents did to buy the crazily expensive property, we're also spending just as much of our incomes to pay off our gargantuan debts.

No, the main issue here is not with Millennials' profligate spending on toast or coffee. The ABS records actual data about this stuff: in 1984, 25- to 34-year-old Australians were spending about 14% of their income on food and another 14% of their income on housing costs; in 2010, food spending amongst that cohort had dropped to 10% of incomes, **while housing costs had jumped to 18%.** We're spending less on food and more on housing than the Boomers did, because housing is so goddamn expensive, so *there*, we win.

Meanwhile, Barnaby's suggestion that young people who'd like to be homeowners should simply get some 'gumption' and uproot their entire lives and move to an outback town like Charleville (population 3,335) is somewhat complicated by the reality that there aren't that many jobs in Charleville – in 2019, the youth unemployment rate in outback Queensland reached 25% – and gumption alone won't pay the bills. *Everyone* wants 'a good job that pays good money', Joe Hockey, you fucking turnip – but even the people who are lucky enough to have those are struggling to afford a house now.

And I'm sorry, but all the twentysomething property tycoons can fuck right off to Jupiter. Your privileged experiences are completely unrepresentative of the horror-show reality of the Australian housing market, and I refuse to accept that in a decent society anyone should have to aspire to become like you just to achieve the 'dream' of having secure shelter.

Screw the deniers: the fundamental issue here is the fact that house prices in this country have become objectively, horrifically, outrageously expensive and unaffordable for a large (and growing) proportion of the population. **So why the fuck is that the case??**

BECAUSE SUPPLY

For many of those who at least won't deny the housing affordability crisis is rooted in the affordability of housing, the answer is simple: **it's all about supply.** Ask the likes of Point Piper resident Malcolm Turnbull ('Housing affordability is the result of there being insufficient supply of housing. You need to have more supply of housing'), girlboss Gladys Berejiklian ('The most effective way we can tackle housing affordability is to increase supply'), former Property Council of Australia employee Scott Morrison ('The principal cause of declining housing affordability is the failure of housing supply to adjust to increased demand') or pretty much any property developer, and they'll all tell you the same thing: **there just aren't enough houses.** If we simply let property developers build more houses – primarily by ripping up the 'red tape' of planning laws and zoning regulations – then there'll be heaps more houses for people to buy, supply will better meet demand, and whack-a-doo, problem solved. *Build, baby, build!!!*

Unfortunately for these Supply Stans – just like the crisis denialists or the smashed avocado shamers – their theory doesn't align with the facts. **Australia does not have a shortage of houses.** It's quite impossible to say that it does, when the 2021 Census tells us there's approximately 10% more dwellings in Australia than households. Of the almost eleven million private dwellings across the country, more than a million were empty on Census night; many of them holiday homes or investment properties sitting there vacant, all while prospective first homebuyers desperately search for somewhere they can afford and more than 110,000 Australians are out on their arses, experiencing homelessness. No, our country isn't being held hostage by Soviet-style zoning regulations that prevent us from keeping up with our growing population, actually; in Sydney and Melbourne, 94% of planning applications are approved, typically within three to four months, and in recent decades Australia has been experiencing record levels of new housing construction, all while prices have continued to rocket.

In fact, the ABS tells us that the average Australian dwelling is home to 2.5 people, and in 2015, ABC business reporter Michael Janda did all the sums to find that **since 1985, Australia has built a new dwelling for every 2.35 extra people added to the population,** even if you factor in demolitions and 'intentionally empty' properties. It's hard to see how the narrative of our cities choking on burdensome evil regulations stands up to scrutiny.[10]

---

10 While it might make me sound an absolute soy boy cuck, it's also worth saying that **building regulations can be quite good** sometimes, particularly when they restrict property developers from replacing every single patch of green public space in your neighbourhood with an overpriced Opal Tower monstrosity made entirely from balsa wood, highly-flammable cladding and hope, which has to be evacuated three days after it's completed.

And yet the 'Supply! Won't SOMEBODY think of SUPPLY!' nonsense continues to be propagated by those in the ruling class and in Big Property – which is perhaps the clearest indication that it's all bullshit. I hate to break your heart here, but **property developers have no interest in land or houses getting any cheaper.** Whenever they're lobbying for the relaxation of planning controls, they're lobbying for the chance to build more homes on the same amount of land, increasing the value of that land (which in turn increases house prices) and allowing them to sell more fuck-off expensive houses whenever they so choose – ideally when the market is fully peaking.

PROPERTY & THE PLAGUE

COVID-19 saw us shut our borders, experience a sharp spike in unemployment and enter a recession. The banks were tightening credit and there was economic uncertainty all over the place. It was a perfect storm for the Australian housing market, and most of the economic Poindexters were predicting that house prices would crash.

The opposite happened. Even as net migration took a hit, tens of thousands of extra homes became available on the market and those dastardly zoning regulations remained unchanged; Australian house prices bloomed. After an initial dip in value at the start of the pandemic, **home prices increased by almost 25% in the two years to February 2022**. Land values increased by 28% ($1.72 trillion) in 2021 – the biggest single jump on record. At some points, houses in our two major capital cities were becoming $800 more expensive every single day.

We'll soon see why this was the case, but the important lesson that this disease-induced housing boom illustrates is that **our monstrous housing market does not abide by simplistic economic ideas of supply and demand.**

Clearly, something else is afoot here. Something *sus*.

And to understand what that is, and to fully appreciate its level of sus-ness, we need to take a quick look back at what Australian housing used to be – and what happened to it.

THE GOODE OLDEN DAYS

Time was when the Australian approach to housing was primarily about people having somewhere to live. Mass home ownership across the population was considered a worthy political goal for those on the Left (social justice yay) and on the Right (people with 25-year mortgages are likely to work, get married, pay their bills, vote conservative and not become communists).

The horny desire for owning one's own home was perhaps best articulated by our longest-serving PM Sir Robert Menzies in his 1942 speech on 'The Forgotten People', in which he opined that 'one of the best instincts in us is that which induces us to have one little piece of earth with a house and a garden which is ours; to which we can withdraw, in which we can be among our friends, into which no stranger may come against our will'.[11]

And so, in the post-war boom years following World War II, both Labor and Liberal Australian governments made housing security a major priority, and they got seriously involved in the business of housing the nation. From 1945, the Commonwealth oversaw and supported public state and territory programs that built thousands and thousands of

---

11 Menzies' former 'little piece of earth' – a five-bedroom, three-bathroom 1912 Georgian Mediterranean fusion house in the Melbourne suburb of Kew, featuring a formal lounge, library, dining room, butlers' pantry, grand reception hall, multiple fireplaces, 'championship-size' tennis court and a Tuscan-style terrace – sold at auction at the end of 2018 for somewhere between $8 and $8.8 million.

No doubt if you, a stranger, ever try to enter those grounds against the owners' will, they will release the hounds and have you ripped to shreds.

new dwellings every year. During the Menzies era, **as many as one in five new houses were built directly by the government.** By the end of his tenure, public housing made up 8% of all dwellings in Australia – the highest proportion it's ever reached.

Silent Generation and young Baby Boomer homebuyers were also helped in this era by the fact that **Australia had one of the most tightly regulated financial systems in the OECD.** Foreign banks couldn't easily get their mitts on our money, our housing sector was protected from the vagaries of global markets and there was a plethora of building and housing societies: **mutually owned organisations** (that is, organisations owned by their members) that were set up so people could pool their savings together and borrow from reputable institutions to buy land and build houses. Some were terminating societies that ended once a particular build was complete, while others were set up permanently. These societies didn't have shareholders; any profits went back into the business for the benefit of members, and the government tended to step in to help if a member defaulted on repayments. Such societies had been around in Australia since the 1840s, but became particularly popular after the War to help build homes for returned soldiers, and they were everywhere in the Eastern states; in the mid-1950s, there were over six hundred such societies in New South Wales with over 60,000 members.

This highly regulated, interventionist approach to housing *fucking delivered*. At the end of the War, barely half of the Australian people were homeowners – by 1966, the ownership rate had reached almost 73%. The population rapidly grew by over 50% with millions of post-war migrants and heaps of those babies during this time, and yet house prices remained stable, and millions were able to gain the housing security they deserved.

It really was a different world. Right up until the 70s and 80s, the majority of young Australians – armed with job security and strong wage growth, thanks to the power of organised labour – were able to become homeowners by their late twenties, just like my mummy and daddy.

DEREGULATE–ARAMA

So it was a nice little housing system we had going there. Be a real shame if something happened to it.

Well, it did. In the 70s, as well as waging a war on workers, the free marketeers of the ruling class used the spicy economic turmoil of the day as irrefutable evidence that heavy regulation and large-scale government intervention in the economy was outdated and bad news. We had to get rid of all that shit to 'modernise' Australia and 'open up' to the world, immediately.

To that end, the Fraser government commissioned businessman Keith Campbell to lead an inquiry into Australia's 'antiquated' financial system, which he eventually handed down in 1981. Over 838 pages, Campbell laid out the case for floating the Australian dollar[12], permitting the entry of foreign banks into the country and deregulating the banking sector in the name of righteous competition and free enterprise, and it was all definitely going to be better for everyone.

Fraser only managed to take a few baby steps towards implementing the agenda before he was kicked out in 1983. Luckily for the deregulators, he was replaced by a Labor government that would take up Campbell's recommendations with gusto. Under Hawke and Treasurer Keating, everything got real loosey-goosey: the dollar was floated, trade tariffs were torn down and there was a bonanza of banks and

---

12 That is, ending the practice of pegging the Australian dollar to the US currency, and
     moving to a market-based exchange rate.

freedom (for banks). By 1987, the number of banks operating in Australia had more than doubled. These banks had fewer restrictions on how much money they could responsibly lend and to whom, and they all soon got to work at fiercely competing against each other in order to help YOU make YOUR dream of owning your own home A REALITY (by lending out shitloads of money). There was now more housing credit than ever before, and **the modern mortgage market was born.**

Most of those nice building societies we talked about couldn't complete with all this big, international, profit-seeking capital, and collapsed.[13] By 1996, the Keating government finished privatising the previously publicly-owned Commonwealth Bank, and from then on all the major institutions you could go to in order to borrow money to buy a home were solely motivated by creating profits for their shareholders, as opposed to facilitating the social good of home ownership. For-profit banks aren't particularly fussed about *who's* trying to buy a property (or how many properties they already own), just as long as they can make the repayments. And banks definitely don't mind at all if house prices just keep going up and up and up and the housing crisis worsens – that just helps them to grow their asset balance sheets, and it allows them to hand out bigger mortgages with better returns.

It's because of evil shit like this that most normal people correctly despise the banks, and why deregulating them was a terrible idea, especially when abolishing them completely and sending all their executives to Christmas Island forever would have been a much more pragmatic approach.[14]

---

13 Some of them, like the St George Co-operative Building Society Ltd., would eventually turn into banks. More banks!

14 There'll be more bank hatred later, in Chapter 4.

$OUND INVE$TMENT$

So as the Age of Deregulation unfolded, there was more credit and opportunities for domestic and foreign investment capital to get a slice of the Australian action than ever before. Soon enough, investors started to eye off the residential housing market, which began to transform into a big juicy T-bone steak before their eyes. It turns out all those 'homes' out there could actually be turned into 'assets' through the joys of **property speculation**: you buy a house (not as a home, but as an *investment*); you rent it out to people who can't afford to buy one themselves for years and years as it appreciates in value (and housing affordability gets worse); then you sell your little homely asset at a higher price, and keep all your winnings. Sick as.

Even sicker, the Australian tax system was only too happy to help this investor class out with a couple of tasty concessions. The tax break/loophole/rort we know and love as **negative gearing** was introduced way back in 1922 as a pro-business measure.[15] It was designed to allow businesses to deduct their losses and outgoings from their taxable income, thereby helping them survive potential early losses so they could carry on and become profitable down the road. This tax break exists in many tax codes around the world, but it tends to only allow you to write off losses against similar income; so the losses you incur on a rental property could only be used to minimise other property taxes. *Our* version of negative gearing is unique in that it allows you to deduct a property loss from *any* income – and pretty soon some top-hatted, monocle-wearing landlords realised what

---

15 To 'gear' an asset is to borrow money to buy it. An asset is 'positively' geared if it makes you money, and 'negatively' geared if it runs at a loss.

this meant: **they could use the properties they owned to pay a lot less tax.**[16]

This was a cosy arrangement, but it wasn't widely used for quite some time. By 1985, however, all that banking liberalisation meant the housing market had started to seriously heat up, and there were enough investors out there negatively gearing it up that Keating identified it as an 'outrageous rort'. He told his cabinet that 'the government cannot continue to tolerate a situation in which the general body of taxpayers effectively subsidises the property investments of a particular group of, usually, high-income taxpayers'.

To its credit, the Hawke government restricted the rules. Losses were 'quarantined' so they could only be written off against income from the same investment that had incurred the loss; if a landlord lost money on the rental property they owned, they couldn't use that loss to minimise their taxable income from their job.

Even this mild reform was heresy for Liberal leader John Howard, who claimed it was 'done in the name of levelling the tall poppies'. The vampires of the Real Estate Institute of Australia agreed with him, and fiercely campaigned against the gearing changes from the get-go, warning that such a move would reduce the number of rental properties in the market which would disastrously drive up rents and it would just be terribly bad for renters, and we all know that if there's

---

16 If, for example, that untrustworthy and unholy Irish Catholic family of eleven living in your tetanus-riddled shanty pays you £40 a year in rent, but the cost of *maintaining* that shanty – paying for repairs, insurance, interest payments on your mortgage, disposing of all their fucking candles, etc. – comes to a total of £60, you can then deduct £20 from the £200 you earned at *The Daily Telegraph* that year writing opinion columns defending the White Australia Policy. Your taxable income has been reduced by 10%, and that may very well drop you down into a lower tax bracket. Hopefully at some point the stupid Irish family will become sentimentally attached to the place in which they've lived for 20 years – the fools! – and offer to buy the shanty from you for three times the price you paid for it (£50, a chicken and a picture of the King).

   You will have been reducing your tax burden for years and now you get to cash in by selling your asset and make a big fat profit. Thanks, negative gearing!!!

one class of people that real estate lobby groups are always fighting for, it's renters. The government went ahead with the changes anyway, investor activity was reduced and rents *did* spike . . . in just Sydney and Perth, two cities that were experiencing particularly low vacancy rates at the time. In the other capitals, rents either remained steady, or actually fell.

But facts have never bothered the property lobby before. Their scare campaign did its magic; Labor state governments in NSW, Victoria and WA were spooked and pressured Hawke to reconsider the policy change ahead of the 1987 election. In the final week of the campaign, he announced that if elected, he'd take another look. Labor won that election easily, negative gearing was restored to its former glory a few months later, and it was enthusiastically embraced by a whole new cohort of investors who had flooded back into the market, hungry for stable investments after they'd been burnt by the Black Monday stock crash earlier that year.

The only thing stopping these speculators from realising their full investment potential now was the dastardly **Capital Gains Tax (CGT)** that Keating had introduced in 1985.[17] Capital gains from properties had been taxed since the early 70s (excluding the family home), but they weren't treated as income until Keating's CGT came along, allowing the public purse to get a bigger slice of your speculating activity. Importantly, the CGT was indexed to inflation. For example, if you:

⇒ bought a house in 1987 for $85,000

⇒ kept it until 1993, when its inflation-adjusted value was $111,500

⇒ and sold it that year for $135,000

⇒ **you've made a capital gain of $23,500 in real terms**

---

17 You make a **capital gain** on an asset – shares, an investment fund, a house – if you sell it for more than you paid for it. Get them gains.

Under Keating's CGT, that $23,500 was taxable income. So from 1987 until the late 90s – as the median house price in Sydney saw a real increase of almost $100k – investors could once again minimise their tax bill by negatively gearing an investment property, but when they sold the property for a (sizeable) profit, a decent chunk of that gain would go to the State.

This was also unacceptable to Johnny Howard, who by 1998 had Lazarus-ed his way into a second term as PM. Howard had opposed the CGT when it was introduced in '85, and in 1999, he bloody well did something about it. Claiming that he wanted to 'enliven and invigorate' the Australian economy, Howard did away with the CGT's indexing for inflation and introduced a 50% discount on all capital gains from the sale of an asset that had been held for at least a year – all to help investors keep more of their cash.[18]

Howard's CGT changes were supported by the ALP, although then-Labor backbencher and future Hungry Jack's patron Mark Latham opposed them, describing the move as 'a multibillion-dollar free kick for the rich' and 'an open invitation for the tax minimisers, the tax avoiders and the capital speculators to do their worst in the Australian economy'.

Latham was as right then as he is right-wing now. **The combination of negative gearing and the CGT discount made property investment too good to refuse.** By 2001, a plethora of Australian landlords had moved their cash into the property market to chase capital gains, insulated by the negative

---

18 Let's just say you're my dad (go with it). You bought a slightly shit house in Ballarat in 1997 for $70k, and you sold it in 2019 for $320k. You've made a *nominal* capital gain of $250k, and a real gain of about $199k.

Under Keating's original CGT, you're paying tax on that $199k. But thanks to Howard's discount, you only have to pay tax on half of the *nominal* gain, which is $125k. **The taxable amount from the capital gain is about $74k less than it would be otherwise,** so congratulations.

gearing system, and the country's total rent collections turned negative. **There hasn't been a year when landlords have collectively made money since.** By 2008, property investors were minimising their tax by a whopping $10.8 billion a year.[19]

Even the pen-pushers at the Reserve Bank of Australia were starting to notice a serious problem: 'With negatively-geared investments particularly attractive to individuals facing high marginal tax rates, a high share of Australian taxpayers are attracted to property investment to lighten their tax burden,' they wrote in a 2003 submission to the Productivity Commission. 'This interaction of high marginal tax rates and negative gearing is frequently emphasised by the property seminar industry.'[20]

The upshot of this sudden influx in landlord demand was a giant leap for house prices. After the CGT changes were introduced, house prices grew from about two to three times typical household incomes to four times typical incomes in just three years. It was the biggest and fastest jump in residential house and land prices Australia had ever seen – and it was just a taste of what was to come.

THERE'S NO PLACE LIKE A COMMODITY

This toxic cocktail – the deregulation of the banking and finance sectors, mixed with generous tax concessions that encourage property investment and speculation – has resulted in our present affordability shitshow. In the Australia that Millennials have grown up in, **housing has become dehumanised, commodified, and financialised.** A house isn't considered a *home*, it's now a 'wealth-generating asset class'.

---

19 Australian property investors now claim about $13 billion in deductions through negative gearing – and make a total of $50 billion in tax deductions – every single year.

20 'Property seminar industry' is the worst possible arrangement of any three words in the English language. It's followed closely by 'social media influencer' and 'body language expert'.

It's a product; an 'exciting investment opportunity' that's 'the key to a happy and secure retirement'. It's not a place to be valued as somewhere to live and raise a family; **it's a place to park and grow capital.**

Baby Boomers typically bought a house so they could have somewhere to live; my generation is told to just 'get into the market'. You don't have to *live in it* – just get your foot on the ladder. Just buy *something*. Start building your portfolio. What are you waiting for? After all, your wages aren't exactly going anywhere anytime soon – why not just try to own something that people need, and watch it grow in value insanely quickly, and reap the long-term gain? And hey, if having *one* house is good, then surely having more than one house will be even good-er? What about two or three times the goodness? Or ten? Ignore all those news stories about how prices are going nuts and an entire generation is getting priced out of housing security: focus on your next purchase. Focus on 'getting ahead'.

Remember: **houses are homes for money, not for people.**

This is the new paradigm Millennial first homebuyers have been greeted with in this century. The residential housing market was supercharged into such an attractive investment opportunity that speculators got involved like never before, pushing prices up and out the wazoo. A decade after the CGT discount was introduced, the ranks of Australian property investors in Australia had swelled by more than 30% – and the median Sydney house price had risen by a third. In the early 90s, around 5% of all home loans were made to investors; around 2015, they made up more than half of all new mortgages.

Investors have been assisted not only by cheeky tax breaks, but by a sustained period of low interest rates. Cheaper borrowing rates encourage people to get into the market and borrow more money to buy a house, which then pushes up demand in the market – from both prospective owner-occupiers, and from parasitic investors – which in turn drives up prices. In 2019, two Reserve Bank researchers estimated that **a single percentage point drop in interest rates could boost housing prices by up to 28%.**

This delightful financial reality was never more apparent than during the pandemic, when the RBA dropped interest rates to a record low of 0.1%, capital poured into the market, and bingo bango house prices went to the moon. While there was an increase in the number of first homebuyers who managed to get a foot in the door during this time, they were significantly outspent by investor activity, which increased by almost a third. Just in November 2020 – while we were all still trying to recover from the weirdest year of our lives and get a handle on our personal and economic futures – Australian property investors were busy taking full advantage of the rock-bottom cash rate, and borrowed a record $10 billion in finance – and the number of houses and apartments sold were the highest on record.[21]

Remarkably, all this money-hungry investor-ing hasn't been super helpful in sorting out all that supply that certain people are so worried about. Twenty years ago, one in every six loans given to investors was used to build a new house, while today, it's more like one in every sixteen. For over two decades now, hungover and confused Millennials have been rocking up to

---

21 The RBA is also responsible for another particularly wonky and cruel twist of the knife for aspiring young homeowners. In the late 90s, the Bank successfully lobbied the ABS to exclude the cost of purchasing a home from the Consumer Price Index. Even though the CPI is the official 'cost of living' measure for governments and business, the RBA believes it should exclude home prices, because 'the purchase of existing housing represents a transfer within the household sector' – that is, it's just an asset changing hands, and not technically 'consumption'.

This small change means that for more than twenty years, **our official economic measure of the cost of living in this country has completely ignored the single biggest purchase most people make in their lifetime: buying a home.** And *that* means the RBA has been *underestimating* the level of inflation in the economy, which has meant it's put itself under greater pressure to lower interest rates to reach its inflation target of between 2 to 3%, which it's done, and *that* has – you know it! – helped to push up house prices even further. WHEEEEE!!!!!

Saturday morning auctions for existing houses and apartments, hoping to secure a place to live – only to be quickly outbid by fresh and sober Boomer property investors who just want to use it for its cash flow and capital growth potential.

G(ESUS) F(UCKING) C(HRIST)

The consequences of propping up your entire economy on the financialisation of housing were plain for all to see in 2008, when the US housing market prolapsed and caused the world to shit its pants.

In the late 90s, Wall Street had successfully lobbied the Clinton administration for the deregulation of the finance industry, arguing that financial institutions could be trusted to regulate themselves lol. The prohibition on commercial banks owning investment banks was ended, and these already massive institutions grew bigger and hungrier to find new investment opportunities with better returns so they could all become even bigger still.

They soon turned to the housing market, which was starting to seriously heat up. In the early 2000s, the dot-com bubble had burst and George Bush had done 9/11, prompting the US Federal Reserve to stimulate the economy by slashing interest rates, which in turn caused a surge in demand for cheap home loans. Thanks to dark Eldritch finance magic (and all that deregulation), these mortgages could be bundled together and traded as **mortgage-backed securities** by hedge funds and investment banks on the market. As long as interest rates remained low and people kept making repayments and the credit ratings agencies kept giving them the thumbs up, it was all considered rock-solid investment activity that just so happened to be making billions of dollars for Wall Street goblins.

Unfortunately, those securities ended up being not very secure at all. In their pursuit of ever-greater returns, the massive banks had begun lending billions of dollars to 'mortgage mills' like Countrywide and New Century, which had sent thousands of property bros with frosted tips into low-income neighbourhoods to offer magical loans to anyone and everyone they met. They didn't check people's incomes or credit histories or IDs or any lame shit like that; they just wanted to sign up as many suckers to these **subprime mortgages** as possible, take their cut and buy a jet ski. This was happening right across the US, and it got even worse as investors happily relaxed their lending practices even further to take advantage of the cheap credit.

The combination of low interests and huge amounts of capital pouring into the dodgy subprime market worked quickly to inflate American house prices. For the three decades leading up to 2000, homes in the US had been appreciating in value by an average of 1.4% a year; now they were shooting up by 7%. This growth made the whole system even *more* unstable, as prospective homeowners and investors took on riskier mortgages, thinking they'd be able to refinance the loans on easier terms later, what with the growth in house prices being a sure thing. The annual volume of subprime and securitised mortgages rose from approximately $160 billion in 2001, to more than $600 billion by 2006.

That's when the bubble burst. Millions of borrowers who had been duped into taking on these loans couldn't keep up with their repayments, and they defaulted on their mortgages, or tried to sell their house and found they couldn't find any buyers at these new, inflated prices. By 2008, house prices had fallen by 20% from their mid-2006 peak. All this sent a massive shockwave through a financial system that was (it turned out) significantly propped up by those toxic mortgage-backed securities. The stock market tumbled, and major investment banks and hedge funds began to collapse, most dramatically with the meltdown of multi-billion dollar outfit Lehman Brothers, which had to declare bankruptcy in September 2008.

In the wake of all this, more than 860,000 Americans lost their homes and homeowners lost trillions of dollars in equity. The ripple effects were so huge, they'd bring on **The Great Recession**: by the end of 2009, almost nine million people had lost their jobs, US unemployment hit 10% and millions had been pushed into poverty.

American Millennials were pwned particularly hard. In a dark irony, the consequences of Wall Street's housing speculation would ensure that tens of millions of young Americans could never dream of being able to afford a home of their own. They found themselves entering a shitty and insecure job market during a massive downturn, and large numbers of them were struggling to pay off their crippling student debts with flat wages: the median income in America was lower in 2015 than it was in 1999. As of 2016, American Millennials were estimated to be 34% poorer than they would have been if they hadn't been GFC'd.

Plus, as you might have heard, this little **Financial Crisis** went **Global.** Thanks to America running the world with imperialism and the insanely risky, entangled nature of international finance, the GFC would eventually wipe 13% off worldwide economic production and 20% off global trade.

Basically, because of the predatory lending practices and rampant greed of American Psychos seeking to extract extraordinary profits from speculating on housing (again – a basic human need), an entire economic system went into crisis and broke down, with massive, devastating consequences all across the world.

'The Bush administration took a lot of pride that home ownership had reached historic highs,' Bush's former economic adviser John Snow told the *New York Times* in December 2008. '**But what we forgot in the process was that it has to be done in the context of people being able to afford their house**. We now realize there was a high cost.'

Whoops! Ah well, I'm sure there are no lessons to be learnt here. Let's just keeping juicing the housing market as much as humanly possible, and let's see how far this baby can go!!!!!!!!!!!

THE LANDED GENTRY

So now we're here: cursed with a financialised, profit-driven housing system that's filled with some of the worst injustices, attitudes, and *people* that one can imagine.

Today, there are more than 2.2 million Australians holding rental property investments. That works out to be about one in five households. We're regularly told that the people who make up this investor class are benign, decent, hard-working **mum and dad investors** who are just trying to 'get ahead'. To be fair, that's not a *complete* lie.[22] The vast majority of these

---

22　In my case, this is quite literally true: my mum and dad negatively geared that Ballarat house for years before selling it off and making a tidy capital gain, so hey – go Team Ballard.

　　Of course, being a 'mum and dad' doesn't necessarily excuse you from dodginess, or righteous judgement. Queen Elizabeth and Prince Philip technically fell into the 'mum and dad' category, but I still have some serious questions about how they've accumulated their wealth.

investors own either one (71%) or two (19%) properties, and with wages and economic insecurity being what they are these days, you can see how plenty of ordinary working people might make the completely rational decision to do what they were being encouraged to do by the government and capital and become a landlord of a relatively humble dwelling.

But to be clear: **a lot of these people are total psychopaths.** There are about 40,000 people in this country who own five or more investment properties, which, to put it bluntly, is just too fucking many. They have absolutely no moral qualms whatsoever about hoarding heaps of these homes during a housing crisis, and for some of them, it's *pretty much their whole life*. In this new sick sad world, you can seriously ask someone 'Hey what do you do for a living?' and they can answer 'I own lots of houses' and even if you tell the police about it, that person won't be sent to jail.

In fact, they'll probably be lauded by our (highly propertied) media class. The MSM loves nothing more than doing fawning profiles on property 'gurus' like Eddie Dilleen, who managed to buy 29 properties by the time he turned 29, or Morgan Kouts, who had 'always dreamt of having 30 properties by the age of 30'.[23] The king of this shit would have to be professional investor Nathan Birch, who's in his mid-thirties, bought his first house at 18, drives a Bentley with the licence plate 'CSH-FLO' and now owns more than 230 properties (net worth $100 million+). For me, a quote on Birch's website best captures the basic, lizard-brain motivation of the property tycoon: 'I love properties. I love being around other people who love properties. **I like buying properties and I like making money.**'

---

23 When Dilleen was interviewed on breakfast show *Studio 10* in 2021, host Sarah Harris was delighted by his efforts.
    'Oh good on you, Eddie – 29 properties by 29!' she said. 'Can't *wait* to see what you do next!'
    What Dilleen did next is buy another 14 properties by the time he turned 30.

The stockpiling of homes for personal gain has now become so normalised and celebrated in our society, sometimes these land barons are deluded enough to think they're just typical Aussie battlers. In August 2022, when the Australian Greens were publicly calling for a nationwide rent freeze to help the millions of tenants in rental stress, an irate man named David called in to Ben Fordham's 2GB talkback show to explain that actually, landlords like him were doing it pretty tough right now. When Fordham asked David how many investment properties he happened to own, he hesitated.

'. . . well, um – okay. 283.'

'*283* rental properties?!' exclaimed Fordham.

'Yeah,' replied David. 'Now I've worked *hard* for that . . .'[24]

These people should be sent to Azkaban, but instead they're free to walk around, carrying on, buying up more 'investments' during a housing emergency, just so they can become richer than they already are. **More than two-thirds of property investors are earning in the top 40% of incomes.** Negative gearing is not a friend of the Common Man; more than 27% of surgeons use it, and when they do, they receive an average yearly benefit of more than $4k – while the tiny number of cleaners who negatively gear get an average benefit of just $41. Meanwhile, over 70% of the benefit of the CGT discount goes to people on the top salaries.[25]

It bears repeating (and screaming): **property investors are not primarily interested in 'providing' housing to human beings.** That's not why they got in the game – first and

---

24 This was too much, even for a capitalist 2GB talkback host.
     'That's amazing – he owns 283 investment properties,' said Fordham, after the call had finished. 'I wonder whether at some point we need to be realistic though about how many homes people need to own . . . that's a lot of homes for one person to own – *283!* And that's the system we've got in place, and you wonder whether that's in the interests of everyone in Australia struggling to get into a home. 283!'
     Ben Fordham – welcome to The Resistance.

25 In 2016, the Australia Institute estimated that just 1% of the total benefits of these concessions were going to anyone under the age of 30.

foremost, they're here to make fucking money. If landlords' driving motivation *was* the altruistic provision of secure housing for their fellow citizens, they probably wouldn't jack up rents just to 'meet the market rate'; immediately turn their rental properties to AirBnBs if they can swap tenants for more lucrative tourists; shit their pants at every new law that might benefit renters' rights; or tolerate **speculative vacancies** – that is, the act of deliberately keeping a property empty to create artificial scarcity while you just sit on your arse and wait for prices to tick ever upwards to eventually deliver you a big fat capital gain.[26]

But that's just the kind of thing that happens when you turn housing into a money-making exercise. You get ridiculously expensive house prices, evil profiteering all over the shop, and an explosion of megalomaniacal property investors. From the point of view of those of us who just want to buy a home to live in, **investors really are the worst of both worlds:** they simultaneously drive up demand for housing (by wanting to buy lots of fucking homes, which drives up prices) *and restrict the supply of housing* (by owning lots of fucking homes, which takes existing homes off the market, which drives up prices), all while being subsidised by the Australian taxpayer for their wonderful service, and generally profiting from the very housing crisis they're helping to make worse.

---

26 Similarly, property developers – motivated by profit, not by a passion for providing housing or doing anything about insane house prices – engage in **land banking**: getting a development approval on the land you own to increase its value, hanging onto it for years while land values increase, then on-selling it with pre-approval for a juicy profit. Big developers like Stockbank and Landlease hold billions of dollars in landbanks on their books.

The same profit motive means these douchebag businesses tend to prioritise development in areas with the highest property prices, so they can get the best possible return – even if that does little to nothing to help provide more affordable housing to regular people.

GENERATION RENT

As more of us are locked out of any hope of achieving serious housing security, Millennials find ourselves banished to the nooks and crannies of the Australian rental market, living in other people's *assets* like the dirty hermit crabs we are. In the early 80s, about a quarter of Australian households were renting their home; **today it's almost a third**, including over half of all 25- to 34-year-olds.

And it's a super awesome deal. Housing costs for Australian renters have increased by about 50% over the past two decades (unlike wages), so now The Rent Is Too Damn High and renters get to spend about 30% of their income paying off some stranger's mortgage in return for not being homeless and quite frequently being treated like shit. In most parts of the country, you'll have zero chance of being able to sign a long-term lease, you'll have to request permission to hang a painting anywhere, your landlord will be able to increase the rent by as much as they like and they can boot you out at the end of your lease period if they feel like it also NO PETS.

If you're not happy with this arrangement, you can simply cry 'This is an outrage! I'm taking my business elsewhere!', but then you must give your four weeks' notice, find somewhere else to live (hopefully with a good rental reference?) and spend a few thousand dollars packing up all your shit and organising a truck to move it. Nice doing business with you.

(Lots of renters would happily stop renting entirely, but they don't have a choice. In one survey from a few years back, the NSW Tenants' Union found that **57% of renters say they rent because they can't afford to buy**. Consequently, more people are finding themselves trapped in the rental market for longer – a quarter of all tenant households are now couples with children.)

The Australian Housing and Urban Research Institute predicts that almost half of younger households today will not have achieved home ownership by the age of 54 and 'will spend most of their working and family life in private rental'. If that's true, we have a collective interest in revolting against the dominance of what scientists call **Landlord Brain**: the bizarre condition that takes over the mind of the mum or dad investor when a tenant moves into their property, and makes them believe that they are an amazing person who's doing the world a great service and are in no way profiteering off a basic human need. Symptoms include whining like a little bitch, and regularly posting in Facebook groups about the *emotional labour* of managing rental properties and the scourge of anti-landlord racism.

There have been massive outbreaks of LB in Victoria since 2018, when the state Labor government introduced a package of reforms that increase protections for renters — including the abolition of no-grounds evictions and rent bidding — and require landlords to do stuff, like ensuring that their properties 'meet safety basic standards' and disclose whether or not their property has asbestos in it.

When the laws came into effect, in a private Facebook 'support group for all those Landlord's [sic] who have had problematic tenants and finds the justice system too much in favour of the tenant' that I may or may not have snuck into, one member claimed this rental reform package 'would have to be the most unfair policy in a non-communist society I have ever seen'.

'I have always said that the less you do in this country the better of [sic] you are,' posted another member. 'If you're a hard worker forget it your [sic] going to pay if you're a drugged up dole bludger you get everything.'

In a different group, one landlord was griping about their new legal obligation to install child safety devices in their property if requested, and one comrade help-fully wrote, 'I encourage [my tenants] to install child safety devices if they need to. It would be my worst nightmare if a child died from something preventable, thats easily patched once they move.

'Alternatively, if someone dies in your house, it affects your property value, so kinda important.'

THE PARADOX

In the face of the seismic housing injustice facing Millennials, Zoomers and millions of others, our political class is, quite frankly, **fucking useless**. They have no solutions to this. Why should they, really? When there's an average of about 120,000 first homebuyers every year (who want houses to be as cheap as possible), compared with the 6.2 million existing homeowners (who want them SWEET CAPITAL *GAINS!!*), those in charge know what's up. They know who they need to look after, and they do; in 2018, the Grattan Institute estimated that **90% of the benefits of major housing policies go to existing homeowners and investors.**

The best the ruling class can possibly do is make some bullshit noises about wanting to do something about housing affordability, **while simultaneously making it 100% clear that they do not want houses to become any cheaper whatsoever.**

'I don't think anyone's proposing that they want to cut the cost of housing,' then-Shadow Housing Minister Jason Clare told ABC's *7:30* ahead of the 2022 election. 'Housing has increased dramatically; you need policies that can adapt and deal with that.'

When asked to clarify if he was saying that it was simply impossible to bring down house prices whatsoever, Clare replied, 'I don't think anyone would *want* to see that. Anybody who owns a home wants to see it appreciate. If house prices were to drop, the economic impact for Australia would be phenomenal.'[27]

It's fucking ludicrous. House prices have exploded out of reach for millions, but they simply *must* keep going up, apparently, otherwise we're fucked. Any reform that might jeopardise the enrichment of homeowners and investors and banks cannot be allowed, even if it makes total sense. Take negative gearing.[28] The widespread economic opinion is that

---

27 Yes, your instincts are correct: Jason Clare is a landlord. In fact, at time of writing, the 23 members of the Albanese government cabinet own 61 properties between them – that's an average of 2.7 properties each.

    Our political class tends to be up to their fucking eyeballs in real estate. A 2017 analysis of the 45th parliament (conservatively) estimated the nation's federal politicians personally had $370 million tied up in the property market. Their number included Nationals senator Barry O'Sullivan, who retired at the 2019 election, perhaps to spend more time with his portfolio of 42 properties, including his eight investment houses.

    And, in case they weren't compromised enough, these sickos happily accept treats from the very people who are making massive profits from our current housing dilemma. Between 2012 and 2018, Labor accepted $5.4 million in political donations from the property industry, while the Coalition accepted over $15 million.

28 Please!

it stinks, and it should go; research from the Reserve Bank in 2017 showed that 76% of Australians would be better off if it was abolished. The Labor Party took a policy of scrapping the concession to the 2019 election and lost, and so they caved and gave up on the idea, even though the Australian Electoral Study that year found that 57% of voters said they supported policies to limit property investors claiming tax deductions (suggesting that most Australian people aren't the greedy idiots that Labor imagines them to be). The ALP folded so hard on this, they ended up doing a complete 180: at a debate ahead of the 2022 election, Anthony Albanese found himself declaring that he now thought 'negative gearing is a good thing'. When the ABC asked Jason Clare if the Party might consider any changes to the insane tax concessions for property investors at the *next* election, his answer didn't leave much wiggle room: 'No.'

'Absolutely not?' asked interviewer Alan Kohler.

'Yes, absolutely not.'

The only 'solutions' our leaders are prepared to seriously offer involve **helping people pour more money into the cooked housing market**, thereby cooking it even further. We should boost supply, they say, so then there'll be more (unaffordable) houses. Or they'll offer up some first homebuyer grants, or some other handout which increases people's purchasing power – only to see it push prices up even higher. It's estimated that successive state and federal Australian governments have spent more than $40 billion on these kinds of grants since the 1960s, and we're living with the results of all that 'help' today.

ROOFS FOR ALL

Before this chapter is through, I should probably disclose that I, Tom Ballard, am now a Millennial home(co-)owner. (Sorry.) After more than a decade of renting – sleeping on a mattress on the floor in a room with no windows, living with dumpster-diving juggling enthusiasts in a sharehouse with no heating and cockroaches, and paying through the nose to be bossed around by passive aggressive property managers – I went in with my much more responsible brother to buy an apartment off the plan in Melbourne's western suburbs, where I now live. We would not have been able to do this without a six-figure withdrawal from the 'bank of mum and dad', owned and operated by my loving, propertied, formerly-negative-gearing Boomer parents.[29]

(If it makes you feel any better, the place is on the fifth floor near a river, so by the time I finish paying it off it'll probably be underwater.)

But hey, don't hate the player – *hate the game*. Because this game sucks arse. Even though anyone with a soul knows that decent housing is a basic human right, **our society has outsourced the provision of shelter to the profiteering private market.** We now have a housing system that doesn't care about creating a society in which everyone can reasonably afford a roof over their head – it cares, first and foremost, about growing capital and getting returns. Australia's young and poor – and, increasingly, even people from the comfortable professional classes – are getting completely shut out of the prospect of home ownership, and are condemned to the exploitative and dehumanised private rental market. Meanwhile, the lucky ones who can afford to get in the game are feverishly encouraged to speculate and invest in the 'financial asset class' of housing; an asset class which, by the way, **doesn't actually produce anything.** I mean, sure, houses are great for shelter, comfort, privacy and storage and everything, but they're not getting more expensive because they're magically becoming better houses. They're just sitting there,

---

29 Nationally, the Australian mum and dad bank is estimated to be worth about $35 billion, making it the country's ninth-largest residential mortgage lender.

appreciating in value as – and *because* – the housing crisis gets worse.[30]

Inevitably, when you primarily hand the job of housing people over to the market, any *non*-market housing that's taking up space will soon get neglected, degraded, or straight up sold off to developers. A major element of Australia's housing affordability crisis is our dearth of **social housing**: that is, public housing (state-owned and run, with affordable rents), community housing (run by not-for-profit community organisations) and Indigenous housing. ('Affordable housing' is used to describe housing that's rented out at around 75 or 80% of market rates.) This is a form of housing that's created to let people live somewhere, not to make money, so you know – it's kind of weird and lame. In the post-war years, we built and owned heaps of the stuff, but since the 70s, governments have chosen to let it slide. Apparently that's not really a government's *job*. As the Hawke and Keating governments deregulated finance and unleashed the banks, they also shifted large amounts of Commonwealth funding away from the construction and funding of public housing and towards subsidising poor and working-class tenants' rents in the private sector. After Howard took over in 1996, base funding for social housing construction dropped by almost a quarter, and over the past twenty years, as our population has boomed, the number of social housing tenants has been cut in half.

Today, social housing makes up just 3% of Australia's total housing stock. There are more than 160,000 people on public

---

30 Our collective obsession with investing in this non-productive commodity really is warping our economy and society in wild ways. Thirty years ago, about two-thirds of bank lending was for business investment, and one-third was for housing. Today, that ratio has reversed. There are now trillions of dollars that could be spent making stuff and actually helping people tied up in the 'business' of house and land prices going up and up and up and up and up.

As the housing market analyst Martin North put it to the *Guardian* in June 2022, 'What we have done as a society and government is to tilt the economy so far towards housing that it's almost a black hole, sucking everything into it.'

housing waiting lists across the country, and at this rate they'll probably be waiting on there for five to ten years. Governments and the market have been obsessing over hou$e$, while these houses have been allowed to fall into disrepair and become stigmatised. We are socially conditioned to look down on not-for-profit housing, and it's often considered to be unfortunate, or a 'last resort', less-than-ideal, unsustainable part of our cities and towns. Growing up in my privileged ignorance in my family's private home in Warrnambool, I'd often join in with schoolmates and make jokes about the city's housing commission, otherwise known as 'The Mish'. If you had a shit haircut or your clothes were a bit dirty you might be referred to as a 'Mish-Rat'. I mean, imagine not even owning your own house lol. What's wrong with you??[31]

Obviously, this country desperately needs more social housing. *Heaps* more – experts estimate we need something like another 730,000 properties by the late 2030s to meet the existing backlog and account for new demand. That equates to something like 50,000 new dwellings built every year for the next 14 years.[32]

---

31   Not all countries have this same relationship to socialised housing. In Singapore, more than 80% of the population live in homes owned by the government's Housing & Development Board. In Vienna, more than 60% of the population are in public housing, and they fucking love it: public housing estates feature courtyards, green spaces, high-quality facilities and renewable energy. In the 1920s and 30s, Viennese social housing even featured bathhouses, swimming pools and public libraries. In Finland, almost three-quarters of the population are eligible for publicly financed social housing, and when new developments are being built in Helsinki there is a legal requirement that there be no external differences beween private and public homes.

     In this European view, public housing isn't there to simply warehouse the poor, but to provide something that everybody deserves: **a nice and desirable place to live.** They give us a glimpse of a world in which there shall be no marginalised Mish-*Rats* – only Mish-Kings and Queens.

32   Our current Prime Minister – who loves to remind us that he himself grew up in public housing, and is now a multimillionaire landlord – has promised to deliver just 20,000 new social housing properties and 10,000 'affordable' homes over five years.

     Truly, with such paltry promises, catchphrases like 'negative gearing is good!' and a full-throated commitment to making house prices climb ever higher, it looks as though finding a stable and affordable home in Australia will continue to Not Be Easy Under Albanese.

But we also need nothing short of **a housing revolution in this country**. If we have any hope of avoiding a dystopian future in which millions of Millennials and almost every Zoomer is spending their retirement posting elderporn on their OnlyFans so they can pay their robo-rent to their robo-landlord, we have to reject and hack away at the commodification and financialisation of this basic human need. Tax breaks for property investors should be abolished, rents should be frozen/capped/moderated/controlled and tenants empowered to live with dignity, with long-term leases and proper rights. The worst landlords should be put on trial and all property managers should immediately be offered free retraining and mental health counselling to make sure they're ok and help them make better career choices. Massive institutional investors buying up housing stock should be declared bankrupt, and any investment property that's ever found to be left empty should be expropriated and given to the first person waiting in line at a soup kitchen.

Collectively, we need to ask ourselves: **do we want a country in which people are adequately housed – or do we want a booming housing market?**

Because it's been made painfully clear that we can't have both.

3

We Want Learn Good

'Universal education is the most corroding and
disintegrating poison that liberalism has ever invented
for its own destruction.'

– Adolf Hitler, *Mein Kampf*, 1925

'The universities are competing commercially, and they
need to have extremely good business management.
It isn't good enough to simply provide
high-quality education.'

– Education Minister Brendan Nelson, 2005

I have always believed that School Is Cool.[1]

This is a big part of the Ballard family brand: my parents are
ferocious readers who have studied and worked as teachers,
and my older brother Gavin is an overachieving nerd who
completed Year 12 with a VCE ENTER score of 99.90. This
would secure him a scholarship to study Law and Software
Engineering at the University of Melbourne, and see him pose
for a photo in a local newspaper displaying his results on his
Nokia 3210:

---

1   No, I was not very Cool when I was at School.

I tried my best to follow in this tradition. During my thirteen years of schooling – from Prep at Warrnambool Primary School to Year 12 at Brauer Secondary College, where I was Public Speaking School Captain no biggie – I was a diligent teacher's pet, who filled every waking moment with extracurricular activities and extension work that I actively requested, like a legend. I finished high school in 2007 with a measly ENTER score of 99.80, which meant that I had failed to outperform my brother, but I still got to pose for a local paper photo with my results so it was worth it.

(Photo: Leanne Pickett © Warrnambool Standard/ACM)

I was offered a scholarship to study law at Monash University. I took a gap year, moved to Melbourne, then started the course in 2009. Six weeks in, I dropped out to pursue my real passion of telling jokes about my genitals full-time.[2] Some critics have described this desertion of higher education for the sake of a puerile comedy career as 'a disgraceful waste of public resources' and 'evidence of everything that's wrong with young people in this country' and 'you should really have a backup, Tom' and 'what do you even *do* all day?', but I disagree. **My public education is surely one of the greatest gifts I've ever received.** It's brought me some of the happiest moments of my life, it fostered my lifelong love of learning, and it's played a crucial role in me being able to lead a decent and fulfilling life, and hey look now here I am writing a bloody book.

Everyone likes education.[3] Some would have us believe that a good education alone is the 'silver bullet' to solve all social inequalities, and while it's definitely *not* that (because capitalism), we can surely all agree that **learning stuff is awesome.** It broadens minds, embiggens hearts, opens doorways, and can generally move the world in a slightly more tolerable direction, as demonstrated in movies like *Dead Poets Society, Billy Madison* and that one where Hilary Swank uses the power of diary-writing to fix racism.

Millennials today are hungry to learn. We've been told *ad nauseam* that getting a qualification of some kind is how you improve yourself and get a decent job and make a valuable contribution to society, and we're all keen to enrich our minds and gain the skills we need to live happy, productive lives. As a generation, we're now credentialed as fuck: about half

---

2   When I called the university to tell them I was stopping my studies to become a comedian, the lady on the phone said, 'That sounds like fun, good luck!' and hung up, bringing my formal academic career to an abrupt end.

3   Except Hitler, I guess.

Year Six!

of all Australian workers aged between 25 and 34 have completed some form of tertiary learning.

But this hasn't come cheap or easy. Even though every politician, business leader and think tanker will tell you that every child deserves a world-class education for the sake of their own souls and for the sake of The Nation, it's not really working out that way. In the Australia that my generation has inherited, just like housing, the **public good of education** has been distorted into a **private commodity**. Knowledge has now become a gold-plated economic asset that you're expected to go into massive amounts of debt to acquire, and increasingly, young people's ability to go to/stay in school and get a good education has become conditional on where you live, who your parents are, what your bank account looks like, and which specific ideas The Market wants you to have in your head this week.

SCHOOOOOOOOL'S OUT
(OF YOUR PRICE RANGE)

The relationship between learning and cash starts early – even when it's not supposed to. Our public primary and secondary education system – primarily funded by state governments, with some contributions from the Commonwealth – is supposed to be totally free, and it totally is, provided you ignore all the money that you have to pay for it. According to the Australian Curriculum and Assessment Authority, Australia's public schools collect more than ONE BILLION DOLLARS from parents in 'term fees', excursion charges and 'voluntary' contributions every year, sometimes just to help cover the costs of basic materials. All up, parents can pay thousands of dollars per annum to put just one kid through a public school, and while that's still a pretty good deal, it's not great, particularly when you consider that almost 90% of the most disadvantaged kids in the country are in the government school system.[4]

But if you *really* want to get serious about haemorrhaging money to help your children learn their times tables and polo, **you simply must go private.** You can exercise your 'parental choice' and send your child to do Year 12 at a prestigious institution like The King's School in Sydney's Parramatta, for example – the *alma mater* of such towering intellects as

---

4 As well as **free**, the system is also supposed to be **compulsory** and **secular,** so we're really only hitting one out of three. You definitely *have to go* to school, but once you're there there's a decent chance you'll hear someone banging on about The Lord, even if you're in the state system. I can still remember the Religious Education classes I inexplicably had to sit through at my government primary school; they were conducted by a silver-haired bespectacled gentleman who would bring in his guitar every week and make us all sing 'God Is Good All The Time' – a song that I refuse to believe has ever been subjected to a second draft.

Since the Howard government introduced the National School Chaplaincy Program in 2007, successive federal, state and territory governments have spent hundreds of millions of dollars funding thousands of chaplains in government schools. Almost all of them are Christians, a tiny percentage are secular and yet not even one of them is a Satanist. Very lame.

former NSW Premier 'Casino Mike' Baird and the current billionaire King of Thailand – provided you're able to pay a cool $40k in fees.

If you don't *choose* to make that choice – because you don't love your child enough, I guess, well then that's *your choice,* but don't judge me just because I happened to make a *different* choice, which also happened to be the same choice made by my father and his father before him (which may or may not have helped me in securing Percy Septimus Frothle-Pip III a place).[5]

This is becoming an increasingly popular choice to make. Since 1976, the proportion of kids in the public education system has fallen from almost 80% to less than two-thirds, while enrolments at 'independent schools' have grown from just 4% to more than 15% today.[6] This means **Australia now has one of the highest rates of private schooling in the world.** One in ten Australian students today switch from the public to the private system in Year 7, and the ones making the move are from disproportionately wealthy families. According to education researcher Barbara Preston, more than 50% of private secondary school students are from families that have a weekly income of $2,500+, while just 8% of them are from families in the lowest income brackets.[7]

---

5   'Labor supports parental choice,' then-Shadow Education Minister Tanya Plibersek told the Council of Catholic School Parents ahead of the 2022 election, as she confirmed her party would be making 'no funding changes to Catholic and Independent Schools'.
       Don't get me wrong: making choices about our lives is cool and fun! But being able to 'choose' to send your kids to a private school is pretty fucking meaningless if it's going to cost you $30k a year you don't have.

6   The remaining 20% of students are in the Catholic education system, which ranges from being Vatican-rich to Mother Teresa-poor.

7   Members of the lower classes are able to sneak into the hallowed halls of these places courtesy of the occasional scholarship.
       When I was 15, I was offered a scholarship to complete Years 11 and 12 at Ballarat Clarendon College (where annual fees for boarding senior students are now around $39k). I declined this offer, because of my principled dedication to a strong welfare state and public services and my heroic solidarity with the working class, and also because moving to Ballarat was scary and I would miss my mum.

Even though many of these independent schools charge exorbitant fees and accept gargantuan donations from loaded parents and generous alumni, **they still receive around $13 billion in public funding from the Commonwealth every year,** which doesn't seem very 'independent' to me, but whatever. This cosy arrangement has been around since the early 60s, when St Brigid's Primary School in Goulburn – run by the local Catholic church and funded by a mix of private fees and charity – was found to be severely overcrowded; at one point it had 84 kids crammed into the one kindergarten class. The state government ordered the school to build a new toilet block to meet health regulations, and St Brigid's demanded the government chip in to help. To show the church was serious, the local bishop initiated the **Goulburn School Strike:** he closed six local Catholic schools, and all the parents re-enrolled their kids in the local state schools, overwhelming the public system. Rather than taking over the operation of these Catholic schools or building more schools for everyone, the government said, 'Ok fair play,' and decided to hand over taxpayer dollars to help them out. Ever since, there's been a bipartisan political consensus on providing 'state aid' to Catholic and independent schools, on what is supposedly a 'needs' basis.

Sixty years later, the King's School apparently 'needs' and deserves a cool $21 million in public money every year, and the discrepancy between the facilities and resources of Australia's richest private schools and the majority of public schools has become truly obscene. Some campuses boast orchestra pits, turrets and plunge pools, while others have leaking roofs, ripped carpets and are still using VHS. In 2019, Australia's four richest schools – responsible for teaching just 13,000 students – spent more on new facilities and renovations than the poorest 1,800 schools *combined*. Melbourne's

Caulfield Grammar, for example, received more than $570k in public money for a multimillion-dollar aquatic centre, featuring an Olympic-sized pool with moveable floors and 'wellbeing spaces' where students can do yoga and Pilates and meditate on the transient nature of material goods. In the early 2010s, millions of dollars of public money were given to Geelong Grammar to help them upgrade their equestrian centre, so that students have somewhere to keep their horsies when they're not being used to hunt kids from Corio for sport.[8]

Back in 2010, the Rudd government asked businessman David Gonski to have a squiz at all this and resolve the 'school funding wars' once and for all. Gonski released his final report in 2012, recommending a 'needs-based, sector-blind' model in which schools were funded to the Schooling Resource Standard (SRS) – a base rate of funding per student, with additional loading to account for student disadvantage (e.g. First Nations heritage, lower socio-economic background, being left-handed). Every school should be given enough funding to meet (at least) 100% of their SRS, said Gonski, and then everything will be fair and hunky dory.

A decade later, this definitely isn't happening. With market-loving conservatives in power and well-resourced lobby groups for the independent and Catholic school sectors being very good at causing headaches for the political class (many of whom are former private school students themselves, who now send their own kids to private schools), any suggestion that substantial amounts of public funding might be redirected away from the posh to the

---

8   Meanwhile, Parramatta East Public School's 500 students had just 10 toilets between them.

poor has been met with fierce resistance.[9] **In the ten years to 2020, federal and state government funding for Australian private schools increased at nearly five times the rate of public school funding.** Many private schools are now *over-funded* relative to their SRS to the tune of millions of public dollars, while most public schools are still falling short of what they deserve. According to ABC analysis, nearly one in three private schools in Australia now get more taxpayer dollars than the typical public school of a similar size and student background.[10]

There is a stark and widening educational divide between the rich and the poor. As more and more members of the elite take their kids out of the public system and divest from public school communities, those schools have to do more with less, while the rich schools get fancier and fancier, and the gap grows even wider. Underpaid public school teachers are struggling to deal with overcrowded classrooms and burnout, and students from the poorest quarter of the population are still on average three years of learning behind kids at the top.

A privatised education system doesn't help reduce society's 'burden' when it comes to publicly educating kids (particularly when so much public money is given to private schools);

9 When she was PM, Julia Gillard explicitly stated that under her implementation/distortion of Gonski's reforms, 'no school will lose a dollar' in funding.

This was an interesting move, as one would've thought it's quite hard to address education inequality by continuing to give rich schools that are getting too much money the same amount of (too much) money. ¯_(ツ)_/¯

10 No matter what the Richie Rich schools might say on their websites, a more expensive education doesn't necessarily produce better academic results. Analysis of MySchool data and tools like the Programme for International Student Assessment (PISA) show that once socio-economic background is taken into account, public school students perform just as well as their privately-educated peers. Sometimes public school kids even *outperform* the toffs: in 2018, Narre Warren South P-12 College – a school where 81% of students come from disadvantaged homes and the cost of doing Year 12 is $258 – averaged better VCE results than prestigious Wesley College, where Year 12 fees cost parents $32k.

rather, it eats away at our collective investment in education, and it redirects resources that could do great public good into the hands of a privileged few. **And *that* is very helpful to the grander, gross project of class stratification and reproduction.** A private education is what economists might call a 'positional good' – something that is often valued more for the *status* it comes with than for its direct utility – and that sort of twaddle tends to be far more popular with people who have enough money to worry about it ('So which school did you go to?'). The high-priced private school fees don't just get you a ridiculous uniform and fencing lessons; they also get you access to a social milieu, a network of alumni connections and all the social capital you need to do very well for yourself out there in the 'real world', even if you happen to be dumb as dogshit. Elite private schools are like giant Sorting Hats, siphoning off the richer kids into different societal orbits, and leaving the poors behind. Never the twain shall meet, and before you know it every single member of the ruling class are old buddies from high school and uni who have definitely *heard* about public school kids, but have never actually seen one in the wild.

⚠ ⚠ PUBLIC HEALTH WARNING ⚠ ⚠

Tragically, Australia's educational apartheid is the leading cause of a debilitating condition known as **Private School Brain**. (This is distinct from – but often a precursor to – Landlord Brain.) PSB is caused when children experience prolonged exposure to sandstone and boater hats, and it can turn even the sweetest little angel into the biggest of pricks.

The sickness hit the headlines in dramatic fashion in September 2020, when *The Sydney Morning Herald* published a leaked document detailing a series of muck-up day challenges that had been concocted by some Year 12 lads at Sydney's Shore School – an all-boys Anglican boarding school on Sydney Harbour that's been educating the children of the elite since the late 1880s. (Total fees for Years 7 through 12 = around $200k.) The challenges made up a scavenger hunt called the 'Triwizard SHOREnament', which required participants to scull 30 beers in 15 minutes, before setting out to earn points by completing tasks such as 'rip a cone on the Harbour Bridge', 'scull 6 Cruisers in 6 minutes' and 'shit on a train' (Ha! Imagine being on a train!!!). Other challenges ranged from the relatively harmless ('steal a street sign', 'get a mullet haircut') to the downright disturbing ('smoke your mate's pubes', 'catch a pigeon and proceed to rip it's [sic] head off', 'spit on homeless man').

One of the tasks was simply 'get a gay man's number'.

(*Haha, gay people are WEIRD!*' laughed the 18-year-old private school boy, as he wore a boater and continued to smoke his friend's pubic hair.)

Exclusive, high-falutin' Shore purports to be an institution which offers a 'world-class education', fosters an understanding of Christian values, and educates its boys to be 'ethical, responsible and caring young people by modelling and teaching good character'. Yet, despite all its resources, the school was somehow unable to protect its students from the devastating effects of PSB, which prevented these future CEOs and Liberal Party presidents from getting their heads around the rather basic idea that poor people are human beings, and you probably shouldn't celebrate your graduation by '[shoving] an egg up ur arse then shit[ting] it out while making chicken noises'.

Don't risk your child catching PSB. Talk to your GP about sending them to a state school *today.*

Millennials have long since left primary school and high school, but we're now starting to wrestle with these issues as parents. *What educational system should we send our child into: the one starved of resources but filled with normal people, or the one with great facilities, that produces cunts?*

This isn't a choice that anyone should have to make. Every single one of the four million primary and secondary students across Australia's 9,500 schools deserves the best possible education that our rich nation can provide, regardless of how much money their parents have, and whether they've ended up at a state school made out of old gym mats that have been sticky-taped together, a private school where the drink taps pump out champagne, a tiny Catholic school where the principal is also the pastor/P.E. teacher/cleaner, or a wealthy selective single-sex public school, which are just weird.

I'm all for our schools having 100% kick-arse facilities and snow trips and small class sizes and well-paid teachers – but a just society would ensure the doors that lead to those resources are truly open to everyone.

UNIVERSITIES 101

Our two-tiered education system at the primary and secondary levels shapes the populations of our higher institutions as well. **Private school kids are nearly 24% more likely to go to uni than kids from government schools.** A 2013 Deakin University study found that while more than 90% of the 2010 graduating class at the expensive Presbyterian Ladies College went on to university, for instance, just over a quarter of those coming out of working-class Hoppers Crossing Secondary College did the same.

Once again – the Sorting Hat did its thing.

Going to uni and being well-to-do have gone hand in hand for a very long time. Back in the day, an Australian (man) who desired a tertiary education had to have the time and money to sail all the way back to England, where he could enjoy all the liberal knowledge and buggery that Oxbridge had to offer. By the 1840s it had become clear the Australian colonies were in need of more educated professionals (to help measure natives' skulls and demonise the Chinese), so in 1850 New South Wales founded the University of Sydney

Future uni dropout

to facilitate 'an increase in the education of the youth of the higher classes'.

When he was advocating for the university in the Legislative Council, Mr William Charles Wentworth expressed his hope that

> *from the pregnant womb of this institution would arise a long line of illustrious names, of statesmen, of patriots, of philanthropists, of philosophers, of poets and of heroes, who would shed a deathless halo, not only on their country, but upon the University which brought them into being.*

Since opening its doors in 1852, Sydney Uni's pregnant womb has given birth to such illustrious poets and heroes as our first prime minister and enthusiastic white supremacist Edmund Barton; traitor/CIA operative Sir John Kerr;

comic book villains John Howard, Malcolm Turnbull and Tony Abbott; party boy Tory Justice Dyson Heydon; normal man Mark Latham; highly-punchable bookie Tom Waterhouse; billionaire demon Gina Rinehart[11] and myriad blood-sucking corporate and banking executives who should all be sent to a prison dimension like The Phantom Zone. The University of Melbourne was created in 1853, and its hallowed walls have since produced monsters like mining CEO and hard-right activist Hugh Morgan, pathologically wrong Sky News host Peta Credlin and Gavin Ballard.

(Yes, these same institutions have also given us the likes of Gough Whitlam, Charlie Perkins, Gillian Triggs, numerous Nobel Prize Laureates and Cate Blanchett, but at what cost?)

Their crimes aside, Australian universities have at least become (slightly) less elitist over the decades and educated more than just 'the youth of the higher classes'. While in 1855 Australia had just two unis attended by 0.004% of the population (all dudes), by 1966, 0.7% of Australians were attending one of the country's 27 institutions (they were still almost all dudes). Higher education was increasingly encouraged and publicly subsidised, and by the early 70s, while less than 30% of kids finished Year 12, those who *did* could expect to go on to tertiary study quite cheaply: around 80% of uni students had some or all of their fees and expenses covered by Commonwealth scholarships and other subsidies. My dad received a government scholarship after the first year of his economics undergrad at La Trobe University, and when my mum was training to be a teacher, she received a small bursary from the Victorian Department of Education to help cover her 1970s living expenses like rent, food, Daryl Braithwaite records and corduroy tunics.

---

11 She studied economics at Sydney Uni for a short period before discovering the course was, according to her father Lang Hancock, 'basically communist'.

So a select few members of our parents' generation were already receiving a pretty sweet tertiary deal. Soon, it got even sweeter. When running for election in 1972, Gough Whitlam declared that his Labor Party believed 'that a student's merit, rather than a parent's wealth, should decide who should benefit from the community's vast financial commitment to tertiary education'. In 1974, his Commonwealth government took over responsibility of funding higher education, abolished university tuition fees completely and introduced means-tested income support for students; payments we recognise today as Youth Allowance, Austudy and Abstudy. Both my parents completed a Diploma of Education at La Trobe in 1975 for exactly $0. After (CIA stooge) Sir John Kerr dismissed Whitlam and a Liberal government was elected, Malcolm Fraser tried to reintroduce fees for postgraduate degrees, but backed down in the face of a national student strike. He did manage to freeze public spending on universities and introduce fees for international students, but at least domestically, **an Australian university education remained basically free for fourteen years.**

More than a million Australian students had their hearts and minds expanded at uni during this time at no personal cost, including the likes of Malcolm Turnbull, Tony Abbott, Scott Morrison, Barnaby Joyce, Anthony Albanese, Kevin Rudd, and former Education Ministers Amanda Vanstone, Julie Bishop, Bill Shorten, Julia Gillard, Brendan Nelson, Christopher Pyne and Dan Tehan. Conservative commentators like Andrew Bolt, Chris Kenny, Greg Sheridan and Miranda Devine got themselves some free university too, as did billionaire balloon-animal Clive Palmer.

AN EXPENSIVE REVOLUTION

But this gravy train would be cruelly brought to an end. In the mid-1980s, popular ideas about what education is for and who should pay for it were dramatically turned on their heads, and the rot started to set in.

The Hawke Labor government was faced with a choice: the big demographic bubble of Baby Boomers and Gen Xers were completing Year 12 at record rates, resulting in a massive surge in demand for higher education, which meant the sector would have to be expanded, which was going to require a bunch of money. Those in power did some big-brained thinking and decided that the funding shouldn't come *entirely* from the State. Being supposed social democrats, they could have perhaps done the social democratic thing and raised (or even just maintained) the levels of tax on big business (which profits from having a highly educated workforce) or on rich professionals (many of whom were now earning lots of money thanks to the university education they had received for free).

But they didn't. That was too *old-fashioned*, and not really what the 80s were all about. Instead, it was decided, a big chunk of the new funding should come from a group notorious for having loads of cash: **students.**

The 'reforms' started slowly. Even though Hawke had been elected and re-elected on a Labor platform that maintained a commitment to 'free tertiary education', his 1986 budget introduced an upfront 'Higher Education Administration Charge' (HEAC) of $250 per student. Uni students these days would probably be delighted to accept such a tiny financial hit to cover their entire degree, but when the HEAC came into effect in 1987, the National Union of Students were (rightly) outraged: an upfront compulsory charge to go to uni was still a clear attack on the principle of a free public education. The Union coordinated national days of protest and mobilised thousands of students to boycott the fee. Six hundred students occupied an administration building at La Trobe for a week in protest, and in Canberra, then-Education Minister Susan Ryan met with a group of angry student leaders, including the President of the Sydney University Student Representative Council, a 22-year-old Arts/Law student by the name of Joe Hockey.

'We will continue to go out onto the streets and to protest,' Hockey told the media on the steps of Parliament after the meeting, 'and actively encourage the public to support us in our campaign for free education.'

Ultimately, this campaign did not go well, even with electric figures like Comrade Joe at the helm. That same year, a Sydney University accounting professor named Murray Wells wrote a piece for *The Australian* suggesting a 'graduate tax' be introduced to help grow the uni sector, and it seems the new Education Minister John Dawkins thought this was an awesome idea. He campaigned hard for a proposal at the 1988 ALP conference to change Labor's commitment from **'free tertiary education'** to **'access to tertiary education regardless of means'**, and it was passed by just two votes, clearing the way for the government to introduce the Higher Education Contribution Scheme – what we now know (and hate) as **HECS**.[12]

---

12 This massive educational reform has now come to be known in political history circles as **'The Dawkins Revolution'**, which makes it sound substantially cooler than it was.

TOM BALLARD'S *HANDY POLITICIAN BULLSHIT DECODER*	
WHEN A POLITICIAN SAYS . . .	**. . . THEY MEAN**
'We believe in **guaranteeing** access to [BLANK].'	'We will give you the opportunity to pay for [BLANK]. You're welcome.'
'We believe that [BLANK] should be **affordable**.'	'We will subsidise [BLANK] a little bit so that we can do a cool announcement about how we're helping you get [BLANK], but we won't subsidise you too much in case it annoys the private market or stops us from cutting taxes for rich people.'
'We will **guarantee access** to **affordable** [BLANK] for everyone.'	'You will have to go further into debt to receive a shittier version of [BLANK]. Better things aren't possible, vote for us, cheers.'

From 1989, Australian uni students wouldn't pay any fees upfront, but they would now be expected to pay back about 20% of the average cost of a degree once they'd graduated: a flat $1,800 per year of study. (If you didn't graduate, you still had to eventually pay off the debt.) These loans would be interest free, but indexed to inflation. They would be made through the tax system, and they were 'income-contingent'; they wouldn't kick in until the graduates' income reached what was then the average worker's annual wage of $22,000.

'People who benefit from participation in higher education will be required to make a small contribution towards the cost of their study,' said Dawkins when introducing the HECS legislation. He argued that it would 'increase the fairness of funding arrangements for higher education, ensuring that the total burden of funding does not fall entirely on the taxpayer'.

Which sounds great! I mean, who *doesn't* love small contributions that increase fairness and ease burdens? *Viva la revolución!*

FEE EDUCATION

Well soon, Dawkins' 'small contributions' began to eat their veggies and grow up big and strong. In just a couple of years after introducing the scheme, Hawke had increased the HECS repayment rates and increased the student contribution to $2,250 per year of study. In 1992, Paul Keating failed to turn Austudy payments into student loans (thanks to militant student opposition), but did succeed in deregulating fees for postgraduate courses in 1994, allowing unis to charge fees for any postgrad course according to 'what the market would bear'. What could possibly go wrong?

In 1996, John Howard proceeded to go hog-wild – just in time to greet the first Millennial uni students with some big fat invoices. Between 1997 and 2005, the HECS repayment threshold was lowered to $10k less than the average wage. Howard slashed university funding, increased HECS fees by 25% and created a tiered HECS fee structure, allowing universities to charge higher fees for courses that were supposed to lead to higher-income professions, like law and medicine. In a radio interview in 1999, he guaranteed Australians that 'we're not going to have $100,000 university degree courses', but by 2004 there were 16 courses that cost at least that much. Plus, in another classic win for the little guy, Howard allowed unis to offer places to students who didn't get the marks for their desired course, but were able to pay the full fees upfront.[13]

By the end of Howard's reign, HECS had become part of the **Higher Education Loan Program (HELP)**, which also included FEE-HELP (the loan program for full fee-paying students

---

13 All of this restructuring obviously triggered many uni students of the time, but in 2005 Howard made it illegal for unis to compulsorily collect fees to fund student unions, which dramatically undermined any student movement's ability to organise a serious opposition to such bastardry. The movement didn't go out without a fight – they protested and rallied and burnt effigies of Howard and cool stuff like that – but was ultimately defeated, and today the power of student radicalism is a mere shadow of its former self, like free-to-air television, or Britain.

whose courses weren't subsidised through HECS, including post-graduate courses). The loans and the costs to students just kept getting steeper. The Rudd and Gillard governments increased university funding significantly, scrapped upfront fee places and introduced a **demand-driven system**, in which universities received government funding based on how many students they'd actually enrolled, as opposed to getting a fixed sum of money and then making do. But it didn't last; in the wake of the GFC, Gillard proposed cutting uni funding by $2.3 billion and converting the Student Start-up Scholarships – which helped poorer kids buy basics like textbooks and learning equipment – into more loans that students would have to repay on top of their HELP debt.

When the Coalition took back power in 2013, it followed through on those (bad) proposals, ended the demand-driven funding and tried to do even more damage. In 2014, Education Minister Christopher *Paaaahn* wanted to remove the cap on how much HELP debt a student could accrue and completely deregulate university fees, allowing the institutions to charge students whatever they wanted and let the market sort the prices out. This was a move enthusiastically supported by the Vice-Chancellors at the biggest universities, many of them salivating at the idea that unleashed market forces and competition would give rise to an 'Aussie Harvard', which they apparently considered to be a good thing. At the *actual* Harvard, yearly tuition fees exceed AU$65k, more than two-thirds of students come from the highest-earning 20% of American households, and 15% are from the wealthiest 1%. The average US college graduate has a student debt of over AU$36k and the total federal loan debt is around US$1.5 trillion.[14]

---

14 Harvard is also rotten with elitist all-male secret societies like The Porcellian Club, which has a long and shameful history of torturing pigs and helping young people become investment bankers.

   Urban legend has it that if a member of the Club hasn't made their first million by the time they turn 30, the 'Piggy Bank' will just give it to them. Another merit win!!!

Pyne 'the Fixer' and his reforms were met with widespread student yelling and a hostile Senate, and like a terrified fresher in Week 5, he flunked out. Fee deregulation was shelved, but later in 2017, the Turnbull government cut base university funding by billions, jacked up student fees by up to $3.5k, and reduced the HECS repayment threshold from $54k to $42k – or just a smidgeon above the minimum wage.

Universities would have to do more with less, and students would have to pay back more of the cost of their degree, sooner.

I PUT A HECS ON YOU

In the late 80s, some left-wing voices objected to the introduction of HECS on the grounds that it would be a barrier to more working-class people being able to go to uni. On this front, they were clearly wrong; the implementation of the Scheme – along with the Hawke government's commitment of almost a billion dollars in increased tertiary funding and 40,000 more university places – brought about a dramatic expansion of the higher education sector. After World War II, Australia had just 10 universities; we now have 43 of them – 36 public, 7 private – educating more than 1.5 million students a year. In 1989, less than 20% of 19-year-olds went to university; today, more than 40% of school leavers are enrolling. More than 130,000 domestic Australian students graduate with a bachelor's degree every year, and more kids from poorer backgrounds, more women and more First Nations kids are getting a university education now than ever before.

But it's also true that the Dawkins Revolution's groundbreaking idea of **charging people money for something good that used to be free** hasn't exactly led us to a fairer world: the 'user-pays' model has meant that the burden of funding

Average Uni Student Debt Over Time

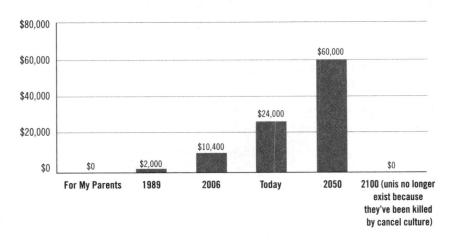

university education has increasingly fallen onto the round, pimply shoulders of individual students.

There are now almost three million people walking around out there saddled with these debts, which now add up to a total of around $69 billion. The average HELP balance is about $24k, but around 280,000 HELPers owe more than twice that, and more than 69,000 have debts exceeding $100k. It will take the average Australian student about a decade to pay off their debt, and that will probably be the same decade in which they'll be trying to go *further* into debt so they can do something ridiculously extravagant like buy somewhere to live (in case you skipped over it, see the last chapter you cheeky bugger). High levels of student debt tend to lead to young people delaying home ownership and starting families (although I still blame hip hop), and debt in general acts as a drag on debtors' economic activity, as well as seriously exacerbating stress and poor mental health outcomes. In some instances, it can even lead to serious issues of addiction and suicide ideation.[15]

Those who recognised HECS as the beginning of a very slippery (and pricey) slope for students were absolutely bang on. As soon as you accept the justification for HECS – that individual students personally benefit from their university education, so they should help pay for it – you're screwed. On that basis, why should students only pay 20% of their degree? Why not 30%? Or 40, 45 or even 51%? For all those four-eyed postgrads, why not 100%? After all, the *student* is the one going to uni, not the bloody government or the taxpaying truck driver or hairdresser or banking CEO, so *the students* are the ones who should cough up. And while we're at it, why am *I* paying for *YOU* to read and borrow books at the library, for FREE? *You're* the one benefiting from all that reading, not me. I fucking hate Patricia Cornwell. If you want to read a bloody book, then you should pay for it, and you alone. Also, why aren't all these free-loading Year 11 and 12 kids chipping in directly for their education, too? They personally benefit from going to school, and they're legally allowed to work. Hit *them* with some loans too, I say, right in the face.

I discussed this matter with political commentator Joe Hildebrand on my podcast in October 2020. Joe's sympathies lie with the right-wing of the Labor Party – he despises anything that whiffs of what he calls the 'radical/extreme/ WOKE Left' – and when I asked him about the notion of Australia maybe offering free (or even just substantially

---

15 Even when they're *at* uni – when young people are supposed to be carefree and laughing and learning and having lots of sex as they slowly accrue those piles of debt – today's students are under the pump. The median income for Australian full-time uni students is just $18k, which means most are living below the poverty line. One in ten uni students defers their studies because they can't afford to continue the lifestyle, and one in three regularly misses lectures or classes because they have to work to earn enough money to cover their expenses and to get ready for their future careers of paying off the debt of their degrees which they might not even get because they're skipping classes or lectures to go to work.

cheaper) tertiary education, he made it clear he did not support any such handouts.

'Even if you're a lawyer, you shouldn't have to pay back money that the taxpayer spent to put you though law school?' he asked. 'Is that fair? I don't know if it is.'

When I pointed out that Australia provided free uni in the past, Hildebrand noted that it was 'only for 15 years' which is 'not exactly a grand tradition.' He then posed a classic hypothetical: 'Do you support a bricklayer paying taxes that are then spent on doctors and lawyers who get a free education and get a profession out of that where they earn three times, four times, five times, *ten times* more than that bricklayer, but never have to pay back the money to the Commonwealth?'

This objection makes perfect sense, until you think about it for three seconds and remember that:

a) bricklayers benefit from living in a society with trained doctors and lawyers[16]
b) doctors and lawyers pay higher taxes on their professional incomes[17]
c) any call for a return to free uni must also include free, high-quality universal vocational education too, to help train the bricklayers and other tradies of tomorrow, paid for by the taxes of wealthy professionals, including doctors and lawyers.

It's almost as if we live in some kind of society.

Yet the individualist, penny-pinching mindset that has shaped the world my generation has entered begs to differ. It has corroded the idea of what a public education is for,

---

16 Obviously not *all* lawyers; we *could* throw 70–80% of the legal profession into the sea and manage perfectly fine.

17 They don't pay enough, and should pay more, which I'm sure members of the Labor Right will be campaigning for vigorously any day now.

and now insists that a tertiary education is not a publicly funded good *in and of itself*, but a 'nice-to-have' commodity that's (begrudgingly) subsidised by the State. Forget the fact that our society *needs* people to be qualified doctors, nurses, dentists, teachers, lawyers, engineers, scientists, translators, architects, city planners, etc. in order to function. Forget the fact that businesses *want* people to be university educated in order to exploit their brains so they can increase their profits. Forget the fact that we're quite fond of having a rich cultural and intellectual life populated by academics, historians, intellectuals and artists. Forget the fact that the OECD has consistently found that **the public ends up benefiting twice as much as individuals from our collective investment in tertiary education.**

And most *certainly* forget the silly idea that a wealthy country should provide the opportunity for young people to spend three or four years of their lives in a nice place learning about history or science or literature or the world around them in general because it's just, you know, *rewarding* and *fun*. All of that is hippy shit. Grow up.

COUGH UP

Even if you reckon the original thinking behind HECS is sound, you'd have to admit that it's long since gone to the dogs. It's hard to argue that getting a uni degree is still some kind of an elite indulgence that will inevitably bestow great riches upon you when it's increasingly becoming a basic requirement for getting a job. Millennials have been lucky enough to start entering the labour market at a time of increasing **credential inflation:** almost a third of jobs today require a bachelor's degree or higher qualification, and about half of all the new jobs being created over the next couple of years are expected to require one, too. But just getting a degree won't necessarily guarantee security; since 2008, graduate employment rates have fallen by more than 12%, underemployment has doubled and wages have gone backwards – but students have still been expected to pay more and more for their learning.

The Coalition government's 2020 'Job-Ready' university reforms represented a complete departure from the original HECS logic. As well as ripping out about $1 billion in student learning, the government argued that it wanted to make courses that would lead to the 'jobs of the future' — like nursing and STEM subjects — cheaper, while making gay shit like humanities cost students more than ever before.[18] Thanks to the Tories, arts, law and business graduates will now be leaving uni saddled with debts of between $40k and $50k.

'Students will have a choice,' then-Education Minister Dan Tehan told the ABC when he announced the policy. 'Their degree will be cheaper if they choose to study in areas where there is expected growth in job opportunities.'

This is mask-off shit. Now it's not

'You kids should help pay for your degree because it's going to get you a good-paying job!'

it's

'You kids should pay more for your degree because it's not going to get you a job at all, you little fucks!'

The modern right-wing dogma — which can be found living happily in both major political parties — is clear: **any fancy learning that isn't going to instantly boost corporate Australia's bottom line is a drain on society.** To the conservative mind, the cost of a university education should now be used as a stick to whip the butts of the country's young people in the direction of profitable enterprise and away from anything else. You don't 'deserve' an education simply because you were born into this very wealthy country — so head down, focus on your work, and stop asking questions.

As *The Australian*'s economics editor Adam Creighton put it bluntly in a piece from June 2020: 'Want to study Foucault? Don't expect a cent.'

---

18 About 113% more, to be precise.

THANK YOU FOR SHOPPING AT UNI

When you start to view higher education as a *commodity*, you inevitably start to look at higher education institutions as *businesses*. A key element of John Dawkins' plan was the reforming of universities' management structures to make them more efficient, innovative, dynamic and soulless, and under his watch, pretty soon unis and colleges were amalgamated and cursed with more executives, more middle management, bigger marketing budgets and more data collation reporting obligations. Our public universities may still technically be charitable organisations, but they've adopted the shiny skins and creepy smiles of corporations; they now have a mandate to use words like 'paradigms', 'outcomes', 'KPIs', 'scalable', 'streamlined' and 'streamlined scalable KPI outcome paradigms'. They don't 'teach' 'students' – they *activate knowledge delivery.*[19]

As we all know, any successful corporation has to be able to stand on its own two feet, and **diversify**. As federal government funding for universities has steadily declined – it's fallen from making up 80% of university revenue in 1989 to just a third today – the sector has had little choice but to hunt for new revenue streams: philanthropic donations, corporate partnerships, and yes, more fees for students. Domestic students were already being shaken down for their lunch money, so we started to look overseas. In the two decades to 2006, the number of international students in Australia grew by 2,000%. Over the past decade, international student

---

19 At quite the premium, too. Private universities like the marbled Bond University charge tuition fees of up to **$17,500 per semester.**

    That particular institution, of course, is named after corporate fraudster and general bastard Alan Bond, who loved to 'stretch' the law, destroy working people's lives during his hostile corporate takeovers and pretended to have brain damage when he was on trial for bankruptcy.

    Bond University's motto is 'Forever Learning'.

fees have doubled. Today, foreign students can be paying up to 400% more than domestic students for exactly the same degree; providing further evidence that placing an objective dollar value on a university education might just be bullshit. This $37 billion international education industry is now one of Australia's biggest exports and accounts for more than a quarter of universities' revenue.

Now sure, there's nothing inherently *wrong* with encouraging people from around the world to come and learn at and contribute to our universities, of course; I'm all for global solidarity and cooperation and sharing knowledge and I once got to sleep with a Colombian guy who'd come to Melbourne to study, so it's a thumbs up from me.

It gets a bit problematic, though, when our nation's higher education system – and its ability to fund and conduct high-quality research – is precariously propped up by our charging an uncapped number of foreign students extortionate fees, as we just cross our fingers and hope it'll all be okay and the students will never notice how racist we are and there'll never be a worldwide pandemic or anything.

As long as those things don't happen (and they never will!), business is good; at least, at the top. Australia's ten highest-earning Vice-Chancellors earn twice as much as the Prime Minister.[20] The workers who really make universities actually *happen*, however, struggle to keep their heads above water. Ballooning enrolments, funding cuts and the adoption of this brutal corporate model have resulted in **Australian unis having some of the worst staff-to-student ratio rates in the world.** In 2020, it was revealed just how casualised the higher education sector workforce has become; billion-dollar institutions like the University of Melbourne and

---

20 They mainly spend this money on bowties.

Monash University were found to be employing over 70% of their staff on insecure terms. We learned of multiple university wage theft cases, involving reports of tutorials being classified as 'practice classes' and tutors being told to 'skim read' student essays to meet impossibly high marking rates and get paid.

So, somewhat ironically, for all the talk on Parler of university campuses crawling with blue-haired genderqueer SJW Marxists, the commies haven't been able to stop their workplaces from turning into managerialist exploitation factories. Nor have they been able to prevent universities from doing very un-Leftist things like putting publicly funded research behind paywalls and collaborating with fossil fuel companies and the arms trade. Various unis have accepted millions of dollars from the Australian Coal Association Research Program, while the University of Melbourne's Peter Cook Centre for Carbon Capture and Storage Research is partnered with the likes of Rio Tinto and BHP Billiton. In 2016, Melbourne University welcomed a new research partnership with the world's biggest weapon manufacturers Lockheed Martin. One Deputy Vice-Chancellor told the media that the uni and the company were looking forward to 'work[ing] together to solve some of the world's most challenging problems'; presumably problems like 'How can we maximise the potential of AI to kill more people in Yemen?' and 'Why aren't there Death Stars?'

LOSING SKILLS

Similar corporate bullshit has been inflicted on Australia's Vocational Education and Training (VET) system. VET is designed to help prepare young people for work through apprenticeships, traineeships, certificates and diplomas, and Australia's publicly funded Technical and Further Education

(TAFE) institutes have been providing high-quality VET to millions of people for more than a century. Something like 70% of Australian workers who currently hold VET qualifications got their training through the TAFE system, including mechanics, plumbers, builders, disability carers, bookkeepers, travel agents, youth workers, hospitality workers, personal trainers and, unfortunately, real estate agents. A 2020 report from the Australia Institute's Centre for Future Work estimated that for the relatively small cost of $5.7 billion a year, the TAFE system adds a total of $92.5 billion to the economy through higher wages, productivity and social benefits. It's very good for alleviating inequality, too; TAFE students are more likely to come from working-class or First Nations backgrounds, and are more likely to identify with having a disability than students in the private or university system.

But our lovely TAFEs are now in crisis. In the late 90s, our approach to VET started getting all market-y as well, and more and more public money went to subsidising private VET providers. Funding for TAFE flatlined, and the number of TAFE institutes across the country has dropped from 84 in 2001 to just 35 today. Since 2012, more than 9,000 TAFE jobs have been cut, enrolments have tumbled, courses have disappeared, teacher workloads have increased, apprenticeship completions have nosedived and infrastructure has been crumbling.[21] Confidence in the system has taken a severe hit, and twice a week every week for the past twenty years we've heard politicians and business leaders bemoan Australia's various crippling 'skills shortages'.

Simultaneously, the always-efficient-and-superior-private-sector has been fucking up vocational education harder than I fucked up my wooden pencil case in Year 8 Woodwork. In 2008, having never met a student loan they didn't like,

---

21 On the upside, I guess having rundown facilities creates more work for tradespeople who probably trained at TAFE.

the Labor government introduced 'VET FEE-HELP': an income-contingent loan for full-fee-paying students studying certain courses at TAFE or at private Registered Training Organisations (RTOs). The Department of Education paid tuition fees directly to the private providers, depending on how many students they had enrolled. After pressure from business groups, the strict requirements and conditions for RTOs were relaxed, and in 2012, providers were allowed to set their own fees.

This set the stage for some truly heinous shit to go down. Dodgy companies with godawful names like 'The Phoenix Institute', 'The Empower Institute', 'Unique International College Pty Ltd' and 'The Galaxy Brains Excellence Foundation Inc.'[22] now had an incentive to enrol/trick as many students as they could, collect free government money and serve up the cheapest version of 'education' imaginable. Tens of thousands of students had loans issued against their name without their consent. Private providers recruited students by using brokers and Facebook advertising, cold calling people, targeting remote Aboriginal communities and offering students $50 in cash and a free laptop on enrolment. Some RTOs would 'layer' students, enrolling them in multiple courses, claiming four times the original amount of funding and charging four times more than TAFE; the 'Australian Institute of Professional Education' was found to have breached consumer laws by falsely claiming that its online diploma was 'free', when in fact it could cost up to $20,000.

Whereas TAFE is a public service dedicated to teaching people stuff so they're able to do important things, these private cowboys were simply in the VET space to make money, and if that meant sending out people to look after

---

22 That's probably a real one.

your grandma or your kids with qualifications flimsier than a pen licence, so be it. Many people didn't even get the shitty piece of paper, because the company went bankrupt before they'd finished their course, leaving them with nothing but tens of thousands of dollars of debt. From 2009 to when it was finally scrapped in 2016, VET FEE-HELP cost the Australian taxpayer $7.5 billion – most of which went to private training colleges – and the government has since had to forgive more than $2 billion in dodgy VET student debts.

The whole thing was a cruel and corrupt shemozzle, which illustrates the disastrous consequences of underfunding public education services, shifting the costs of learning onto individual students and sacrificing the provision of crucial skills and training to market logics.

In 2017, the Coalition government chose to replace VET FEE-HELP with the 'VET Student Loans program'.

DUMB COUNTRY

(Source: https://www.memeatlas.com/images/brainlets/brainlet-brain-meat-grinder.jpg)

Over the past thirty years, the philistines in our ruling class have made their disdain for public higher education very clear, and are perfectly happy to leave the dissemination of knowledge, like everything else, to market forces. When the COVID pandemic hit, public universities almost immediately started losing hundreds of millions of dollars in revenue, but the Coalition government locked them out of receiving the JobKeeper wage subsidy. By mid-2021, the sector had lost 40,000 jobs.

PM Morrison treated the situation with his trademark sensitivity and compassion, telling the *Herald Sun* that if unis were so sad about not being able to continue to exist or whatever, then maybe it was 'time for [them] to consider their economic model'.

'I wouldn't expect universities to respond [to the crisis] any differently to any other business,' he said, because that's the kind of shit that he says.

Indeed, during their time in office, **the Abbott/Turnbull/Morrison governments really tried to do everything they could to make Australia dumber than it already was.** Even as student enrolments grew by 23%, federal funding for higher education suffered a real terms decline. The Coalition cut public research and development funding in our unis to its lowest level in four decades; it cut or froze funding for bodies like the Australian Research Council, the National Health and Medical Research Council and the National Collaborative Research Infrastructure Strategy; and it ripped funding and jobs out of the Commonwealth Scientific and Industrial Research Organisation (CSIRO).

Turns out free-market ideologues especially don't like **pure basic research** (that is, research conducted for the sake of increasing human knowledge, rather than a commercial outcome). They'd much rather give cash to **applied research** that gives 'value for money' and has 'impact', like the sort of thing that helps Ashley & Martin achieve their cutting-edge hair-based technology, or allows yoghurts to claim their bacteria has been 'clinically and scientifically proven' to help you do better shits.

FREE (AGAIN) AT LAST

In June 2022, SBS News ran a profile on 25-year-old Tori Tennant, who graduated from her veterinary studies in 2020 with more than $180k in combined student debt. (Thanks to recent inflation, that's now been indexed up to $193k, while wages across the economy continue to stagnate.)

Tori is now working in regional Victoria on a salary of $55k a year after taxes, and is making HECS repayments of $75 per week.

'The optimist in me wants to say at some point [I could pay it off],' she told SBS, 'but I think I worked out a rough estimate . . . I should pay it off when I'm 76.'

This is insane. As corporate profits soar and as we slash taxes for the rich, **our society chooses to mount piles of debt onto the backs of young people for the crime of wanting to learn.** Over the past forty years, young Australians have been constantly encouraged to get a so-called 'priceless' education, only to learn that it's come with an ever-increasing price tag. Education is now a product to be bought and sold, teachers are retailers and students are either customers to be marketed to or soulless products themselves, laden with debt and subjected to market-oriented standardised testing. Learning for learning's sake is now considered a decadence, and attending an educational institution is more of a kind of job skills program, and nothing more.

I think it's important to acknowledge just how truly *weird* this 'You Learn It, You Buy It' attitude has made us, as a country. Professor Bruce Chapman, the public servant who was the architect of the HECS policy, recalls that in a 1992 HECS-related meeting he had with the ATO, an official offered him a HECS-branded pen sporting the slogan, '*HECS – the ATO Working for You*'. The official also excitedly informed Chapman that the ATO had a HECS video that they showed to high school students, and '[t]his was followed with some HECS balloons and a HECS board game'.

Within three years of being introduced, government-enforced student debt collection had become so normalised and celebrated that it had its own fucking merchandise. I'm not totally sure what a 'HECS board game' designed by ATO officials might involve, but it's safe to assume that playing it would have to be one of the most boring activities a living human being could possibly undertake.

Over thirty years, we've created a system dedicated to squeezing as much cash out of the young as possible. During their brainstorming sessions on fresh ways to be evil back in 2013, the Abbott government was seriously considering charging students interest rates on their HELP loans and selling off the country's $23 billion HECS debt, putting it in the hands of the Ringwraiths and Dementors of the private finance industry. Christopher Pyne floated the idea of changing the rules so that outstanding HECS debts could be collected from students *even after death* – a measure that could apparently improve the budget position by about $2.8 billion over three years.[23]

The prevailing Boomer/Gen X wisdom seems to be that the Australian era of free university education was 'never going to last'; that it was simply unrealistic/unfeasible/impossible to maintain, and **the only way to expand higher education was to make students pay.** Even figures like the Chief Executive of Universities Australia, Catriona Jackson, praise the HECS system today, claiming it 'opened the doors of opportunity to hundreds of thousands more Australians of modest means who would not otherwise have had the chance to go to university'.

This was bullshit in the 80s, and it's bullshit now. It's entirely possible for us to give lots of people high-quality,

---

23 At the time, Minister Pyne was being advised by a Professor in the Practice of Higher Education Policy at the Australian National University, Andrew Norton. I spoke to Norton while researching this chapter, and learnt that he stands by the death debt collection idea to this day.

'Unfortunately, every year there was going to be a few students that wrapped their cars around trees, etc.' he told me. 'And what do you do with their HECS debt? Do you want the ATO claiming the few hundred dollars left in their savings account? That's not a good look. So let's just write it off. And in those days, when relatively fewer people went to university and they didn't borrow much, writing it off wasn't really very costly at all.

'Whereas now, when you've got 40% plus of the cohort borrowing – and borrowing more than they did in the 80s and 90s – well, now we're talking *serious money*.

'I still think it's a no-brainer. It's just like dying with your credit card debt. Pay it back.'

tuition-fee-free public tertiary education, as they do in not-dumb countries like Norway, Ireland, Sweden, Germany, Finland, Greece, Scotland and Slovenia. Yes, we do have lots of people in our higher education system, but according to OECD data, the Irish have an even *higher* tertiary participation rate than us, and they've had fee-free full-time undergraduate degrees since the mid-90s. Greece spends about the same proportion of GDP on tertiary education as we do and offers universal free public university courses, while everyone from the Canadians to the Swiss to the Scandinavians invest a higher level of their GDP into higher learning, and it seems to be going quite well for them.

What's the price tag? Well, even though he's much more on board with the whole HECS thing than I am, Andrew Norton kindly took the time to lay out how much providing truly free higher education might set us back. He laid it out like this:

- In 2020, domestic uni students either paid or borrowed about $5.3 billion in HECS-HELP money.
- We can assume that 15% of HELP debt won't be repaid anyway and can be counted as existing government spending.
- Therefore, **making public university tuition free for Australian students would cost the federal government something like an extra <u>$4.5 billion</u> a year.**

We spend well over twice that amount in annual subsidies and tax breaks to the fossil fuel industry, and tbh we always seem to have hundreds of billions of dollars to spare when it comes to buying missiles and underwater surveillance systems and probably something like the S.H.I.E.L.D. helicarrier from *The Avengers* that we'll have to get the French to make and definitely won't even work.

We must reclaim the vision of an Australia in which a genuinely free, universal, world-class public education system is possible and righteous and good. The student debts of Xers and Millennials and Zoomers should be wiped, all of our public educational institutions should be fully funded and yes, the opulent swimming pools and equestrian bungee-jumping facilities of the private schools should be available to everyone, forthwith.

If we don't fight for that better world, the educational apartheid will only grow wider, and the price of knowledge will only grow steeper – all to the exclusive benefit of those boater-wearing pricks at the top.

4

From Our Warm, Public Hands

'If you put the government in charge of the Sahara Desert, within five years there'd be a shortage of sand.'

– Conservative aphorism

'Qantas asks executives to volunteer to fill in as baggage handlers'

– *Guardian* headline, August 2022

Take a squiz in the stationery drawer in the Ballard family home today and you might come across a treasured relic from my primary school days: **my holographic Dollarmites ruler.**

From what I can remember, the Dollarmites came to our planet from another galaxy to teach Australian kiddies about the importance of financial literacy. If you joined the 'Dollarmites Club' you were rewarded with bank books and free merchandise like toys and stationery, and if you had any pocket or lunch money that you wanted to put away for a rainy day, you could put it into the yellow plastic coin pouch, hand it to your teacher, and trust that it would be deposited into your very own Dollarmites account at the **Commonwealth Bank of Australia (CBA)**. You'd taken the first step on your lifelong journey towards economic security, you got

What the fuck were they supposed to be?
Irradiated mermaids? Space crabs? Obese starfish?!

a free ruler, and you got to hang out with some weird, financially prudent alien parasites, who were also your friends.

The CBA started running its School Banking program more than 90 years ago. Back then, it was Australia's publicly owned and operated central bank, tasked with keeping the government's cash and providing savings accounts and general banking services to the people, via its own various branches and through the (public) post office. Providing an educational financial literacy program to schoolkids was considered part of the Bank's mission and a social good, and by the mid-forties the program was operating in 4,000 schools across the country and the Pacific. The Dollarmite mascots arrived 'from Outer Space' in 1988, and continued to delight me and millions of other young Australians throughout the 90s as the School Banking program continued, even after the bank was fully privatised by the Keating government by 1996.

Two and a half decades later, CommBank announced that the Dollarmites program would be coming to an end.

This was fair enough; by the late 2010s, a number of gross scandals had come to light and exposed the scheme for what it had become: **financial grooming**. In 2018 we learned the bank had paid hundreds of thousands of dollars in kickbacks to public schools in Queensland for participating in Dollarmites and for getting students to open accounts, and retail branch staff had fraudulently set up YouthSaver accounts for schoolkids in order to meet aggressive KPIs and receive performance bonuses. We'd later learn the program involved promoting credit card products to kids as young as five.

A 2019 inquiry by the Australian Securities and Investments Commission (ASIC) into 'school outreach' schemes like Dollarmites found the banks that ran them were 'unable to demonstrate that these programs in and of themselves improve savings behaviour' and they consistently 'fail to effectively disclose that a strategic objective of these programs is customer acquisition'.[1]

In the wake of all the bad press, Queensland, Victoria and the ACT announced they would no longer allow Dollarmites in their schools – a move which CommBank thought was very 'disappointing' – and the little aliens were sent back to their home planet.

This was just one of many disgraces that the CBA has been involved with since it was sold off. Over the years, the bank has happily financed climate-wrecking fossil fuel projects, denied life insurance to people with terminal illnesses, made hundreds of thousands of dollars in political donations to both political parties and punished whistleblowers trying to expose its wrongdoing. At the same time as CHOICE was raising the alarm about Dollarmites, the Banking Royal Commission

---

1   In its defence, Dollarmites was *extremely fucking good* at achieving this objective. According to consumer advocacy group CHOICE, 46% of people got their first bank account with the Commonwealth Bank through the program, and more than a third of them still had that account as an adult. It was a massive cash cow; in 2018, one analyst estimated the program was worth about $10 billion to the bank's bottom line.

was hearing about how CommBank's sales-driven, profit-at-all-costs culture had led to widespread, greedy predatory behaviour. It charged more fees for no service than any other major bank, deceived regulators, did some money laundering for drug syndicates, ignored terrorism financing, had a bit of dodgy foreign exchange trading going on and even knowingly charged fees to dead people for planning advice, which is very rude.

Way back in 1911, Labor Prime Minister Andrew Fisher established the Commonwealth Bank of Australia with an act of parliament, declaring that it would be '**a bank belonging to the people,** and directly managed by the people's own agents'.

But like so much else, 'The People's Bank' is no more. Now it's just a bank belonging to shareholders, and its agents have 'directly managed' to rip The People off.

ALL STOCK HAS GONE

One of the starkest contrasts between the Australia that Millennials know and the one that Baby Boomers were born into is the ubiquity of **privatisation: the transfer of public ownership and control of institutions, infrastructure and services to the private sphere.**

We've already seen how the economic revolution of the past forty years subjugated workers' rights to market forces and hacked away at the government's provision of housing and education. But it's fucked up plenty more than that, and as a result, we have a society that has thoroughly hollowed itself out. Assets, services and responsibility have been sold, leased and put out to tender, and everything has been identified as a potential source of profit extraction, from the skies to your grandma.

I think it's difficult for my generation to appreciate just how much of our public inheritance has been flogged off. By the time the oldest Millennials were entering adulthood in the late 90s, the national fire sale was well underway, and today people my age are totally conditioned to watching ads on SBS and having to talk to six different people in an offshore call centre to sort out the details of our dogshit internet contract. That's just *how things are*. When you've never known anything else, it's quite hard to imagine a different world – one in which almost every single facet of life isn't mediated by a business trying to make a buck out of you and your needs. It's hard to imagine a world in which your bank, your employment service, the planes, trains, trams and buses you catch, the telecommunications you use, health services, the electricity grid or your national airline are owned by a democratically elected government, and run for their own sake, not simply for profit.

But that world isn't Stalinist Russia or an episode of *Black Mirror* – **it's our very recent past.**

GETTING OWNED

For as long as there have been nation states and governments, private actors have been trying to muscle in to get a slice of the action and 'help' run society. In Ancient Greece, for example, things like banking, trade and even tax collection were regularly performed by the private sector.[2] In the late 1700s, the East India Company (EIC) even used a massive private army to seize political control over vast tracts of India and ruled like a government for more than 40 years, torturing the Bengali people to extract taxes and pillaging the country's wealth. This resulted in very poor levels of customer satisfaction; an Indian official at the time asked, 'What honour is left to us when we have to take orders from a handful of traders

---

2 There was also quite a bit of slavery going on, which, from the slave's point of view, is about as privatised as you can get.

who have not yet learned to wash their bottoms?', which I guess means that the voracious sociopaths of the EIC were not only murderers, they didn't even know how to douche.

Thankfully, humanity's fate hasn't been (entirely) dictated by such profiteering maniacs. After heaps of painful struggles and bloodshed we've been able to come up with elected governments that are given democratic control over various parts of the economy and society, and we expect those governments to run all that shit properly for our collective welfare – especially the stuff we all know to be **essential** – otherwise we'll boot them out at the next election, and give a new bunch of people the chance to fuck it up.

For most of the 20th century, the scope of what was expected to be included in this 'public sector' was very wide. Across Western capitalist societies, public ownership and control was all the rage, and governments owned and looked after various **natural monopolies** and ran **government-owned enterprises** to manage things and deliver services.[3] These enterprises were often run in competition with private business, and were expected to be 'model employers'.

Australia bloody loved these things. Thanks to the work of Labor (and some Nationalist) governments, Australians got that Commonwealth Bank, as well as a public broadcaster in the Australian Broadcasting Commission (later 'Corporation'), the Commonwealth Line shipping company and the Commonwealth Oil Refineries. At the state level, governments owned and ran everything from cattle stations to sawmills, coal mines, smelting works, hotels, plant nurseries, insurance offices, clothing factories, brickworks, building

---

3 A 'natural monopoly' refers to an area in which there can be little to no competition, because of massive barriers to entry and economies of scale and logistics, e.g. the electricity grid, the water supply, the railway system, national communications infrastructure, airports, tax collection, law enforcement, and so on.

companies, flour mills, bakeries, timber yards, metal quarries, motor garages and more.[4] Governments across the world ended up taking over even more stuff after the epic market failure that was the 1929 stock market crash; the State was expected to come to the rescue, and lots of countries either briefly or permanently **nationalised** major industries to save them from collapse in the Great Depression.[5]

Indeed, the only people who were super passionate about privatisation in the 1930s were the goddamn Nazis. While these 'national socialists' brought almost 500 companies under government control, they simultaneously did a shitload of *Reprivatisierung*: they 'reprivatised' much of what the Weimar Republic had brought into public hands. The Nazis sold off public ownership of steel, mining, banking, railways, public utilities, and social services, often to the private benefit of members of the Nazi Party and a few wealthy industrialists who had helped the Führer rise to power.[6]

Meanwhile in the West, the US, Britain and Australia brought everything from the steel industry to aviation to banking to food production under public control in order to fight those blasted Nazis in the War. This approach worked quite well; large-scale government ownership and economic intervention continued to be considered 'jolly neat', and helped give rise to that big fat post-war reconstruction Long Boom that we're familiar with. Curtin and Chifley's welfare state massively expanded the concept of what a government's role should be in a good society; it turns out the State could actually help you find work, or maybe provide your mum

---

4   At various points in its history, the Queensland state government owned a fruit cannery, a fishing trawler, multiple fish shops and almost 90 butchers.

5   That is, they brought those industries under government control. Nationalisation (yay) is the opposite of privatisation (boo).

6   So now, if you ever hear someone say, 'I think privatisation is GREAT!' you can be like, 'Ok cool so you're basically Hitler'.

with a pension in her old age, or build you a house, and it was a very good thing that it was doing that, because **those are basic things that everyone deserves.**

As well as running such services, the post-war government decided it could totally build and own crucial national infrastructure. Chifley's government began construction on the publicly owned, nation-changing Snowy Mountains Hydro Scheme, created the publicly owned domestic national carrier in Trans Australia Airlines (TAA) and nationalised the private airline Qantas Empire Airways Ltd to offer international flights for the country, which Qantas did, under public ownership, for 46 remarkably successful years.

YOU'VE HAD ENOUGH NOW

But by the time the Cold War starts cooking in the late forties, the political Right and the forces of capital were viewing this sort of Lefty authoritarian #DictatorDan shit as completely unacceptable. Socialism and communism were now the ultimate evils, and the militant traitors in the ALP and the union movement were often championing all this public ownership nonsense on explicitly anti-capitalist, socialist-ish grounds.[7]

So, for the likes of Robert Menzies and Australia's business lobby ghouls, nationalisation was a one-way ticket to Stalin's Russia, and it had to be resisted at every turn. These arseholes were quite good at said resistance, and managed to repeatedly thwart Labor's ambitions for greater public ownership. Chifley had originally wanted to outlaw private

---

7 To this day, the ALP's constitution states that it is '**a democratic socialist party and has the objective of the democratic socialisation of industry, production, distribution and exchange**'.

It's fair to say that this has become a bit, er, *outdated* in recent decades, and there are plenty of Labor figures – especially from the party's Right – who have tried to get this objective 'modernised' (i.e. ditched, to be replaced by some vague sentiments that most Liberals would be perfectly comfortable with).

airline licences entirely and give the government a monopoly on air travel, but the Liberals and business groups mounted a High Court legal challenge against the plan, and the Court eventually ruled that such an act would be in breach of the Australian Constitution, which insisted that all trade and commerce among the States be 'absolutely free'.[8]

Similarly, when Chifley announced his plan to nationalise the country's private banks, all hell broke loose. The leader of the Country Party described the move as a 'communist ramp', while a hysterical Menzies declared it to be indicative of 'a coming dictatorship in Australia' and said that if Chifley was successful, his next steps would be to 'socialise the shops or the newspapers, or even, heaven knows, the Churches'. A fierce and well-funded public campaign was launched against the legislation, as well as another successful legal challenge on 'absolutely free' trade grounds, and the humiliated Chifley government lost the 1949 election to Menzies by a landslide.[9]

Over the next few decades of the Cold War, the same anti-Communist paranoia would inform the West's zero-tolerance approach to *any* sovereign government that looked like it was interested in exerting greater democratic control over its own economy – especially if that was going to upset international capital. The freedom- and democracy-loving United States used the CIA to do heaps of political assassinations during this period, and to orchestrate coups to overthrow democratically elected leaders in various countries, including Iran (where

---

8   Having completed Year 11 Legal Studies, six weeks of an undergraduate law course and a fair bit of reading of Australian history for this book, I am now of the firm opinion that **our constitution sucks big fat wombat balls**. It's an explicitly racist, anti-democratic document that doesn't allow us to have nice things, written by the ruling class to protect the ruling class, and we should probs tear it up and start again.

9   Sydney's 42-storey 'Chifley Tower' is named in honour of the former prime minister. (It was originally named after Alan Bond, but then he went bankrupt, so they changed it.)
     Ironically, the Tower has long been used as a trading floor for a succession of investment banks and private equity firms, which is not so much dancing on Ben Chifley's grave, as it is setting up a bunch of fucking banks on there, which is worse.

Prime Minister Mohammad Mosaddegh wanted to nationalise the Anglo-Iranian Oil Company), Guatemala (where moderate reformer President Jacobo Árbenz had helped end exploitative labour practices and was trying to redistribute some land from the rich to the poor), South Korea, Indonesia and, as we've discussed, Australia. It's estimated that between the late 1940s and the late 80s, America successfully inflicted regime change on other countries 26 times from a total 72 attempts.

One of its biggest 'successes' in this effort took place in Chile. When the Chilean people had the gall to elect the uppity socialist Dr Salvador Allende as their president in 1970, the US government wanted to teach them a lesson.[10] The Yanks waged an aggressive economic campaign on the country, deliberately stoking inflation and slapping Chile with brutal trade embargos, and they used the CIA to funnel weapons and cash to Allende's political enemies and actively foment political dissent during his presidency.[11] The US finally saw this Marxist bastard overthrown in a military coup in 1973, when the fascist General Augusto Pinochet violently seized power, and began chucking Leftist dissidents out of helicopters.

As soon as he got the top job, Darth Pinochet was conveniently gifted with a detailed economic plan for Chile's future, lovingly prepared for him by the '**Chicago Boys**': a group of Chilean economists who had studied at the University

---

10 In September '70, then-CIA director Richard Helms met with President Nixon and National Security Advisor/Nobel Peace Prize recipient/war criminal Henry Kissinger to discuss the disastrous news of this hippy's electoral success. The Allende government – with all its crazy plans of redistributing the country's wealth for the benefit of working people – simply could not be allowed to succeed. According to Helms' notes, Nixon wanted the US to make Chile's economy 'scream'.

　　'**I don't see why we need to stand by and watch a country go Communist due to the irresponsibility of its own people,**' Kissinger had said in June, beautifully illustrating the American commitment to spreading freedom and prosperity all over the world, whether the people of that world fucking want it or not.

11 They were helped out in this effort by their buddies in the Australian Secret Intelligence Service, who opened a base in Santiago to help the CIA with its destabilising operations. Straya!

of Chicago under old mate Milton Friedman, and whose maverick agenda had been too much even for Allende's right-wing opponent during the 1970 election. (Yes, they were also helped out by the CIA.) The Boys recommended sweeping deregulation of the Chilean economy and the privatisation of public assets (including all of Chile's water resources) and services (like education, health insurance and pensions). Pinochet – who declared his dream was 'to make Chile not a nation of proletarians, but a nation of entrepreneurs' – dutifully carried out the mercenary plan, the capitalist class cheered, the rich got richer at the expense of everyone else and today, Chile holds the title of the most unequal country in the OECD. The wonderful liberalising economic reforms squeezed working Chileans so hard for so long that in 2019, more than a million of them hit the streets in *El Estallido Social* ('The Social Explosion'): widespread mass protests that voiced the people's rejection of the Pinochet legacy, and would eventually see a complete re-writing of the Chilean constitution, filled with legally enshrined public services and lovely political and ecological rights for The People.[12]

SELL! SELL! SELL!

Any normal person would look at the pillaging of Chile and recognise it as evil and wrong and gross. But for some sickos, it was The Future – they wanted to see the Chicago Boys' vision go global. By this point, Milton Friedman – who described Pinochet's Chile as an 'economic miracle' – was everywhere in the Western media popularising his dogma, and he and his ilk were using the stagflation crisis and the supposed failure of Keynesianism as proof that **government was way too big.**

---

12 At least, that was the dream. The new, progressive constitution was thoroughly rejected by the Chilean people in September 2022, and now they all have to go back to the drawing board. I blame the CIA.

There was too much public ownership and State intervention in Western economies, and that was very bad, because
governments simply aren't that good at running stuff. They
needed to get out of the game as much as possible, the privatisation zealots argued, and allow the free market and individual
consumers to take care of the rest. After all, private companies
are bound to deliver goods and services way more efficiently;
not because of any sense of public duty or service, but **because
they're driven solely by the magical profit motive.**

In Australia, Malcolm Fraser was quite sympathetic to these
kinds of ideas. Although he was still basically a Keynesian
and wasn't as gung-ho about economic liberalisation as some
of his fellow Liberals, he had no time for the big-spending,
redistributive agenda of Gough Whitlam's government and
its attempts have the Australian people own more of, you
know, Australia. When he was Opposition Leader, Fraser
vehemently resisted the Whitlam government's Minerals and
Energy Minister Rex Connor's campaign to 'buy back the
farm' and exert more public ownership and control over
the country's mineral resources.[13] After Gough was dismissed

---

13 Whitlam and Connor tried to do this by establishing the **Petroleum and Minerals
Authority (PMA)**, which was basically a government-owned mining company. The
PMA was able to explore for, extract, process and market Australia's minerals, and was
tasked with cooperating with and regulating private mining outfits. Unlike the private
multinationals that dominated mining at the time (and still today), the PMA would
actually share its massive profits with the Australian people, not just foreign shareholders, which would be fucking nice.

'Just as it has been stated that war is much too serious a matter for generals to
control,' Connor told the Parliament in 1973, 'so a Labor Government says that exclusive control of Australia's fuel and energy resources is much too serious to be left to
individual companies.'

The whole project went to shit in 1975, when Connor was trying to raise a multibillion-dollar loan to help the government fund some big juicy resource projects. Finance
capital wasn't interested, and Connor ended up turning to a dodgy Pakistani deal maker
named Tirath Khemlani. Khemlani never came through with the cash, the story came
out publicly, Connor had to resign for misleading the parliament about it, and this
'**Loans Affair**' fed into the sense of rolling political crisis that was used to justify Gough
Whitlam's dismissal in 1975.

But mainly, it was the CIA. Khemlani had CIA links, and Sir John Kerr was a prominent member of the Australian Association for Cultural Freedom, which was a CIA
front group. Just saying.

(by the CIA), Fraser's government quickly went about mutating Whitlam's **Medibank** – a compulsory, universal health insurance scheme designed to provide coverage for any medical expense, with the government covering 85% of the cost – into **Medibank Private:** a voluntary scheme that would offer private medical and hospital insurance. It was government-owned and not-for-profit, but it would still compete with private health funds. Fraser's Health Minister Ralph Hunt assured Australians that the government intended 'to operate the Medibank private insurance as a completely commercial operation, with no subsidies, no help at all. It will have to stand on its own feet entirely'. So, thanks to the Tories, the 'business' of helping sick people to avoid financial ruin would once again have to follow the rules of business.

By Fraser's second term in the early 80s, the privatisation craze had really taken off across the West. British PM and Pinochet-admirer Margaret Thatcher was privatising anything that moved (council housing, British Airways, British Telecom, British Gas, the British Paedophile Factory, etc.).[14] Similar transformations were underway in France, Canada and New Zealand, while US President Ronald Reagan was using his inaugural address to inform the American people that **'Government is not the solution to our problem, government *is* the problem.'**

Fraser tried to do his part, convening a group nicknamed **The Razor Gang,** which sounds pretty badass until you find

---

14 By the time she left office in 1990, Maggie had shunted off 40 state-owned businesses (employing 600,000 workers) and £60 billion worth of state assets, including the buses and even the country's water agencies. She claimed that all this privatisation was done to ensure 'the State's power is reduced and the power of the people enhanced', and to realise her vision of a shareowning 'popular capitalism', whatever the fuck that means.

After Thatcher was rolled, her Conservative party went on to privatise British Rail, while future PMs Tony Blair and David Cameron would later privatise air traffic control and the Royal Mail, and all of this has helped to make Broken Britain the flourishing, confident island it is today, where an hour train journey costs more than a flight to Italy and almost every single creek or pond is filled with dumped spotted dick sewage.

out that it was just a government budgetary review committee and it involved John Howard. The Gang identified government spending and jobs that could be slashed and investigated a few privatisations (including selling Medibank Private) – all of which was described by then-Labor leader Bill Hayden as 'a wholesale slaughter of national responsibilities' – but ultimately, it failed to move much off the government books before Fraser lost to Hawke in '83. Later, John Howard would become Liberal leader and boast that his party had a 'full-blooded privatisation policy that will offer enormous incentives and benefits', and he'd call for the selling of public enterprises like TAA, Qantas, the Housing Loans Insurance Corporation and the Commonwealth Bank, as well as the deregulation of the government's telecommunications service, Telecom. Paul Keating, now Treasurer, attacked such outrageous demands, claiming the conservatives wanted 'simply to indulge ideologically in a Thatcherite vandalistic splurge to try and destroy these authorities', while Hawke described the policy as 'a one-off fire sale; **a "sale of the century" of your assets**, the assets of the people of Australia. [The Liberals] would transfer them into the hands of a privileged few to the cost of every one of us.'

Haha, *yes!* Go off, King! Cop THAT, Little Johnny!

WELCOME TO THE THATCHERITE VANDALISTIC SALE OF THE CENTURY

Not long after saying those cool things, **Hawke and Keating would effectively turn into Tony Barber and Alyce Platt and host the Sale themselves.** Along with disciplining the labour movement, unleashing finance and sending students into debt, the 'modernised' ALP of the 80s and 90s gave up the fight, put the whole 'we're about democratic socialisation' thing in a drawer, locked it, and fully embraced the Liberals' privatisation agenda, radically transforming the landscape of Australian life for the worse.

Hawke started out in 1987, announcing a billion dollars' worth of Commonwealth asset sales, including some overseas embassies and the sale of Williamstown Naval Dockyard to defence contractor Tenix Defence.[15] This was promptly followed by the privatisation of the Commonwealth Accommodation and Catering Services and the Australian Industry Development Corporation, all justified on the grounds that the government needed the money from the sales to do all the nice social stuff it wanted to do. Around this time, an editorial in *The Australian* argued that **'governments should get on with the job of governing undisturbed by the problems of running banks, airlines or telephone companies'**, and Labor seemed to pretty much agree; in the face of widespread public disapproval and vocal resistance from the union movement, the party changed its platform regarding public ownership at a special National Conference in 1990, and the garage sale could begin.

By the end of the Hawke–Keating years, the ALP had fully privatised the Commonwealth Bank for $14.4 billion (in today's dollars), Commonwealth Serum Laboratories ($574 million) and Trans Australia Airlines, which was merged with Qantas and sold off (total $4.5 billion).[16] More private childcare providers were encouraged to enter the market, SBS was showing ads, and the process to privatise the country's major airports had begun. Keating wanted to fully privatise the 'bloated and arrogant and uncompetitive' Telecom, but he lost the argument in Cabinet; instead, Hawke merged Telecom with the Overseas Telecommunication Commission

---

15 Tenix would later be acquired by the Australian arm of BAE Systems, a company that likes to bribe dictators and sell fighter jets to Saudi Arabia, the country that did 9/11, kills journalists, and is currently turning Yemen into soup.

16 The government handed Qantas a sweet injection of $2.5 billion before it was floated on the stock market, just to help make it look extra pretty.

to form 'Telstra' and sold the government's satellite company AUSSAT to the Optus Communications consortium, initiating some sweet competition between a publicly owned government business and a business using assets and infrastructure that used to be owned by the government.

Later, Keating's reforms to open Australia up to international competition not only let in a flood of foreign banks, but a bunch of other bloodthirsty players, too. His government signed legally binding deals like the World Trade Organisation's General Agreement on Trade in Services, which aimed to encourage international trade in services like banking, transport and telecommunications, and actively discouraged governments from doing (or heavily regulating) such things. These kinds of Free (but unFair) trade agreements were very popular with global services corporations like Serco and private water companies like Veolia and with foreign investors, who were more than happy to get a slice of the lucrative action when Australia opened its doors and began selling assets and services willy-nilly.

When he finally got the top job in 1996, John Howard looked at all this ruthless ransacking and marketisation of everything and said, 'Hold my beer'. His government – featuring David Kemp, the 'Minister Assisting the Minister for Finance for Privatisation' – asked the National Commission of Audit to report on the state of all the businesses and enterprises under government ownership, and it suggested *very strongly* that the Commonwealth get divesting. Howard proceeded to privatise everything from the Commonwealth Employment Service to the aged care sector to Medibank Private (even more so than before). Howard sold off billions of dollars' worth of Telstra shares and finished the job of selling off the airports ($5.9 billion), as well as the National Rail Corporation and Freightcorp, chunks of the telecommunications and radio spectrum and 59 Commonwealth properties.

Meanwhile, Liberal and Labor state governments were busy privatising electricity, gas, public transport, hospitals, ports, mines, jetties, lotteries, betting agencies, radio stations, hospitals, insurance offices, prisons and their souls. In the 90s alone, Australia sold off government-owned assets and services valued at more than $108 billion, without even asking us if that was really such a great idea.

GOVERNMENT INC.

Central to this hot new privatisin' ideology was a passionate belief in the ability of *KOMPET!T!VE MARKET$!!!* to make things better and cheaper and gooder, pretty much always and everywhere. Under this new mindset, any kind of bloated government-owned authority or business that wasn't privatised should immediately be **corporatised:** that is, it should be subjected to market logics.

We've already seen how this was inflicted upon the modern university, but the rot spread everywhere. Labor's 1995 **National Competition Policy** (NCP) recommended that statutory entities – responsible for delivering services like electricity, gas and telecommunications to people (now known as 'consumers') – be restructured to be more like private corporations, so they could compete in the market against private firms on a 'level playing field', with no special treatment or nothing. The NCP introduced a 'competitive neutrality' policy to ensure that 'government businesses do not enjoy unfair advantages when competing with private businesses', which meant they now had to turn a profit and pay taxes, and they wouldn't be able to borrow money from the government at a cheaper rate.

This new push would lead to the corporatisation of everything from utility commissions to port authorities to sections of the defence force and Airservices Australia. Such a transformation inevitably changes an outfit's DNA. Priorities shift away from delivering a public service to people, and towards the pursuit of profit and commercialisation. Before it was corporatised in 1989, for example, **Australia Post** was the **Australian Postal Commission**, and was run by representatives of customers, workers and the wider community, not directors and CEOs. It was primarily concerned with meeting 'the social, industrial and commercial needs of the Australian people for postal services', and it provided good solid public sector jobs with good conditions.

But once it became the 'Australian Postal Corporation', it started doing weird things, like selling off post office buildings to private companies, which would then rent out those post office buildings – to the fucking post office. Today, AusPost is a mess. The salaries of senior executives are truly obscene, while many of their employees are treated like dogshit on low-paid, insecure work. When online shopping exploded during the pandemic, AusPost put a call out for 'volunteers' to help clear a backlog of parcels with their own cars, while executives were in line for around $7 million in bonuses. My parcel *still* hasn't arrived, the people who work in my local post office seem to be constantly pissed off at everything about their lives, and I'm sorry but all the cheap novelty tat they sell in those places should be illegal, because I shouldn't be looking at a Peppa Pig Bubble Machine or a Wiggles 'Potty-Time' interactive training toilet when I just want to get some fucking stamps.

IT'S NOT A COMPETITION

So: the privatisers won. Comprehensively. They delivered all their 'reforms', and they completely remade the Australian economy in the process.

Quite frankly, **it's been fucking disastrous**. Privatisation has screwed over Australian consumers, workers, the environment and – to get a little bit *West Wing* about it – the integrity of our very democracy. It regularly fails to live up to its own promises of reducing inefficiency, lowering prices, improving services or sparking innovation, and yet it's just allowed to continue, accepted by the political class and the 'experts' as solid and good economics that can never be challenged or reversed.

The failures are never more apparent than when we look at the privatisation of natural monopolies, where 'competition' is a mirage. Take electricity. I speak on behalf of everyone when I say that we couldn't give two flying shits about competition and 'choice' when it comes to making sure the stuff in our houses work. Electricity is not simply another optional product for us to enjoy at our leisure; **it's essential for us to live, and for the economy to function**. We need it to do basic things like charge our phones, keep our beers cold and watch *The Masked Singer*. It's not exactly a *dynamic* product, either; there's literally no qualitative difference between electricity that's provided by Origin or electricity provided by Alinta. There's no 'premium electricity' called 'Electricity+' that will *revolutionise* the way your microwave works, and if you're a private energy company executive working on something like that, please stop. We don't care. Electricity is a public utility, and we just want it provided to us as cheaply, simply and fairly as possible, please and thank you.

That's what privatisation was supposed to deliver. After he was elected Premier of Victoria in 1992, Jeff Kennett's Liberal government decreed that the State Electricity Commission of Victoria, which had been providing Victorians with power since 1921, was too laden with debt and simply had to be privatised to be made fit for purpose. Kennett laid off a whole bunch of highly skilled engineers and blue-collar workers, broke the whole operation up into private companies and sold it for a cool $20 billion, which I assume he then spent on his two favourite hobbies.[17] Other states soon followed suit, and throughout the 90s, the generation, transmission, distribution and retailing of Australian electricity in various states was disaggregated and sold off to private companies, while electricity authorities and regulators were corporatised.

This was the birth of our **National Electricity Market (NEM)**, which has since grown to include all the Eastern states and territories. The NEM is now a vibrant hive of capitalist

---

17 Demolishing hundreds of government schools and maintaining his personal Museum of Golliwogs.

competition between a bunch of (mainly foreign-owned) corporate behemoths like the 'Big Three' (EnergyAustralia, AGL and Origin), all of it overseen by the Australian Energy Market Commission (which maintains the Australian National Electricity Rules, which are enforced by the Australian Energy Regulator, while the day-to-day management of the actual Electricity Market is performed by the Australian Energy Market Operator wow thank God privatisation helps us get rid of red tape).

The experts assured us that all this competition would herald a new age of low prices and convenience. They were violently wrong. According to The Australia Institute, between 1996 and 2016, as consumer prices increased by 64%, **electricity prices soared by 183%.** When the NEM was formed in the late 90s, Australians enjoyed the lowest retail electricity prices in the world – today, we pay some of the highest, and dealing with energy companies has consistently been voted at number one in Tom Ballard's Annual List of the Least Convenient Things of All Time.

Private energy companies, y'see, really aren't interested in providing energy as *cheaply* as possible, because their whole thing is about profit maximalisation. They're going to charge you as much as they possibly can, and you pretty much have to cop it, because, well, *electricity*. These oligopolistic douchebags can (and do) wield their market power to 'game' the system and price gouge us in the face. Some will jack up their prices when another company's power station shuts down (because they can); others will even deliberately withdraw their capacity from the market to drive up prices; and many will engage in 'shadow' pricing, in which a coal-fired power generator will make sure their power is only *slightly* cheaper than that of their gas competitors, but still as high as possible. It's thanks to this kind of profiteering that the Big Three retailers are able to make about $3 billion in pure profit every year, and rather than spend that money on making all our bills cheaper, it's spent on advertising or lobbying or being sent to overseas shareholders or invested in doing the bidding of Satan.[18]

Then there's public transport. You really don't get much more of a natural monopoly than a metropolitan train system: there's one company that's been given a twenty-year contract to operate the train you have to catch, and that train runs on the one line that exists, and if you don't like it, how about you go fuck yourself. Kennett privatised Victoria's train and tram systems in 1999, creating two Melbourne train operators, two city tram operators and a regional train operator, each in charge of its own set of routes. These franchises were sold to British and French multinationals, who immediately began to view each other not as nice friends all working together to help Victorians get around, but as rivals. One would assume that maintaining the city's *integrated* transport network would make the most sense in getting around, but these individual companies ended up creating their own individual tickets and produced maps showing *only their half* of the train system. While Kennett promised that taxpayer subsidies to run the trains would gradually disappear as business boomed, they absolutely did not: the franchisee Connex received $651 million

---

18 In July 2022, the Ukraine conflict, unplanned outages at coal plants and a particularly bitter winter coalesced to push wholesale electricity prices through the roof. It got so bad, the Energy Market Operator had to step in and impose a price cap to protect customers. Several power generators responded by making the 'rational commercial decision' to withdraw their capacity from the market, because the cap meant they'd be operating at a loss (even though they'd still be eligible for government compensation for lost revenue).

Eventually things got so bad that AEMO had to shut the Market down entirely, and for about a week, the whole thing ran like it did before our grids were privatised: a central authority told the generators how much electricity to dispatch and when. The only catch was that the Commonwealth had to pay these massive companies more than $1 billion for doing their fucking jobs, and for not plunging the entire Eastern seaboard into darkness and chaos during a cost-of-living crisis.

So yes, our privatised Electricity Market system is extremely efficient, except when it's required to provide electricity.

from the state government to run the trains in 2007, and by 2016 its successor Metro Trains was getting $1.18 billion.[19] It wouldn't cost the government any more to run the system itself – it might very well be able to do it cheaper, considering these companies often report hundreds of millions of dollars in profits – but bringing things back into public ownership is generally verboten. In 2017, the commercial operators' contracts were up and unions called on the Andrews Labor government to put the system back into public hands, but those calls were ignored, and the contracts were extended until at least 2024.

Sydney had one of the biggest and most efficient publicly owned tram networks in the world until the 60s, when pressure from private interests compelled the state government to rip up the system and replace it almost entirely with buses.[20] Tram lines would be closed in the dead of night to avoid being seen by an outraged public, and carriages were then taken to the tram yards and literally set on fire, which as a Melburnian, I consider to be a hate crime. Decades later, the NSW government would realise that trams are good, actually, and it leased the operation of the surviving light rail out to a private company – which it would then have to buy out in 2012 in order to build the CBD Light Rail. Over the years, the state government has also privatised huge chunks of the city's ferry, bus and train systems, and all this rational and efficient activity has resulted in Sydney becoming the fun, easy-to-get-around and congestion-free metropolitan utopia that we know and love today.

---

19 Metro Trains is majority owned by the MTR Corporation, which is majority owned by the Hong Kong government. So Melbourne's trains *are* publicly owned, just not by the Victorian public.

20 While technically there's no 'evidence' that it was the oil companies who pressured/bribed the NSW government to get rid of Sydney's trams, that's exactly what was happening in the US, where such companies bought up tram networks just to scrap them. Efficient!

While we're at it, why not privatise all of our roads, too? May as well. In 1995, Kennett signed Victoria's first private road deal with a group of bankers and builders that would eventually Megazord themselves into the giant toll road company, Transurban. The road was CityLink, a $1.8 billion project that has since delivered rivers of revenue for the company and its shareholders. The original contract included a clause that allowed Transurban to claim compensation if infrastructure was built that 'competed' with CityLink, so if the Victorian government wanted to build road or rail projects that might help make Melbourne a cleaner and less congested city – what some might describe as *a state government's fucking job* – they'd have to pay a financial penalty to protect Transurban's profits.

This is not 'competition' or anything like a 'free' market – **this is a grift**. Time and again, crucial services and pieces of infrastructure have been put up for sale, the private sector has cosied up to the political class, they've all started sucking and fucking each other to come up with a sweetheart deal, and we're all left to deal with the soggy leftover mess. When Sydney airport was privatised in 2002, the government rolled back regulation of the airport to boost its price, then it gave the Sydney Airport Corporation the right of first refusal to build and operate any second airport in Sydney at a later date, thus gifting them a dominant monopoly and the ability to charge you $14 for a fucking muffin. The Corporation turned down the chance to build and operate the Western Sydney Airport in 2017 because of the 'considerable risks' involved, but the state kinda *needed* a second airport, so now the state government is going to take on that risk, build the airport, and then probably lease it to some other company that will charge you the price of a house deposit for the pleasure of parking your car.

bUt It'S gOoD bEcAuSe It'S mOrE eFfIcIeNt

For the privatisers, something under public ownership is 'fat', 'bloated', 'flabby', 'lazy' and 'slow', while things in the private sector are 'lean', 'sleek', 'flexible', and 'a daddy' who can 'absolutely get it'. Release a public service from the molly-coddling hands of government and throw it into the colosseum of the marketplace, they claim, and the profit motive will ensure that service undergoes a cool training montage and emerges on the other side looking more ripped and cut than ever before.

This is indubitably bullshit. The private sector is filled with giant, bloated, bureaucratic companies that are wasting resources all over the joint. These fucks regularly commit various crimes of 'inefficiencies' in their quests for profit, and when they take over a privatised essential service, *we lose*. Since the electricity industry was privatised, for example, the number of workers involved in the actual production of electricity has grown by just 21%, while the ranks of the managerial class have doubled and the number of sales staff has quadrupled. Investment in the grid and infrastructure has withered away. Actual output per employee has fallen and productivity growth has been worse than almost any other industry. The sector now spends more on finance and banking costs than on, you know, *making fucking electricity*, and for us customers, navigating power bills is an inefficient nightmare. Jeff Kennett or the wonks at the Productivity Commission might get off on filling out paperwork, but normal people dread the hassle of having to get connected or change providers when we move house or when something goes wrong. We resent the fact that we're expected to spend valuable hours of our short time on this planet scrolling through websites to compare different offers from the various energy companies to find out which one will gouge us the least, instead of simply receiving the essential service that we need and deserve.

How efficient is our privatised telecommunications network, when companies like Telstra and Optus build and maintain their own set of mobile phone towers around the country, often with the help of government funding? Telstra has balked at suggestions that it should have to share its regional infrastructure with its competitors, because that would eat into its profits, so the only sensible alternative is for other telcos to build their own (superfluous) towers, or let the company maintain its coverage monopoly. Our privatised national carrier Qantas, meanwhile, has sacked and outsourced more than 13,000 workers since 2010, all in the name of cutting costs and streamlining efficiencies, and now flying Qantas is brilliantly efficient, provided you're not on one of the 42% of Qantas flights that don't arrive on time and your luggage isn't sent to Norfolk Island. If you have any issues with Qantas' service, please feel free to ring one of the call centres that the company has sent offshore to South Africa and Fiji, and they'll be happy to help within five to eight hours.[21]

But *even if* a privatised company can prove itself to be an efficient operation, that doesn't change the fact that in plenty of areas of life, **running things for a profit isn't the most efficient option for society**. Replacing the government/citizen relationship with that of a business and customer can seriously backfire, as people have been learning the hard way for ages. Until the 1860s, for example, the business of firefighting in London and New York was managed by private insurance companies; a brigade would only extinguish the ferocious blaze destroying your home or business if you'd prepaid the appropriate premium. This approach was eventually abandoned when people realised that fires don't tend to check

---

21 In September 2020, as thousands of stranded Australians were priced out of return flights home, Qantas announced a seven-hour 'flight to nowhere' departing from and arriving in Sydney, which is an extremely efficient use of resources and a good use of everybody's time.

paperwork, and they'll quite happily leap from an uninsured building to an insured one. For the sake of public safety, the cities created publicly owned and funded metropolitan fire services, because they made actual sense.

When we take a broader, social view, can we really say it's more 'efficient' for us to collectively rely on a market in which entire airlines can collapse like Ansett and Virgin have, or as more than 370 airlines did after the GFC? How *efficient* is it when the for-profit childcare centre you send your kids to goes into liquidation, like ABC Learning did back in 2008, only to then be bailed out by government? How are you better off if you live in a regional area and your local bank branch, hospital or public transport options are shut down because some cost-cutting corporate executive with suspenders 600 kilometres away in The Big Smoke decided those services just aren't profitable for shareholders anymore?

Or take private health insurance. In the years after Fraser made Medibank optional in the late 70s, more than half of all Australians had private health cover. Then the Hawke government introduced the 'universal' public insurer Medicare in 1984, and over the next thirteen years, the proportion of people choosing private coverage dropped to a third, because most people will trust the public sector over massive private health funds to look after them when they're ill, because they're not idiots.[22]

---

22 It is nice that we have Medicare and everything, but it can't genuinely be called 'universal', because it still costs a lot of people a lot of money to access healthcare, which they need, because they're alive. Thanks in part to Labor freezing the Medicare rebate in 2013, there is a large and growing 'gap' between what doctors are charging and what they're funded for, resulting in more out-of-pocket costs for ordinary people. As the system continues to be chronically underfunded, it's getting harder and harder for people to find doctors that actually bulk bill at all, and in 2021, 1.5 million Australians reported to the ABS that they had missed recommended medical specialist treatment due to cost.

Plus there's the fact that Medicare doesn't cover dentistry or mental health services (more than 3.7 million people avoided going to the dentist in 2021 because of costs), which is kind of crazy seeing as how last time I checked **TEETH AND BRAINS ARE DEFINITELY PARTS OF THE HUMAN BODY.**

Free-market loons like John Howard hated this system, of course, and when he came to power, he tried everything he could to reverse the trend and push as many of us back into the arms of private insurers as possible. He introduced a surcharge to the Medicare levy, which actively encouraged rich people to leave the public health system and go enjoy rich medicine in the rich hospitals for rich people, and he offered billions of dollars in subsidies to the private health industry. He also created the 'Lifetime Health Cover' policy, which effectively penalises you for every year you don't have private health insurance once you turn 30, and blackmails young people into signing up to a private system in which premiums for shit policies get more expensive every year, while private health funds make billions in profit, all just so we can avoid going bankrupt when we get sick.

But not only is it generally evil, **ruthless private health insurance isn't even more 'efficient'.**[23] In the public Medicare system – backed up by the State's vast resources and expertise, with no profit motive – 94 cents of every dollar is spent on actual medical services. In private health insurance – thanks to 'administration fees', advertising, the need for profit, etc. – it's 84 cents. Our private health industry isn't exactly 'easing the burden' on the public health system, either; our public health systems are more crowded and underfunded than ever, and some private hospitals have been found to be specifically focussing on treating patients with more straightforward medical conditions (i.e. cheaper ones) and leaving more complicated (and expensive) cases to the public system, thereby putting public hospitals under greater strain and increasing wait times even further. I regret to inform you that this tactic is known as **'cream-skimming'**, which is a term

---

23 You'll know this if you've ever had to navigate your way through an increasingly complex world of different private funds and plans and premiums and exclusions and excesses and then for some reason you have to consult a fucking meerkat.

that makes me want to vomit, but I'm worried that won't be covered by my private health insurance.

CUTTING CORNERS

Sometimes, **private capital's obsession with 'efficiency'** *is the fucking problem*. Privatised companies' drive to make as much money as possible out of everything has led to shoddy work, gas explosions, prison riots, water contaminations and lethal fires, and there are now multiple formerly-privatised hospitals across this country that had to be reverted to public ownership because the market could only deliver poor service, high costs, and crappy working conditions.

Just look at the national shame job that is our aged care sector. Since the Howard government further privatised, deregulated and marketised the sector in the late 90s, private operators have consistently prioritised making bank over providing quality care and dignity for the elderly. Giant companies like Bupa and Opal Aged Care receive hundreds of millions of dollars in public funding to spend at their discretion, and as long as they meet the sector's lax and often unenforced accreditation standards, any unspent money can be kept as profit. Government funding for aged care is on a per resident basis, creating an incentive for companies to jam-pack a facility with as many residents as possible, while at the same time reducing staffing hours and cutting costs on food and medical supplies. Successive pro-market governments have decided that legally requiring 'nursing homes' to have actual registered nurses on duty would be super inefficient, so they've just become 'residential aged care facilities' that don't necessarily have a trained nurse on hand. Instead, cheaper, less qualified and more insecure workers have been employed to attend to the needs of frail dementia patients, who might not be stoked about the high turnover of strangers coming into their home and helping them with some very intimate activities. It's way more *efficient* to have fewer staff working at any one time, of course, even if that means those staff are expected to get an elderly person up, out of bed and showered within six minutes, which I struggle to do every morning, and I'm 33.

It's these efficiencies that have been resulting in widespread, sickening neglect across the sector for decades. The first major national scandal broke in the year

2000, when nurses at Victoria's for-profit Riverside Nursing Home were found to have given 57 aged residents diluted kerosene baths as a cheaper alternative in the treatment of scabies. Some residents suffered second-degree burns as a result, and one 84-year-old woman died two days after receiving the treatment. This wasn't Riverside's first controversy, either; previous investigations of the facility had reported cases of weevils being found in residents' cereal, bedpans being washed in buckets by staff without gloves and maggots being found in a patient's wound.

Twenty years later, **almost half of Australia's aged care homes are run for-profit**. We have turned caring for the elderly into a multibillion-dollar industry featuring some of the country's biggest corporations and some extremely shonky small-time operators. (In 2021, *The Sunday Age* reported that Gerry and Chris Apostolatos were involved with the private aged care company Chronos Care and had played secret roles in the company's acquisition of two Melbourne aged care homes. The brothers were previously commercial poultry farmers, but were both banned from the industry for 17 years in 2015 after they starved more than a million chickens to death.)

Both Labor and Liberal governments have continued to accept donations from private providers and sat back and watched the market forces work their magic. Despite numerous inquiries and reviews and exposés and public outcry, these corporate people-farms continue to cash in; the recent Royal Commission into Aged Care Quality and Safety found that as many as **one in three people living in Australian aged care experience neglect, physical or emotional abuse**. The Commission heard horrifying stories of grandmas and grandpas being chemically restrained, served inedible slop for food, slapped because they 'weren't getting dressed fast enough', financially abused and left to sit for hours in their own urine and faeces. In one case, a 95-year-old resident at for-profit home Epping Gardens was yelled at so badly by a staff member she 'retreated to her room and vomited violently'.

In contrast, the Commission was presented with overwhelming evidence that highly regulated government-run aged care providers outperform both non-profit and for-profit providers on almost every indicator. Residents in privately run homes were four times more likely to be hospitalised for weight loss or malnutrition than those in government-run aged care, and five times more likely to register a complaint about the home's cleanliness or safety.

'The aged care system has suffered from sequential attempts by governments to define it as a market in its own right,' the Commission's final report reads, 'which can and should behave like any other market in our economy.'

And yet, it seems, that suffering is just going to continue, because pretty much no one in the political class is prepared to say that **there are some areas in which profit-making is very bad.**

'So are you saying there should be no profit-making in aged care?' David Speers asked then-Shadow Minister for Government Services Bill Shorten on *Insiders* in 2020. Shorten had come on to discuss the crisis in the sector, and had suggested that it simply wasn't possible to 'serve two masters' of profit and care at the same time.

'I'm saying that we need to put people before profit,' Shorten replied. 'I'm saying that if you can make a profit, that's good. But the problem is here, that we're seeing profit being made but people not getting looked after.'

'But when you just said, "You can't serve two masters" –'

'You've got to make a choice,' said Shorten. 'In a beauty parade, you've got to make a choice who you want and I want us to look after our elderly Australians.'

Speers tried again. 'But you're not saying there's *no* place for profit?'

'. . . no.'

There you have it, folks: in a hypothetical beauty parade in which the competing contestants are 'profit' and 'caring for our elderly', Bill Shorten would definitely choose 'caring for our elderly'. But *also* making a profit is 'good'. You can't serve two masters, but you can sort of try to make those two masters team up and work together towards a common goal, even though the masters have diametrically opposed interests, and the past two decades have made it painfully clear that that 100% does not – and cannot – work.

---

bUt It'S gOoD bEcAuSe iNnOvAtIoN

When it's not cream-skimming the sick or keeping Nanna in a cage, apparently privatisation is busy unlocking public services' creative potential. Without the profit motive and competition driving every single decision an organisation makes, how will it ever come up with fresh new thinking and become its best self?

Certainly, private businesses are innovating all the time. Apple, for example, has brought us the Apple Watch, which is kind of like a phone, except it's a watch.[24] Not even a raving Lefty like me could deny that the wild chaos of capitalist markets can and does often produce cheaper products and services for us to enjoy (as long as you can afford to pay for them).

But that doesn't mean private enterprise has a monopoly on coming up with new ideas. Don't listen to the Right's slander – the truth is that public sector and state-owned businesses have been innovating their butts off for centuries, funding and creating things like the microchip, space travel, penicillin, the internet, renewable energy, barcodes and the Google algorithm. The Soviet Union made groundbreaking discoveries in satellite, spacesuit and LED technology, while Japanese National Railways pioneered the Shinkansen 'bullet train' when it was a fully state-owned company. Cuba's publicly owned health and medical research system has seen it become the first country in the world to eliminate mother-to-child transmission of HIV and syphilis and develop a vaccine for lung cancer. Under public ownership, Qantas became the second round-the-world airline on the planet, effectively invented business class and helped make the first inflatable escape slide raft.[25] The Commonwealth Serum Laboratories (now privatised as CSL Ltd) was established in 1916, and for more than 70 years it developed and provided life-saving vaccines, sera and antivenoms to the Australian public, often for free, while public institutions

---

24 For the record, Apple received substantial amounts of US government funding when it started out, and key features of the iPhone like touchscreen and GPS began their lives in the public sector.

25 Qantas was still government-owned in 1988, when the film *Rain Man* was released, featuring Dustin Hoffman's autistic Raymond character insisting that he was only prepared to fly Qantas because of its impeccable safety record.

In a hilariously bitchy move, embarrassed competing airlines would cut the key scene out of the film when they played it on their inflight entertainment.

like the CSIRO, our universities and libraries are constantly helping to expand human knowledge and keep up with international best practice. Just because you're not run for profit, doesn't mean you're not ahead of the game; the ABC launched its ad-free catch-up streaming platform iView in 2008, putting it way ahead of the commercial networks. Channel Ten didn't launch 10Play until 2013, and even then, it was shithouse, and remains shithouse to this very day.[26]

---

26 The privatisation of the ABC is a long-held dream of all the Right-wing Sky News gremlins, IPA turds and Coalition hacks. In 2018, the Liberal Party's Federal Council passed a motion from the Young Liberals calling for the 'full privatisation of the Australian Broadcasting Corporation, except for services into regional areas'; Young Libs Vice President Mitch Collier even told the Council that the broadcaster shouldn't remain in public hands because of 'blind sentimentality' and dismissed *Play School* as 'rubbish', which is hate speech.

Of course, no matter how efficient and professional the organisation might try to present itself as ('We only cost 4 cents a day! Please be nice to us!'), no matter how many lives it might save through its emergency broadcasting, no matter how much valuable journalism it produces or how many Gold Logies it might take home, the ABC will always be resented and despised by those with an unshakable ideological belief that *government simply should not do anything that can be done by the private sector*. Sure, they hate all of its Marxist and non-binary content, too, but it goes deeper: **they hate its very existence**.

Thankfully, selling Aunty off is still way too politically toxic, because the overwhelming majority of Australians – including a majority of Coalition voters – trust and value their public broadcaster. Instead, conservatives have just tried to attack, stack and starve the ABC as much as they can; according to progressive think tank Per Capita's *It's Our ABC* report, its operational funding is almost 30% lower today than it was in 1985.

In response, Aunty has been forced to shed hundreds of jobs, slash budgets, cancel journalist cadetships and often pull its punches for fear of political blowback, and is generally left with the task of creating awesome content with no money that everybody has to love (but doesn't compete with commercial media) and doing journalism that fearlessly holds to account the same people who control its budget and don't think it should exist.

Don't get me wrong: #TheirABC isn't perfect. It's given me a job on several occasions, and for that alone some heads should roll. But generally speaking, **it's a very very good thing to have**. I love the ABC, and SBS too. I fiercely believe that strong, dynamic and independent public broadcasters are vital, particularly when we have one of the most concentrated media markets in the world, and that market is concentrated in the reptilian hands of Rupert Murdoch. It's crucial that we have a fearless news service that doesn't defer to commercial interests and doesn't have its nightly bulletin breaking 'news' about Coles' latest discounts on honey and soy chicken kebabs.

The ABC is one of the few remaining places in the public square where everyone – young and old, rich and poor, Black and white, city and country and yes, even Left and Right – can go to be informed, educated and entertained for free, without being bombarded with ads for Dodo or Sportsbet. It's been delivering world-class children's programming for more than 50 years ad-free, and quite frankly the idea of future Aussie kids having to watch episodes of *Play School* or *Bluey* that are brought to them by KFC makes me want to scream and jump out the Round Window.

In fact, the privatisation wave has, in many cases, **actively sent us backwards.** Just before Jeff Kennett sold off Victoria's energy grid in the early 90s, the State Electricity Commission had published a discussion paper on ways to address the climate crisis, including the promotion of energy efficiency and the use of renewable energy – only to see those plans shelved by its new corporate owners, who probably considered them boring expensive nerd shit. State and federal governments chose to turn to the exciting innovation and expertise of the private sector during the pandemic, and that choice delivered us the COVIDSafe app (which failed to identify a single positive case in Victoria, a state where you could barely fucking move for all the coronavirus whizzing about the place) and contact tracing systems composed of private laboratories and poorly trained call centre staff, who used pens, paper and fax machines to record and communicate test results, much like your aunty would do.[27]

Or there's the mongrelised, sloth-like joke of our National Broadband Network. When John Howard sold off Telstra, he sold off the Australian government's capacity to design and build major communications infrastructure. When Telstra later refused to build an NBN for internet services because it might hurt their bottom line, the Rudd government had to start again from scratch, and set up NBN Co. – a government-owned corporation tasked with building a super-fast, national, end-to-end, Fibre-To-The-Premises network to bring Australia into the internet

---

27 While the Liberal NSW government conducted its coronavirus contact tracing and quarantine regime in-house with public servants, Labor's 'Socialist' Victoria spent more than $115 million contracting out COVID-related work to private businesses. The Andrews government even awarded a $4.2 million contact tracing contract to IBM, a company with a proud history of exciting public-private partnerships, particularly in Germany circa the 1930s.

age.[28] This Big Government project was viciously attacked and undermined by Rupert Murdoch (whose pay-TV monopoly in Foxtel was and remains threatened by emerging internet streaming services) and the free-market-loving Coalition government of Mr Tony Abbott, who dismissed Labor's NBN as a 'video entertainment system' and instructed his Communications Minister and best friend ever Malcolm Turnbull to 'demolish' it. The Coalition came up with a cheaper version of the NBN – a Fibre-To-The-Node model that would continue to rely on the existing copper network and pay-TV cables, and would allow for more competition between private providers – which Abbott proudly endorsed by declaring, 'We are absolutely confident that 25 megs is going to be enough, more than enough, for the average household', displaying the same visionary 21st-century instincts that would later compel him to give a knighthood to a 94-year-old racist prince.

The end result of all that was our pathetic status quo. By the time 99% of the compromised NBN rollout was completed in July 2020, it cost more than Labor's original model, we had a slower average internet speed than Thailand, Romania and Madagascar, and complaints to the Telecommunications Industry Ombudsman had increased by over 200%. Our country is now home to the fourth-slowest internet speeds in the OECD.

'The NBN was a nation-building activity, not a money-making scheme,' telecommunications expert Paul Budde told the *Australian Financial Review* in 2019. 'The government went wrong by trying to make it a semi-commercial activity. **It would be impossible on a commercial basis.**'

---

28 Labor's original NBN was designed to be able to deliver speeds of up to 1 gigabyte per second. It was supposed to be completed by 2021 and would cost $45 billion – but that money would eventually be recouped by NBN Co.'s commercial activity and its eventual privatisation after completion. From the very start, the NBN was never intended to remain in public hands, because Labor.

Not turning a massive infrastructure project into a money-making exercise is a very cute idea, Paul. But we don't do things that way anymore. Instead of a properly funded, game-changing, publicly owned piece of national infrastructure that could equitably provide a vital utility to every human being on the continent for our collective good, we got an expensive and embarrassing turkey, and every night across the nation you can hear people screaming at the heavens in righteous frustration as we suffer through the stutters and shakes of endless buffering and the constant pinging of internet error messages, while executives at NBN Co. award themselves millions of dollars in bonuses for all their awesome work.

SUPER VILLAIN

Outside of its most direct failures, one of the more insidious consequences of privatisation is the way that it takes things that we should consider to be **universal, guaranteed social rights** and turns them into optional 'treats' that you may or may not receive, depending on how capitalism is feeling today. As the State handballs more and more responsibilities to the market, it shrinks the list of things that you and I can say we are *entitled* to, by virtue of the fact that we are citizens and goddamn human beings.

That's pretty much what's happened with Australia's **compulsory universal superannuation scheme**. Super is often hailed as a shining progressive achievement of Labor's Accord era, but that really ignores what it effectively boils down to: **a privatisation of the pension system**. While some countries have generous, (truly) universal old age pensions that are guaranteed to everyone when they retire, in Australia, our stingy, means-tested pension is considered a last-resort safety net, and we've once again turned to the market for better answers.

'The Treasurer [Joe Hockey] talks of ending the age of entitlement,' wrote Paul Keating for the ABC in 2014. 'I gave substance to that notion 30 years ago, when I first asked Australians to **provide for their own retirement** – to move beyond reliance on the age pension as the default anti-destitution measure.'

(Someone should probably tell Paul that 'Fuck you Joe Hockey I was hacking away at the social solidarity of the welfare state *before* it was cool!' is not quite the own that he thinks it is.)

Under Keating's privatised, individualised system, a decent retirement is not something you're entitled to, but something you really should have to provide for yourself, you lazy bugger. Ever since Keating legislated the **Super Guarantee** in 1992, bosses have been legally required to confiscate a chunk of your wage over your working life and put that cash into an accumulation account with the private capital super fund of your choice. The fund then hangs onto that cash, and invests some of it in the stock market and infrastructure projects and other things over time, so it can make financial returns and grow your balance. In theory, this means you'll have a big fat pool of savings to draw from during your wrinkly years, and you won't have to suck so much from the public teat. (As Keating put it, the super system was created to help 'save future generations from the budgetary stress' of having to pay for the country's ageing population in the form of a bigger welfare bill.)

So we've shifted the job of ensuring that old people aren't living in 'destitution' away from being **a collective duty** to **an individual responsibility,** and propped the whole thing up on the continuing health and wellbeing of capitalist markets. In the process, **we've created a monster**: superannuation assets are now worth more than $3 trillion (that's almost $1 trillion more than the value of everything on the Australian Stock Exchange), and they're expected to be worth around $10 trillion by 2040, which could certainly buy plenty of retired Boomers a shitload of resin jewellery and tickets to see James Taylor.

But, like most market-oriented systems, **super replicates and exacerbates inequality.** In a scheme that's based on lifetime earnings, low- and unfairly paid workers (including most women) and those who've experienced long periods of unemployment will end up with measly or $0 super balances, and they'll suffer shittier retirements as a result. Meanwhile, wealthy pricks are hoarding hundreds of millions of dollars in the Self-Managed Super Funds that they've been able to transform into tax shelters. Retail, for-profit super funds have been found to be ripping their members off with particularly exorbitant fees and slippery commissions, and *all* super funds – even the not-for-profit 'industry' funds – are strictly guided by their 'fiduciary duty' to accumulate as much cash as possible for their members, even if that means investing in weapons manufacturers, immigration detention centres, fossil fuel bastards or companies like Amazon and Uber, which basically means millions of workers' retirement savings are tied up with the flourishing of companies that regularly screw over their fellow workers and drive down conditions.

(Plus, thanks to super, when markets don't flourish at all but actually do one of their regular backflips and crash, **it's individual workers who are exposed to the risk**. In the wake of the GFC, Australia's pension system was the second-hardest hit in the world, with 21% of the superannuation savings pool – representing a market value of $270 billion – going bye-byes. Some workers were forced to postpone retirement or go back to work as a result, and some suffered mental breakdowns, depression and even suicide.)

Bizarrely, all the tax breaks embedded in the super system are now causing the Commonwealth some 'budgetary stress' of more than $41 billion every year. **The forgone revenue from these concessions is projected to exceed the total cost of the age pension by 2050**. Meanwhile, the age pension has consistently been undermined by cuts, a raised retirement age, tighter eligibility tests and general meanness; Australia spends just 3.5% of its GDP on the aged pension, when the OECD average is closer to 8%. The full pension rates for pensioner singles and couples both sit below the Henderson poverty line, and according to National Seniors Australia, **one in four Australian pensioners are living in poverty**.

For millions of vulnerable people, Keating's market-friendly approach to retirement income has guaranteed them sweet fuck all, and it's hacked away at our sense of what we can rightfully expect from the State and society. The government's 2020 Retirement Income Review found that according to various surveys, **less than half of the Australian population – and less than 40% of people aged under 55 – think that the age pension will still exist when they reach retirement**. Out of fear of spending their final years eating cat food in the cold, many of these people hoard as much money in their super accounts as they can, and end up barely even touching it by the time they pass away.

Things might have gone a different way for Australia. We could have accepted the fact that paying for generous, universal pensions for the elderly is not a 'burden', but the duty of a civilised society, or we could have constructed super in a more collective, less market-y fashion. The idea of a national, publicly owned superannuation scheme was rejected by conservative Australian governments in 1928, 1938 and 1976, and by the Hawke government in 1989, which at that point was committed to the 'twin pillars' system of pension and private super funds. We could now be the proud owners of a single, big-ass, democratically accountable national investment pension fund like Norway, with lower fees, lower risk and better returns (thanks to no duplication of effort from multiple funds, no advertising bullshit and economies of scale).

But that wasn't part of the Keating vision.

'If you look at the Norwegian fund or the Dutch fund . . . your wages are levied at a certain amount,' he told the ABC's *7:30* in 2021. 'It goes into a national fund. The fund is managed by the government and you get a pension from it. I didn't want that. What I wanted was [that] you got your pension from it, but you own the capital.'

And that's what he got — rather inconveniently entangling trade unions, workers, retirees and trillions of dollars in wages up in the capitalist machine along the way.

CUI BONO?

In sum, privatisation has been a catastrophe for our infrastructure, services, people and the social contract. It's a real shame.

On the upside, **it's worked out brilliantly for the ruling class.** Selling off national icons was supposed to turn us into a 'shareholder democracy', but today, the largest shareholders of Telstra, Qantas, CSL, and the Commonwealth Bank are multinational hedge funds like BlackRock Inc. and The Vanguard Group, AKA the bloodthirsty colossi of global finance. Privatisation has stolen public wealth and transferred it to the private clutches of these shareholders, while simultaneously enriching multimillionaire Stonecutter CEOs like Alan Joyce, CommBank's Matt Comyn, Telstra's Andy Penn and the owners of Serco and Chevron. The CEO of CSL, Paul Perrault, is one of Australia's highest paid CEOs, with realised annual pay of more than $58 million, which, as you know, is far too much money for anyone to be paid for doing anything.[29]

The corporate behemoths that have been birthed from privatisation's pillaging of the public sector turn out to be just as evil as all the other corporate behemoths. They're always telling us about how they love serving the 'national interest', but that's balderdash: **they're first and foremost serving the interests of their shareholders.** Qantas is the 'national carrier' bursting with the 'Spirit of Australia', but Alan Joyce hates the idea of government-owned airlines and has campaigned hard against the foreign ownership laws that require Qantas to be majority Australian owned. Commonwealth Serum Laboratories was created to help Australia independently manufacture vital medicines for the public good, but when it was privatised in '94 its Chief Executive made its new mission clear: 'All our business activities will continue to be consistent with CSL's key objective – the growth of shareholder wealth'.[30] CSL has since stopped producing certain vaccines and antivenoms because they're 'unprofitable', and in 2014 it chose to build a new plant in Switzerland because Australia's tax arrangements weren't 'competitive' (i.e. low) enough. But their grift continues, of course, because we want and need medicines; at the end of 2020, the Australian government agreed to pay a subsidiary of CSL nearly $1 billion over the next ten years to produce a number of pharmaceutical products that were developed when the Laboratories were publicly owned.

---

29 Governments, meanwhile, have happily opted for privatisation because they're cowards. Rather than consider raising taxes on big business and the wealthy, plenty of politicians are happy to put the kitchen sink on eBay and collect the windfall so they can do what they think is the most important thing in the world: pay down debt and balance the budget.

   (In the case of the Howard government, they mainly did this so they could cut taxes for, wouldn'tyaknowit, big business and the wealthy. More on this in our next chapter.)

30 They've been extremely good at this. Keating sold it for about half a billion dollars in today's money, and the company now enjoys a market capitalisation of $140 billion.

These supposed patriots are also extremely bad at doing their national duty in paying their fucking taxes. In the four years to 2018 – as power prices continued to climb across the country – EnergyAustralia (whose parent company is incorporated in the tax haven of the British Virgin Islands) recorded a total income of $30.2 billion, and paid exactly $0 to the ATO. Transurban has grown so big over the years it now effectively holds a monopoly over the country's toll roads in Melbourne, Sydney and Brisbane, but thanks to complicated trust structures, in the five years to 2020, it brought in $11 billion in revenue and managed to pay zilch in company tax.

Strangely, such ATO-dodging dicks always seem to be able to find some cash to hand out to the people running the country. These are not 'neutral players' in Australia's political life. Origin Energy and Transurban regularly donate heaps of money to both sides of politics, as do the big consultancy firms like KPMG, EY, PriceWaterhouseCoopers and Deloitte, who (coincidentally) receive multimillion-dollar contracts as governments increasingly outsource the work of the public sector. The privatised employment services industry is terrible at helping unemployed people find jobs, but it's great at sucking up billions of dollars in public money and creating super-rich CEOs like Sarina Rosso, who has donated tens of thousands of dollars to the Coalition over the years while her job agency business has been 'winning' hundred-million-dollar contracts.

When capital wins this hard, **labour inevitably loses**. During the big sell-offs in the early 90s, the public sector share of employment across the country fell by more than 5%, which meant the loss of not just some jobs, but *good jobs*. Thanks to the overriding collective mission of public service and its greater union density, the public sector has always averaged better pay and conditions, which makes public sector jobs a fucking hassle for those at the top. As soon as public services and government-owned businesses are privatised, new private bosses are quick to liquidate jobs, cut conditions and outsource and casualise labour as much as they can. Telstra has cut thousands of jobs in Australia, automating them or offshoring them to call centres in the Philippines and India, where workers are treated to shit wages and regular racist abuse from your uncle who just wants to top up the bloody credit on his pre-paid flip-phone and speak to someone who speaks bloody English for fuck's sake. Privatised Qantas has gone to war on the transport workers' unions over the years, using labour hire companies, freezing wages and threatening to bring in scab workers during industrial disputes, while Centrelink has outsourced thousands of call centre jobs to companies like Serco, who pay and train their workers poorly, leaving them ill-prepared to deal with the calls they'll inevitably be receiving from all the people who have become unemployed because they got fired because of all the fucking privatisation.

In total, this rort is a massive cash cow for the rich and helps to smash workers' power. It really is a capitalist's wet dream, and it's no wonder that the private sector wants more of it, please. In a submission to a government panel in 1995, Serco Australia argued that 'all government services can be delivered by contractors, even if the services are of a social nature and involve activities which are hard to specify in empirical terms', and suggested governments should consider privatising services in everything from health to education to social services to tax collection and justice. Many of these wishes have since been granted. The rollout of the National Disability Insurance Scheme has seen state governments hand over the responsibility of hundreds of disability services to the private sector. After Medibank Private was fully privatised in 2014, its services arm Medibank Health Solutions carried on running the national sexual assault and domestic violence helpline 1800 RESPECT, effectively turning a profit from the provision of rape counselling. Over the years, everything from the administration of veterans' affairs to the conducting of local government elections has been outsourced to private actors; we've even put control of our water supply in the hands of private and foreign interests by selling and trading water licences, while statutory bodies like Infrastructure Australia have called for the privatisation of state-owned water utilities.

If the ruling class has its way, it's highly likely there'll be more of this trash to look forward to. In 2016, the Productivity Commission called on Australian governments to consider introducing more 'competition' to the provision of social housing, public hospital services, public dental services, services in remote Aboriginal communities and even palliative care. No matter if you're poor, sick, Black or dying, it seems, The Market is always ready to help.

OI GIVE US IT BACK YA DOGS

Back in 2005, the Howard government was all set to sell off the Snowy Hydro Scheme. The historic piece of national infrastructure had been corporatised in 2002, and now, with the support of the Victorian and NSW Labor state governments and the Federal opposition, Howard was ready to privatise the entire thing.

Unfortunately for him, most people thought this was an extremely shit idea. Even after 15 years of being told by politicians and economists that privatisation made everything better and was good for you so stop complaining, the Australian public drew a line. Farmer groups and concerned citizens from across the political divide let their MPs know that despite the fire sale of public assets that had been going on lately, they would not stand to see the Snowy go, too.

'I've been surprised by the level of public disquiet – it's turned out to be much greater than I expected,' Howard told reporters as his government announced that the sale wouldn't be going ahead. 'For whatever combination of reasons, there is over-whelming feeling in the community that the Snowy is an icon.'

No shit, Sherlock.

This backdown in the face of democratic outcry enraged the voices of capital. One stock analyst told the *Sydney Morning Herald* that the backflip meant that Australia had become 'a laughing stock on the international stage' and '[w]hat this shows is that the government is standing in the way of commerce'. Similarly, in 2019, when Labor announced its policy to limit the increase of private health insurance premiums, the chief executive of health fund nib, Mark Fitzgibbon, decried it as 'absurd'.

'[It] may be politically popular but it's an affront to how the free market operates,' he said. 'What next? [Price limits on] food, clothing, car insurance, school fees and petrol?'[31]

These people just don't get it. Their wallets are full, their brains broken. They simply can't comprehend that privatisation **is despised by the very public that it constantly rips off**. Essential Polling has been tracking this issue for years, and the results have been consistent: more than 70% of Australians think that 'privatisation mainly benefits the corporate sector', 'utilities like water and power suppliers are too important to be sold off' and 'prices always increase more when services are privatised'. One Essential survey from 2011 found that 74% of Australians opposed privatising Medicare, and there was even substantial majority support for the public buying back Qantas, Telstra and the Commonwealth Bank. People can clearly see and regularly suffer from privatisation's failures, and we don't want any more of it, thank you, even if

---

31 Yes please, cheers.

that means 'standing in the way of commerce' to prevent our entire society being handed over to greedy oligarchs.[32]

Now to be clear, **I can to some degree appreciate the view which says 'government sucks'.** As someone who has had to renew a driver's licence, tried to use the MyGov website, visited the post office, worked for a public broadcaster and watched the news for the past 15 years, I would never suggest that the government and the public sector are perfect and consistently nailing it in all areas. There are millions of ways that government services, bureaucracies and publicly owned bodies could be improved, updated and made more democratically accountable – probably by being de-corporatised and properly funded, for a start.

But the claims that government is always, inherently and irredeemably inefficient and bad – and the only possible way to fix it is to sell off as much of it as possible – **is an evil lie.** The ruling class has repeated that lie for forty years now, and they still refuse to reckon with the result: a seriously weakened society that rips people off and doesn't work very well, and the transfer of enormous wealth and power from public hands – from *our* hands – to unelected and largely unaccountable private interests. That's the society that's been delivered to Millennials and Zoomers, and by this point we're like 'Thanks, I hate it'.

If you ask me (and by getting this book you basically have), **the privatisation, marketisation and outsourcing of everything around us has to end.** Most of it should be reversed, immediately. Give us our stuff back. Providing care and dignity for our elderly, for people living with disabilities and for our kids shouldn't be a money-making exercise. Crucial national infrastructure – electricity, gas, water, the Snowy, roads, public

---

32 More recently, the ABC's *Australia Talks* survey for 2019 found that **90% of people in this country agree that 'Big businesses care more about profit than they do about what's best for Australia'** – and that included 82% of Liberal voters. Solidarity, Tory comrades!

transport and the NBN – should be in public hands. No one should be incentivised to leave our universal public health-care system, and Medicare should cover **all** healthcare, for everyone, everywhere, always. We deserve a reliable, not-for-profit public bank that wants to help you manage your money, not feast on your blood. Public services should be carried out by public servants, and the ABC and SBS should be publicly owned and well-funded enough to keep taking risks on Tom Ballard-based projects until I reach retirement.[33]

Championing public ownership and resisting the menace of privatisation isn't easy, as Ben Chifley or Salvador Allende or millions of unionists will tell you. When socialist French President François Mitterrand nationalised major industrial groups, defence manufacturers and thirty-six banks in the early 1980s, big business screamed and went on a **capital strike,** pulling billions of dollars of investment out of the country, prompting an economic crisis. The Swedish social democrat Olof Palme pushed back against the power of capital and fought for a strong and growing public sector during his time as prime minister, and in 1986 he was assassinated for his trouble. And yes, a huge amount would have to change for Australia to look anything like a social democratic country like Norway, where the State owns 74 companies which account for nearly 60% of GDP, and employs 30% of the nation's workforce (our public sector makes up just 15% of workers).

But what's the alternative? Continue to allow the vampires at the top to keep pinching all of our stuff? Stand back and watch as our future is determined by the whims of the market forever? Keep selling everything we have until there's nothing left?

Fuck that. We need to call off the auction. Now.

---

33 Also, in the interests of public safety, Twitter should be nationalised and permanently shut down, and we should all go outside.

5

The Wealthening

'Let me tell you about the very rich. They are
different from you and me.'
— F. Scott Fitzgerald, *The Rich Boy*, 1926

'The only way that I can see to deploy this much financial
resource is by converting my Amazon winnings into space travel.'
— Amazon CEO Jeff Bezos, 2018

March 2020 was chaos. This mysterious, lethal virus was changing everything; economies were being locked down, and our freedoms and plans were disappearing all around us. We were an anxious nation, yearning for some leadership and some hope in these dark, uncertain times.

So *60 Minutes* interviewed Gerry Harvey.

'This is an opportunity!' gurgled the octogenarian billionaire retailer. 'Our sales are up in Harvey Norman in Australia by 9% on last year. Our sales in freezers are up 300%. And what about air purifiers? Up 100%!'

This was great to hear. The pandemic wasn't *all* bad news; sure, thousands were dying and millions were being fired, but at least Gerry was still able to sell a bunch of shit to scared people doing frantic retail therapy in lockdown.

By the end of the year, the explosion in online sales (and the bonus of $22 million in JobKeeper wage subsidies) saw Harvey Norman profits double to over $462 million. Gerry Harvey reaped $70 million in dividends, his personal wealth blossomed by 24% and, quite frankly, hearing that makes me just want to plug in my Harvey Norman Sunbeam Tribeca 4-Slice Toaster, hug it to my chest and leap straight into the bath.

The world's 2,600+ billionaires have found these pandemic years to be a time of great dynamism and growth. After an initial stock market collapse wiped out a bunch of their cash, the global shift to online living, cheap credit, massive government stimulus and surging commodity prices ensured that these plutocrats were able to quickly get back on their feet and go Super Saiyan mode. By the end of 2020, their collective wealth had grown by almost US$2 trillion, and by March 2021 twenty new 'pandemic billionaires' had emerged in Asia. Jeff Bezos became US$13 billion richer over the course of a single day. In July 2020, his ex-wife MacKenzie Scott announced that she had donated US$1.7 billion to various charities on a Tuesday; by the Friday, her Amazon shares had surged by so much, their value had more than replaced what she'd given away.

The World Bank estimates that COVID-19 has pushed more than 160 million people into poverty, but the super-rich refused to let any of that bum them out or stop them from living their best lives. During the worst of 2020, entertainment mogul David Geffen shared an image on Instagram of his $590 million superyacht (complete with wine cellar and basketball court) with the caption 'isolated in the Grenadines avoiding the virus'; Kylie Jenner let us know she bought her two-year-old daughter a pony named 'Frozen' for just $200,000 (plus shipping); and Kanye West had a very normal one by self-funding his run for President, declaring that if he was elected, he would run his White House on the governance structures of Wakanda, which is a country that doesn't exist.[1]

Not even the coronavirus itself could defeat these pricks. COVID managed to gain VIP access to the bodies of many members of the global ruling class, including Boris Johnson, Jair Bolsonaro, Hillary Clinton, mining billionaire Andrew 'Twiggy' Forrest, Prince Charles, Donald Trump and P!nk, but sadly, they all made a full recovery. They received the best available medical care and were showered with sympathy and prayers, and any hope of Comrade Corona wiping out the planet's elites like an international microscopic guillotine were dashed.

Even when our society is completely turned upside down in a generation-defining crisis, it seems, the same rules apply: **the system is rigged to make the rich even richer, no matter what.**

RICH THEM, POOR US

Millennials have come of age at a time of gobsmacking, mind-blowing, mega-X-treme inequality. Extraordinary levels of wealth are concentrated in the hands of a tiny few. You've probably heard some version of the stats before: **the top 1% owns more than the bottom 99% and it's all 100% fucked.**

In their 2021 Wealth Report, property consultants Knight Frank found the earth is now contaminated with more than 610,500 'Ultra-High Net Worth Individuals' – that is, people with assets of more than US$30 million. Squatting at the top of this group is the global billionaire class, whose collective wealth is now around US$13.5 trillion, which means they own more than 4.6 billion of their fellow human beings. According to Oxfam, **the ten richest men in the world alone own more than two-thirds of humanity.**

---

1 Yeezy received just 0.04% of the national vote on election day. He immediately tweeted 'Kanye 2024', which is pretty baller.

Most of these oligarchs own, run and profit from the gargantuan corporations that now dominate the global economy. Big Business has used its Bigness to make itself ever Bigger; as profit sheets and asset portfolios have fattened, they've thrown off the shackles of regulation, reduced competition with various mergers and hostile takeovers, and formed a bunch of duopolies and monopolies and monopsonies and now, **70 of the world's 100 biggest economies are corporations, not countries.**[2] In 2018, the Commonwealth Government of Australia raised less revenue than Walmart, which is quite embarrassing. If current trends continue, it's easy to imagine a day when Amazon or Apple or Samsung are recognised as sovereign nation states, and we'll have no choice but to give them seats at the UN and let them compete in the Olympics.

We're told that Australia is The Fair Dinkum Lucky Country & Official Home of The Fair Go Pty Ltd ®, but it's absolutely not. **Here, the top 1% owns more wealth than the bottom 70% of the country combined.** According to the *Australian Financial Review*'s Rich List, the number of Australian billionaires has more than doubled from 49 in 2015 to 137 today, and during the pandemic years these buggers have seen their collective wealth double, too. At the executive level, millionaire CEOs like Qantas' Alan Joyce and Woolworth's Brad Banducci are paid more than 125 times the median Australian worker's salary, even though there's no way they work 125 times harder than their baggage handlers and shelf-stacking workers who are exploited for profit.[3]

---

2   The US Institute for Policy Studies says the majority balance tipped in corporations' favour for the first time in the year 2000. They've only been growing their majority ever since.

3   In 2022 we learned that the co-CEOs and co-founders of Afterpay, Anthony Eisen and Nick Molnar, received a combined $264.2 million in realised pay, which is about 2,800 times the average full-time wage.

Big Capital dominates the Aussie economy, too. In 1960, family-run and small businesses made up more than quarter of national income, but today their share has dwindled to less than 9%. We live in one of the most monopolised countries in the world; the biggest four firms in Australian retail, newspapers, banks, health insurance, domestic airlines and internet provision hold 80% market share.

Meanwhile, more than 3.2 million Australians are living in poverty. That's one in eight Australian adults and one in six kids skipping meals, facing housing stress, and missing out on the security, education and healthcare they need, as the richest ten Aussies sit on $219 billion between them and air purifier sales are up 100% and Gerry Harvey is in his mansion, rubbing honey all over himself and rolling around in a pile of money so that the money sticks to his sticky, golden body, laughing maniacally.

RICH PEOPLE ARE NOT SENDING THEIR BEST

We're regularly assured by corporate media, business leaders and politicians that the one-percenters are products of our glorious meritocracy. We should all worship them, for they are impressive brain geniuses who take risks and create jobs and wealth and do innovation. Truly, they are the best of us.

These rave reviews are hard to reconcile with **the scientific fact that many of these people are cunts**. Yes, they may be highly intelligent, industrious or even personable and charming cunts, but they are cunts nevertheless, and their ridiculous levels of wealth clearly make them crazy, which therefore makes them crazy cunts. Polite society and the media lavish them with praise and deference, and we're all supposed to listen and clap as these arseholes never stop banging on about how they're going to disrupt death or clone the Moon or whatever.

Here's a short list of the most egregious of these cunts, and some ideas about how we might deal with them:

RICH CUNT	NET WORTH	WORST QUOTE	PUNISHMENT?
KIM KARDASHIAN (famous lady?)	~ US$1.8 billion	*'I rented my mom a monkey for the week because she had a syndrome where she missed children in the house.'* On *The Late Show with David Letterman*, 2009. I don't know the context, and I'm okay with that.	• Getting back together with Pete Davidson • Having to watch my sex tape
CLIVE PALMER (mining & graphic design)	~ US$2 billion	*'The spirit of Rose and Jack, Romeo and Juliet, lives in all of us.'* Palmer in a video released in 2018, trying to keep people excited about his plans to build Titanic II, a $500 million replica of the notoriously successful original boat. Titanic II was announced in 2012, but is yet to exist.	• Being eaten by an animatronic dinosaur • Forced to travel on the Titanic II but in steerage • Stairs
JAMES PACKER (casino magnate)	~ US$3.7 billion	*'Whoever dies with the most toys wins.'* Believed to be James' motto for life. This is also what a greedy child in a Roald Dahl novel would say.	• Ocean's 11-style heist of all his money • A mirror
JACK MA (Alibaba co-founder)	~ US$23 billion	*'I personally think that 996 is a huge blessing.'* Ma in 2019, endorsing the e-commerce overtime work schedule of 9 am to 9 pm, six days a week.	• Being #blessed by working 247 • Having to do a corporate comedy set at a union Christmas party
GINA RINEHART (iron ore-ligarch)	~ US$29 billion	*'Is our future threatened with massive debts run up by political hacks / Who dig themselves out by unleashing rampant tax?'* From Gina's poem, 'Our Future'.	• Hanging out with Barnaby Joyce

RICH CUNT	NET WORTH	WORST QUOTE	PUNISHMENT?
BILL GATES (MS Paint)	~ US$113 billion	*'Of course, I have as much power as the president has.'* According to *Wired* magazine, Gates said this during a dinner party conversation about Bill Clinton in 1993. He tried to pass it off as a joke, but it wasn't a joke.	• Spending eternity trapped in a room, having to use Microsoft Teams
JEFF BEZOS (Amazonian)	~ US$163 billion	*'If we're out in the solar system, we can have a trillion humans in the solar system, which means we'd have a thousand Mozarts and a thousand Einsteins.'* Bezos in 2019, describing his vision of future Elysium-like space colonies, packed with thousands of geniuses (all of them working on zero-hour contracts).	• Immediate liquification • Being fed to sharks with frickin' laser beams on their heads
ELON MUSK (Tesla CEO, SpaceX founder, leading cunt)	~ US$260 billion (i.e. more than the GDP of New Zealand or Vietnam)	*'The coronavirus panic is dumb . . . based on current trends, probably close to zero new cases in US too by end of April.'* Tweeted March 2020. (By the end of April, the number of confirmed US cases had risen past one million, including the deaths of 58,000 Americans.)	• Getting strapped to a rocket by his (unionised) employees and being blasted in the general direction of Mars • Going to Tesla jail, where he has to serve a decades-long sentence alongside all the Tesla cars that have killed people

GILDED AGE 2.0

Humans have been divided into The Haves and The Have-Nots throughout history. But the massive disparity between the rich and poor that we see today is *uniquely* shithouse, and represents a reversed trend. **In the post-war decades, inequality was falling across the developed world,** including in Australia. Our parents were born into a country in which there were certainly still wealthy elites, but the gap between them and the common man was the width of a river, not an ocean.

As we've already seen, everything really went to pot in the wake of the stagflation crisis. Since that time, the human race has increased its *overall* wealth, but we've been terrible at sharing it: **between 1980 and 2016, just 12 cents in every dollar of global income growth went to the poorest 50% of humanity.** The top 1% nabbed 27 cents from every dollar, which they probably then used to buy some members of the bottom half. A 2020 paper from the RAND Corporation found that if the level of income inequality in the US had remained constant since 1975, the median full-time American worker would be earning $42k a year *more* than they are today. This effectively amounts to a gigantic wealth transfer of $50 trillion from the hands of the American working class to the top 1% over the past 45 years, perhaps constituting the greatest *yoink!* in human history.

The yoinking hasn't been quite so bad here in Australia, but we've been trying our best. Since the mid-70s, while the incomes of the bottom tenth of Australian wage earners have increased by 15%, **the incomes of the rich have grown by almost two-thirds.** The rich are getting a bigger slice of the national pie; according to the World Inequality Database, the wealthiest 10% of the country were getting less than a quarter of national income 50 years ago, but today they're getting more than 30%.

We're regularly told that our free-market economic settings are super rad because since the recession period of the early 1990s, they've let us all enjoy '**three decades of uninterrupted growth!!!**'. But that doesn't give us the full picture: this growth hasn't brought us a fairer society. Even after the lucrative mining boom years, inequality has grown substantially worse: we've got more billionaires than ever, while our poverty levels have remained steady. (In fact, poverty in Australia actually shot *up* during the mining boom.) The rising tide of wealth simply isn't lifting all boats; according to ACOSS, between 2003 and 2016, the average wealth of the top fifth of Australians rose by more than 50%, as the real term wealth of the bottom fifth declined.

How the devil has this occurred? you ask, sitting in your dingy sharehouse, crying into your bowl of Maggi Noodles that you had to buy with Afterpay. *How in the living fuck have these greedy bastards managed to get away with hoarding such obscene levels of wealth?!*

It's a very fair question. In part, we already know the answers: this is the culmination of the capitalist nonsense we've covered so far in this book. The defeat of organised labour, the financialisation and commodification of housing, warping the provision of education into a user-pays model and the privatisation of everything everywhere has certainly helped to ensure that bosses, owners and investors can afford more lobsters than ever, while ordinary people just keep treading water, or are pushed further and further into debt.[4]

But what's been just as important is **The R Word.**

---

4   During those much-lauded decades of 'uninterrupted economic growth', Australia's level of private debt exploded, in no small part due to those blossoming house prices. In 1970, Australian households' debt as a percentage of their income was about 40%; that is, they owed less than half of what they earned each year. Today, that debt-to-income ratio is more than 180%.

(NO, NOT THAT ONE)
WE'RE TALKING
REDISTRIBUTION

As long as we're sticking with our current shitty economic arrangement of private ownership of the means of production, we should insist that the spoils of that production be shared fairly. Ideally, this is done mainly through workers' wages, but we've already seen how that system's been royally screwed by the ruling class in recent times.

The other alternative is the redistribution of wealth by the State, via collecting and spending taxes. This can help us work towards creating a vaguely functioning, non-feudal society, and should work to reduce the proliferation of uber-super-rich godkings. **This is a central part of the pitch of living in a 'market society':** we allow private enterprise to do its thing, but in exchange, the government gets a slice of the action and redistributes that wealth to make our lives better. In the interest of fairness, our income tax system is designed to be **progressive:** the more money you have, the more tax you're expected to pay, which makes total sense, because the rich can afford to pay more taxes because they have more money, because they're rich.

This used to be bog-standard common sense. Granted, in the first half of the 20th century, the introduction of taxation was mainly about redistributing wealth so we could go kill people overseas. At the time of Federation, the Commonwealth tax-to-GDP ratio was just 5%, but then Franz Ferdinand went and got himself shot, and a federal income tax was introduced to fund our efforts in World War I (a wonderful, noble war that was definitely worth getting involved in for the sake of proving our love and loyalty to King George V). By the end of World War II, federal tax revenue had reached

22% of GDP, although now it wasn't just funding the war machine, but also the growing modern welfare state in the form of widow pensions and unemployment benefits.[5]

The burden of paying those taxes fell most heavily on the wealthy, as is right and proper. In the early 1950s, **the top marginal tax rate was around 75% for Australians on annual incomes over £10,000** (about $425k today). Robert Menzies cut this down to 67% in 1955, but it stayed above 60% for the next quarter of a century. Our company tax rate was above 40% in 1940, and it stayed there for almost 50 years. This was very much the norm across Western capitalist societies; from the mid-1940s and throughout the 1950s and 60s, the top marginal tax rates for individuals in the US and the UK were above 90%.[6]

But then came the 70s and the end of the Keynesian consensus and the ensuing political and economic upheaval, which brought with it some radical new ideas about how wealth redistribution should work. It shouldn't really be determined by the *State* anymore, apparently, so much as by natural market forces. Big government just *got in the way*, you see, and it should keep its filthy, taxing hands to itself, because that's going to be better for everyone.

TRICK-LE DOWN

In the fallout from the Great Depression, Republican President (and former businessman) Herbert Hoover refused to expand the size of government to tackle the economic devastation facing the country. Instead, he turned to the private sector. His administration bailed out the big banks, provided

---

5 Federal government tax revenue has hovered around the same level pretty much ever since. In 2021, the Commonwealth tax-to-GDP ratio was 23.4%.

6 To be fair, a huge chunk of this money was being spent on waging the Cold War, making it slightly less of an awesome Leftist 'win'.

government-guaranteed loans to private capital and waited for the market to do its thing. This didn't work (at all), and Hoover would eventually have to sign a US$2 billion public works bill that would later form part of Franklin Delano Roosevelt's historic **New Deal**.

The humourist Will Rogers roasted Hoover's approach in 1932 when he wrote, 'The money was all appropriated for the top in the hopes that it would trickle down to the needy.'

Forty years after the joke, **'trickle-down economics'** was about to be taken very seriously. In 1974, Republican President Gerald Ford proposed raising taxes to curb stagflation, and this pissed off a small group of right-wing politicos: economist and University of Chicago professor Arthur Laffer; members of the Ford administration, Dick Cheney and Donald Rumsfeld; and conservative journalist Jude Wanniski. These disgruntled ghouls bitched about the tax hikes over dinner at a Washington restaurant one night, and Laffer was inspired to sketch out on the back of a napkin something that would come to be known as **'The Laffer Curve'**: a simple graph designed to show the relationship between tax rates and revenue.

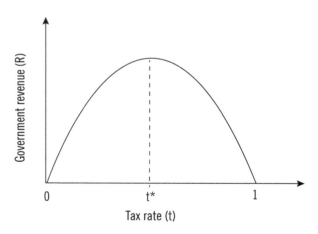

You'll just have to imagine the napkin.

According to Laffer's sketch, if tax rates were at zero, government revenue would be $0 (obvs), and if tax rates were at 100%, revenue would be $0, because no one would bother working, because that's basically slavery, or being an intern. Thus, Laffer reasoned, there must be a **tipping point**, where the level of taxation gets so onerous that it disincentivises people to work, invest and be entrepreneurial, and that's bad for the economy.

'Whenever you redistribute income, you take from those who make a little bit more and you give to those who make a little bit less,' says Laffer. 'By taking from those who make a little bit more, you reduce their incentives, and they work a little bit less and produce a little bit less. By giving to those who make a little bit less, you provide them with an alternative source of income other than working, and they *too* will produce a little bit less.

'Now this is math. It's not left wing, right wing, Republican or Democrat, it's not liberal or conservative; **it's just plain economics.**'

Laffer's theory held that below the tipping point must be a **sweet spot**: a level of taxation that allows the government to raise sufficient revenue, but will still incentivise people to work hard; *so* super hard and brilliantly, in fact, that the economy will boom. Laffer argued that current US tax rates were definitely higher than the sweet spot, so the government should immediately slash them, because that would create more incentives and economic activity, which will spur economic growth and prosperity that can be taxed and shared and it'll all 'trickle-down' from the top to everybody else. In fact, the resultant economic growth will be so great, Laffer claimed, that miraculously **these tax cuts for the rich will pay for themselves.**

Wanniski went on to write about the Laffer Curve in his 1978 book *The Way The World Works* (bit arrogant). It's considered to be the definitive work on **supply-side economics:**

the macroeconomic theory that increasing the supply of labour, goods and services at lower prices (by cutting taxes and regulations) will spur economic growth.[7]

Now this all sounds great and I'm sure it was really fun for Arthur to do the drawing on the napkin and everything, but the only issue is there's no evidence that this theory actually works here, on Planet Earth. It's not for a lack of trying. Laffer joined Republican President Ronald Reagan's Economic Policy Advisory Board in the 80s and supply-side/trickle-down/Laffer-nomics quickly became implemented as **Reaganomics**. Reagan enacted sweeping tax cuts for the rich in 1981 – the top marginal rate was cut from 70% to 50% – and shockingly, this resulted in hundreds of billions of dollars in lost government revenue, prompting a budgetary crisis. Reagan initially refused to raise taxes, for that would anger The Almighty Curve. Instead, his administration responded by making savage cuts to Medicaid, food stamps, disability insurance and school lunches, and by introducing harsher means-testing for welfare cheques, during an economic recession, no less.

Reagan was finally forced to raise taxes in 1982, and did so again in 1983, 1984, 1986 and 1987 (although in '86 he still cut the top tax rate for the rich down to 28%). After the two recessions early on in his first term, the US economy recovered quickly (and unevenly) for the rest of the 80s; productivity continued to rise, and unemployment fell, but wages remained flat. By the end of Reagan's presidency in 1988, taxes for the rich were lower, debt was up, and the country was more unequal: more Americans were living in poverty, and a greater share of the nation's wealth had gone to the top 1%. Over in the UK, British PM Margaret Thatcher enacted a similar revolution under the counsel of

---

7   As opposed to Keynesian, **demand-side** economics.

Mr Laffer, with similar results. As taxes were slashed and the British elites' share of national income grew under her rule, so too did child poverty and the proportion of pensioners living below the poverty line.[8]

CUT TAX, FUCK UP, REPEAT

So all in all, a pretty solid F– for the validity of trickle-down theory, right out of the gate. But that hasn't stopped the same boot-licking supply-sider ghouls from trying it out again and again and again.

President George W. Bush passed huge tax cuts in 2001 and 2003, slashing marginal tax rates, cutting taxes on capital gains and dividends and inheritances.[9] 'You bet I cut taxes at the top,' he said while spruiking his tax-cut plans during the Republican primary debate in 2000. 'What we Republicans should stand for is growth in the economy. *We ought to make the pie higher.*'

The Congressional Budget Office and the US Treasury have consistently reported that Bush's tax cuts didn't raise the pie at all. They did not 'pay for themselves', and in fact added trillions of dollars to the US deficit while the economy stagnated throughout Bush's second term, until finally exploding

---

8 Reagan and Thatcher were also advised by our old mate, the anti-Keynesian, free-market loving, libertarian, monetarist, anti-taxing supply-sider, Milton Friedman.
    Ironically, Friedman worked for the US Treasury in his youth and helped to invent payroll taxes, so the government could pay for the war; taxes which have remained in place ever since, much to Milton's chagrin. Pretty massive self-own there.

9 When George's daddy H. W. Bush ran against Reagan for the Republican nomination in 1980, he labelled this trickle-down theory a '**voodoo economic policy**'. H. W. then went on to become Reagan's Vice President, deny that he'd ever said that 'voodoo' thing, then when the media showed him the footage of him saying it he said he was 'only kidding' about denying it, then he backed Reagan's economic plan in full, then he helped his son George become president and watched on with pride as his special little boy passed massive tax cuts for the rich, too. Great family.

in 2008.[10] Then, during the Great Recession that followed, Arthur Laffer encouraged the Republican Governor of Kansas to slash the state's business and income taxes to send a 'shot of adrenaline into the heart of the Kansas economy', which the Governor did, promptly throwing his state into a prolonged and brutal fiscal crisis that resulted in widespread cuts to public services.

But Laffer didn't have time to give a hoot about *that*, because by 2016 he'd already moved on to serve as economic adviser to the presidential campaign of Donald Trump.[11] Under Laffer's excited guidance, Trump delivered the *Tax Cuts and Jobs Act*: a 'revolutionary change' that was going to act as 'economic rocket fuel'. Passed in 2017, the Trump tax cuts reduced income tax rates for all individuals (except those in the lowest income brackets), which is exactly the kind of thing that working-class opioid-addicted #MAGA Americans had been crying out for. This was, unsurprisingly, a total bonanza for the rich: in 2018, the bottom half of US households paid an average effective tax rate of 24.2%, while the richest 400 families in America paid an average rate of 23%. Thanks to Trump, billionaires were now paying a lower effective tax rate than teachers, nurses, firefighters or truck drivers, and America was becoming Great Again.

Trump's package also enacted the biggest corporate tax cut in US history. The trickle-down lie tells us that when you cut corporate taxes and let companies keep more of their profits, it'll

---

10 Arthur Laffer, for the record, believes that the *real* cause of the GFC was the election of Barack Obama.

   'As he got closer and closer to winning,' Laffer told Fox News in 2019, 'the markets collapsed.'

   Top economic advisors in the Bush White House were being warned as early as 2006 that the US housing market was inflated and that a crisis was coming. Barack Obama didn't receive the Democratic nomination until August 2008. This is the economic brain genius we're dealing with here.

11 2016 was a great year for Donald Trump: he became the most powerful man in the world, and he only paid US$750 in federal income taxes.

definitely lead to a boost in wages and productive investment and more jobs, but that isn't at all what happened. Approximately just 6% of the corporate cuts went to higher wages, and half of that went to one-off bonuses, never to be repeated. Corporate giants like Walmart and AT&T announced they would spend some of the billions of dollars in tax windfall they'd received on handing out $1,000 bonuses to eligible employees, while simultaneously firing thousands of other employees who had become surplus to requirements. (Walmart literally announced the bonuses and laid workers off on the same day.)

The cuts also inspired an orgy of **share buybacks**: a dirty practice in which existing shareholders use a company's profits to buy up more shares in the company, thereby jacking up the share price and boosting collective shareholder wealth. These buybacks don't make the company more productive or help workers get a greater share of the fruits of their labour or anything, but if you're an executive who gets bonuses for jumps in the business' stock price, you're going to think they're pretty fucking great. After the Trump cuts, buybacks in the US surged by more than 50%, reaching a record $806 billion in 2018.[12]

In a twist that no one could have possibly seen coming, the Trump/Laffer tax cuts led to a sharp fall in government revenue. Corporate tax receipts alone fell by a third, and the Congressional Budget Office predicted the cuts would add $1.8 trillion to US debt over the next decade. Just like Reagan, Trump responded by proposing sweeping cuts to Social Security, Medicare, Medicaid, food stamps and the Environmental Protection Agency, while still increasing spending for border security and defence.

---

12 Buybacks were considered a form of illegal market manipulation until 1982, but then everyone chilled out about them in the 'Greed Is Good' years and now they're part of the financial furniture. Since 2012, companies on the S&P 500 have spent more than US$4.5 trillion buying back their own stocks.

I gotta say, it really is an elegant strategy the Right has managed to perfect here. You cut taxes for the benefit of you and all your wealthy mates and donors, then use the consequent fiscal shortcomings to justify hacking away at all the lefty social programs you've always wanted to destroy anyway. I fucking despise this agenda with every fibre of my being, but hey – you've gotta respect the commitment to the bit.

TRICKLE-DOWN UNDER

Australia hasn't been immune to the supply-side disease. This snake oil is so popular around here that back in 2015, the Australian Chamber of Commerce and Industry even brought Arthur Laffer to our shores to help spread the good news of his Curve, just as the Abbott government was trying to make the case for a cut to the company tax rate. Laffer met with the likes of Scott Morrison, Josh Frydenberg and Kelly O'Dwyer, spoke at all the usual right-wing free-market think tanks and chirpily summed up his general vibe for Fran Kelly in an interview on the ABC's *RN Breakfast*: 'All taxes are bad, Fran, and some are worse than others.'

This has been a popular mindset for our political class for decades. While they were disciplining the labour movement and deregulating and privatising their brains out in the 80s and 90s, Bob Hawke and Keating proudly cut the top marginal tax rate down to 47%, and they'd eventually bring the company tax rate down to 36%, all in the name of making Australia 'competitive with east Asia in attracting business investment'. Inequality worsened accordingly.[13]

---

13 As Treasurer and PM, Paul Keating was all about 'broadening' the tax base. This led him to introduce that Capital Gains Tax, which was very cool, but it also saw him advocate for the introduction of a 12.5% consumption tax (not unlike the GST). Keating was pushing for the tax in 1985, but couldn't get it past unions, welfare groups and public opinion, and it was shelved.

In 1997, Keating's advice to the fresh New Labour PM Tony Blair was, '**Don't ever put up income tax, mate**. Take it off them anyhow you please but do that and they'd rip your fucking guts out', which seems like quite a cucked position for the leader of a supposedly working-class party to take.

Not to be outdone, the Howard government arrived in 1996 and promptly went about passionately cutting taxes for the wealthy. Howard cut the company tax rate to 30% and the top marginal income tax rate to 45%, and dramatically lifted the threshold at which it cut in from $50k to $180k by 2007. He introduced that 50% discount on the CGT, as well as a batshit franking credits policy which now effectively works to give retired shareholding Boomers free government pocket money as a little reward for being good capitalists and voting Liberal.

FRANKING INSANE

A **franking credit** is issued to shareholders to avoid supposed 'double taxation'.

Companies pay dividends out of their after-tax profit, so the money that a shareholder receives has already been taxed, and a shareholder can use the franking credit against their other personal tax obligations. This is known as **dividend imputation** and was introduced to the Australian tax system by Keating in 1987.

But in 2001, the Howard government allowed shareholders who received more in franking credits than they had to pay in tax **to get a cash refund**. Thanks to other tax loopholes, many retired shareholders have a taxable income of $0, but under Australian tax law they're still able to receive little cash treats from the State. Handing out these rebates for excess franking credits costs the country about $10 billion a year, more than 74% of the benefit goes to the top 10% of income earners, and it leads to some truly perverse outcomes; multimillionaire Dick Smith claimed in one year he received a $500k cash refund from the ATO thanks to the magic of franking.

In the 2019 election, Labor ran on ending this bizarre and inequitable tax measure (with exemptions for charities and pensioners) and using the money to boost social spending instead. The Coalition labelled this a 'RETIREE TAX!!!', and outraged franking credits beneficiaries attended inquiries, called in to talkback radio and wrote numerous letters to many editors. Steve, a 71-year-old retiree in Fremantle who had $500k in super and owned his own boat, told ABC's *7:30*, 'The franking credit proposal is the most unfair and hostile proposal I've ever seen or heard of in my life', suggesting he hasn't read a lot of history.

Although the issue received a ridiculous amount of coverage and clearly hurt Labor in a few key marginal seats, the Australian Electoral Study found that 54% of all voters in the 2019 election supported limiting franking credit cash rebates to shareholders. But Labor still lost, the stinking Coalition government was returned and in January 2021, Anthony Albanese announced that Labor wouldn't be taking any changes to franking credits to the next election, and they're still a thing now.

Heartbreakingly, after the 2019 poll, there were reports of confused pensioners calling up government authorities to ask when their franking credits were going to come through, only to be told that they *needed to own shares* to get them, which they didn't. Excuse me, I'm heading off to walk directly into the sea.

While he was helping out the toffs, Howard was slugging everyone else with the 10% GST, which now covers about 47% of Australia's consumption and makes up about 13% of government revenue. This fucker is a **regressive tax**: as a flat tax on consumption, it means the poor have to spend more of their income on essentials in order to eat, clothe their kids, survive, etc., so they're paying a higher proportion of their income in GST than those who earn more.[14] Finally, to round out his tenure, Howard went to the 2007 election promising further tax cuts of $34 billion, and 'fiscal conservative' Kevin Rudd said, 'Yeah sure, me too.' Labor won government, passed on the cuts, and 42% of the benefit went to the top 10% of income earners, in yet another Labor victory for The Little Guy.

The political class has continued to inflict this horseshit on us all for the past decade and a half. They've gone to war on almost all taxation of capital, all of it justified on the nonsense of trickle-down ideology. The Gillard government went to the 2010 election promising to cut the 30% company

---

14 The Tax originally included no exemptions for fresh food, healthcare, medicines or education services and 'non-essential' items like tampons.

Most shamefully, Howard claimed in September 1998 that the GST would result 'in no more than a 1.9% rise in ordinary beer', but following its introduction in July 2000, the price of beer rose by 4.8%, and the cowardly Howard has never apologised for this outrageous attack on the Australian people and our way of life.

tax rate, arguing that 'a lower company tax rate will increase investment, raise productivity, and increase the real wages of working Australians', while then-Assistant Treasurer Bill Shorten went on the parliamentary record in 2011 arguing that 'cutting the company income tax rate increases domestic productivity and domestic investment'. The Abbott/Turnbull/ Morrison Coalition desperately wanted to bring the rate down to 25% for all businesses, even though it would forgo $65 billion in revenue that could be redistributed to fund healthcare, alleviate poverty or help the ABC to #BringBack-Tonightly. Letting the likes of Qantas, Wesfarmers, BHP and the Big Four Evil Banks keep more of their (record) profits, the nation was told by its (multimillionaire) Prime Minister Turnbull, would definitely trickle down to the rest of us in the form of more foreign investment and jobs and growth and higher wages and growth and also jobs.

This was all poppycock. Firstly, there is simply no serious correlation between Australia's level of company tax and our ability to attract foreign investment. Private business investment in Australia as a share of GDP slowly declined between 1960 and the early 1990s, then climbed steadily, hit its highest point in decades during the mining boom of the early 2000s, then started to fall again, and during all this, the company tax rate has been high, cut, flat for extended periods, raised (briefly) and then, since the late 80s, progressively reduced, so it's clearly not that important. In fact, a 2017 report from the Australia Institute found that **97% of applications to the Foreign Investment Review Board came from countries with lower company tax rates than ours.**

Secondly, the supply-siders' claim that '[r]educing the burden of tax on these Australian employers will improve their cash-flow and allow them to reinvest in new equipment and machinery, to take on new staff and to pay higher wages to their employees', and the Finance Minister Mathias

Cormann's prophecy that if the cuts went through, 'wages will increase as certain as night follows day', were total bunkum. They were spouting all this at a time when corporate Australia was making bigger profits than ever before, as workers' wages continued to flatline. Australian companies haven't been using their proceeds to pass on more cash to workers or to invest in nation-changing levels of equipment; they've been doing what corporate America has been doing, i.e. just bumping up their bottom line.[15]

Thankfully, Turnbull failed to get his Big Business tax cuts through parliament. Not to be discouraged, these free-market freaks immediately turned to 'reforming' Australia's personal income tax rates by setting them on fire. Across Stages 1, 2 and 3 of their unholy tax agenda, Turnbull and Morrison managed to rip the guts out of our progressive system. They've lifted the tax-free threshold and the top marginal tax rate, and reduced the total number of tax brackets to three, so that by 2025, all Australian workers earning between $45k and $200k will be paying the same marginal tax rate of 30%. Thanks to Stage 3 of the cuts – fully supported by the ALP during the 2022 election – **those earning more than $200k a year will soon be getting an annual tax cut of about $9k,** all for the low low total cost of about $243 billion in forgone revenue over the next decade. If these cuts go ahead, by the time we hit the 2030s, this turd of an arrangement will be costing the budget a cool $37 billion per year.

These cuts will not magically un-quash the 'aspiration' of millions of Australian workers (who are already working quite hard, thank you very much), nor will they inspire a flood of the

---

15 By 2019, Australian share buybacks were up 140% on the average of the past four years, and had become so rife they'd even unnerved Liberal Treasurer Josh Frydenberg.
   'With Australian corporates enjoying healthy balance sheets, record low borrowing costs and strong equity market conditions,' he pondered at a BCA breakfast, 'the question is: are corporates being aggressive enough in the pursuit of growth?'
   Hmm. Really makes you think.

world's best and brightest to come to our shores so they can trickle down all over the rest of us.[16] What these cuts *will* do is supercharge inequality, widen the gender pay gap between men and women and enact yet another massive wealth transfer to CEOs, bankers and media tycoons and other Liberal Party donors; the richest 1% of Australians will get as much benefit from the Stage 3 tax cuts as the poorest 65% combined.

BOO-DOO ECONOMICS

It's all such an obvious, evil, toxic con job; one that capital has pushed on ordinary working people for half a fucking century. The elites have managed to get away with telling a 'convincing' story about how you should allow *me* (a man with a monocle) to keep more of my money, because it'll totally actually work out better for *you* (someone who watches *The Block* or whatever). This is especially remarkable when the evidence is so overwhelmingly, consistently, crystally clear: **tax cuts for rich people don't 'trickle' anywhere, they just make rich people richer.** Back in Arthur Laffer's homeland, the US Congressional Research Service looked at this in 2012 and it could find no conclusive evidence of 'a clear relationship between the 65-year reduction in the top statutory tax rates and economic growth'. A major research paper from the London School of Economics' International Inequalities Institute analysed data from 18 OECD countries – including the US, the UK and Australia – over the past five decades and found that 'economic performance, as measured by real GDP per capita and the unemployment rate, is not significantly affected by major tax cuts for the rich. **The estimated effects for these variables are statistically indistinguishable from zero.'**

---

16 Even with a godforsaken top marginal income tax rate of over 45%, Australia has been the number one destination for the world's migrating millionaires in 2015, 2016, 2017, 2018 and 2019.

In fact, these kinds of tax cuts do *precisely the opposite* of what they're supposed to do. By simply increasing the share of national income that goes to the aristocracy, they increase the gap between the rich and the poor – **a gap which the OECD has repeatedly told us is 'harmful for long-term economic growth'.** A 2014 OECD report estimated that in the two decades before the GFC, rising inequality knocked up to 9% off GDP growth for the US and the UK, and 10% for New Zealand and Mexico. Another report, prepared for the International Monetary Fund (IMF) in 2015, *Causes and Consequences of Income Inequality*, showed that when 'the income share of the top 20 percent (the rich) increases, then GDP growth actually declines over the medium term, suggesting that the results do not trickle down.

'In contrast, an increase in the income share of the bottom 20 percent (the poor) is associated with higher GDP growth.'

And yet, trickle-down bullshit refuses to die. Even though his Curve and his theory about wealth redistribution and his little fucking napkin have all been so objectively, catastrophically wrong for so long, Arthur Laffer hasn't been banished or incarcerated. Not even a little bit. In fact, in 2019, he was awarded the Presidential Medal of Freedom by Donald Trump in recognition of his contribution to the field of economics, because we live in a godless universe.

ANTI-TAXXERS

Full credit to these supply-side fuckers: they've been very effective. Personal income rates for the wealthy have been slashed across the world in the trickle-down era, and Oxfam reports that the global average statutory corporate tax rate has fallen from 49% in 1985 to just 23% in 2019. When you add up our state and federal taxes, Australia's total tax-to-GDP ratio is now around 29%, **which makes us one of the lowest-taxed**

countries in the OECD. We are ranked 29th out of 37 countries in terms of tax revenue, with lower rates than the likes of Japan, the UK, Canada, France, and Germany. Our top marginal tax rate of 47% (including the 2% Medicare levy) is lower than the top rates in Canada, Germany, Austria and all of Scandinavia.

So the rich have basically won the low-tax world they wanted, but they're still not fucking happy. Their taxes are still too damn high, and if you even *dare* suggest raising them any further, they will chuck a massive tanty. In October 2020, rapper Curtis James '50 Cent' Jackson III (net worth approx. US$40 million) was so scared that he'd have to pay a top marginal tax rate of 62% if Joe Biden became president, he took to Instagram to encourage his fans to re-elect Donald Trump.

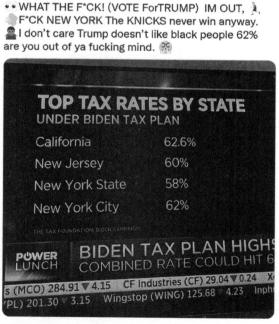

Fiddy even doubled down on his position the next day, tweeting, 'Yeah, i don't want to be 20cent.'[17]

This is typical of the prevailing attitude towards wealth redistribution now – it's considered to be **EVIL**. Toffs and businesses have never exactly been *stoked* about having to pay money to the government on a regular basis, but the trickle-down revolution has hailed an altogether new paradigm, in which taxes are viewed not as a fundamental part of the social contract, but rather as an 'attack' on 'success'. In a society geared towards the never-ending accumulation of wealth, the ever-wealthier plutocrats demand to keep even more of their heaps of money and big business is driven to minimise anything and everything that hurts their profits, tax included. These plutocrats will happily deploy their resources to whinge about the horrors of taxes to anyone who will listen; supply-siders in the political and media classes have dedicated hundreds of political speeches, millions of column inches, and thousands of hours of airtime to the notion that government taxation is an illegitimate cancer, eating away at our (read: their) freedom. Society's entrepreneurial LIFTERS are all cruelly 'saddled' with taxes that are a 'handbrake on the economy', we're told, and they desperately need 'tax RELIEF' now. Any form of mild wealth redistribution is 'a great big new

---

17 This was quite confusing, as it's well documented that 50 Cent named himself in honour of Brooklyn gangster Kelvin '50 Cent' Martin, and not as a way of accurately describing his financial position. Plus, Biden's proposed marginal tax increases were expected to only affect those making over $400k a year, so if 50 Cent's total net worth was a mere 50 cents, he'd surely be well below the threshold.

  I know I'm being pedantic here, but I guess I just expect a more sophisticated level of understanding from the artist responsible for albums like *Power of the Dollar* and *Get Rich or Die Tryin'* and for songs like 'I Get Money', 'Straight to the Bank', 'Chase the Paper' and 'Too Rich for the Bitch'.

tax' that needs to be repealed/cut/axed/dumped/scrapped yesterday.[18]

Some will even tell you that taxation is really a form of *theft* – you know, the kind of theft in which the thieves are supposed to give the money they stole *from* you *back* to you, your fellow citizens and future generations in the form of welfare, services and infrastructure via a (theoretically) transparent process with democratic oversight. (The perfect crime!) In a submission to the Parliamentary Economics Committee in 2018, the free-market think tank the Institute of Public Affairs (IPA) even went so far as to suggest that our progressive income tax system was as bad as racism: 'Other forms of discrimination, such as by skin colour, race, or ethnicity, are rightly abhorred,' the submission read, 'yet the income tax system openly discriminates against people by income.'[19]

---

18 For example, there was the **Resource Super Profit Tax**: Kevin Rudd's 2010 attempt to tax 40% of the chunky profits the mining companies were making as they dug up and sold off our mineral resources. The idea came out of Treasury Secretary Dr Ken Henry's wide-ranging Tax Review, and was projected to raise billions and billions of dollars that could be reinvested into super, cutting the company tax rate (yuck) and building large-scale infrastructure.

True to form, the forces of extractive resource capital were seriously pissed off by this. Gina Rinehart and Twiggy Forrest held rallies calling to 'Axe the Tax!', the Coalition labelled it unbridled socialism, *The Australian* called it 'Robin Hood economics' and the mining industry spent $22 million over 53 days on a brutal advertising campaign about how we were all 'gonna get WHACKED! / By the Mining Tax!'. (These ads referred to 'The **Extra** Mining Tax', I guess to avoid the use of the term 'super profits', because that might have been a bit awkward.)

Labor got WHACKED! in the opinion polls as a result of the campaign, and things became so dire that Rudd's colleagues removed him as PM, in what *The Australian* described as 'the coup we had to have'. Julia Gillard took over, renegotiated the design of the tax with the likes of BHP and Rio Tinto and came up with the **Minerals Resource Rent Tax**, which taxed the profits at a lower rate, and was narrowed to just apply to iron ore and coal. Gillard claimed the tax would raise $2 billion in its first year; we soon found out that in its first six months, it had brought in a paltry $126 million. After they returned to power in 2013, the Coalition repealed even this pathetic shadow of a tax, like the cads they are.

What can you say? Taking money from the rich has never been – and never will be – easy.

19 Normally the IPA would reject this kind of talk as the Left's virtue-signalling idpol wokeness, but if you happen to 'identify' as a high-income earner, your lived experience is valid, and you deserve trigger warnings and a safe space.

After four decades, this demented anti-tax ideology has become so entrenched in our political 'common sense', its adherents barely even feel like it needs to be backed up by anything at all.

'What's your evidence that higher taxes weaken an economy?' *7:30* host Leigh Sales asked Scott Morrison back in 2019, as he was campaigning against Labor's economic 'sheet anchor' of a policy platform.

'Well, I think it's just **fundamental economics 101**, Leigh,' Morrison replied.

Except we know that it's not, because other countries exist. Switzerland, Iceland, Norway and Denmark all have higher tax-to-GDP ratios than Australia, but they also have a higher level of GDP per person. The Norwegians tax their economy 10% more than we do, yet Norway has about US$75k for every citizen, while we have US$56k, which, according to economics 101, is less money.

'By your logic,' Sales responded, 'if higher taxes in and of themselves generally weaken an economy, a country like Norway should be weak, but it has some of the highest taxes in the world, and yet the average Norwegian is richer and has a higher standard of living than the average Australian.'

At this point, Scomo's brain appeared to go into 'Danger Mode' and automatically spat out the classic right-wing retort to any critique of the supply-side dogma: 'Australia has had 27 years of continuous economic growth.'

That's it. Stop looking at and learning from other countries that aren't Australia, Leigh. That's unAustralian. No further questions.

WHAT EVEN *IS* 'RICH', THO?

The anti-tax malarkey becomes seriously offensive when the suited buffoons in charge try to argue that the rich deserve to have their taxes reduced – or at the very least, never raised – because actually, they're *really not that rich at all.*

'I don't regard someone who's earning $200,000 a year as being from the top end of town,' Anthony Albanese told Sky News in 2019, shortly after being elected the new party leader. His new shadow treasurer Jim Chalmers agreed, celebrating Australians who were 'on a good wicket' and trumpeting Labor's commitment to 'aspiration'. In 2020, Scott Morrison rejected the idea that his precious tax cuts were just for the wealthy because many FIFO workers would be earning more than $180,000, and he didn't 'think they should be penalized and treated like they're some merchant banker in Sydney'.

(A merchant banker in Sydney earning $180k or more would also be receiving the tax cut, of course, as would everybody else on that income, including Scott Morrison, because that's how taxes work.)

Around the same time, Albanese claimed that many people on a family income of $180,000 'will be struggling with a mortgage, with the bills they have to pay'. *Sunrise* host Samantha Armytage agreed: 'It depends on where you live in Australia as to whether or not you are wealthy on that,' she said, on national television, as part of her job, for which she was reportedly paid $500k a year. 'In Sydney, probably not.'

This shit is bananas. On the latest figures, the typical Australian worker makes around $48k a year, *before tax*. Even in the exceptionally expensive, higher-waged city of Sydney, the median income is around $65k (or approximately 13% of a *Sunrise* host's salary). The typical Australian household makes $91k. So **the vast majority of Australian workers and families are earning less than $100k a year.** Just over 3% of workers are earning over $180k, and good luck to them or whatever, but *they are not normal.* They're earning more than three times the typical worker's wage, and they deserve way less attention and sympathy and tax relief than pretty much everybody else beneath them.

Hands down, the most warped expression of sympathy for the rich I've ever heard came from former Labor MP Joel Fitzgibbon in 2013, when he told the media, 'In Sydney's west you can be on a $250,000 family income a year and you're still struggling – particularly given property prices.' Jesus Christ.

The anti-taxxers can never rest. Back in 1998, the British New Labour Secretary of Trade Peter Mandelson told a US industrialist that he was 'intensely relaxed about people getting filthy rich **as long as they pay their taxes'**, which is kind of like saying 'I'm fine with the Komodo dragon being let into the maternity ward, as long as it signs a non-aggression pact'. The filthy rich have not only spent the past fifty years cutting the amount of tax they're *supposed* to pay, they've been very busy dwindling the amount of tax they *actually* end up paying, too; the ATO estimates that across corporate Australia, small business and high wealth individuals, the gross 'tax gap' in the 2019/20 financial year – the gap between what they should be collecting in taxes and what they actually got – was something like $33 billion. In that same year, **sixty Australians earned more than a $1 million and paid precisely $0 in income tax.** The average income of these people was $3.5 million, and they claimed an average amount of $250k in 'tax management litigation costs' deductions.

Spend hundreds of thousands of dollars to fancy accountants and lawyers, it seems, and they'll help you keep millions.[20]

Across the world, thanks to loopholes, tax havens, complicated corporate structures and sexy tricks like 'profit-shifting' and 'strategic transfer pricing', multinational corporations are today able to live their best, profitable, tax-free lives. In its annual report for 2020, the Tax Justice Network used OECD data to conclude that multinationals shift US$1.3 trillion worth of profits into tax havens every year, and all the international tax-cheating costs governments around the world around US$427 billion in lost revenue. About a third of Australia's biggest companies didn't pay *any* tax in 2019 and seven of them paid more in political donations than they did in company tax. Fossil fuel giant Chevron Australia Holdings,

---

20 Churches paid $0 in tax during this year and in all other years, because in Australia they're considered to be charities doing the important work of 'advancing religion', and are thus tax exempt.

   The Hillsong Church rakes in more than $80 million per year and the Catholic Church in Australia holds a business and property portfolio worth more than $30 billion, which is all definitely the kind of vibe that Jesus was going for.

for example, had a taxable income of $900 million, paid $0 in tax, and still managed to find around $130k to donate to both major parties in the same year.

This is not to say that rich people and companies aren't occasionally benevolent and happy to share a bit of their good fortune around. Since 2000, the Gates Foundation has given away $45 billion and helped to vaccinate more than two billion children against malaria, for example.[21] Other times, they are diabolical: the billionaire industrialist Koch brothers have poured hundreds of millions of dollars into political candidates and causes that are climate denialist, anti-union and pro-tax cuts for billionaire industrialists. One day Dick Smith gives a hundred grand to a homelessness charity; the next, Clive Palmer tries to buy a federal election.

The point is, the redistribution of these hogs' masses of wealth is **entirely on *their* terms, according to *their* priorities.** The rest of us are just left to watch and covet these freaks as they privatise space exploration, buy up newspapers and sports teams, get appointed to fancy boards, run for (and win) elected office, and passionately *Eyes Wide Shut* each other's brains out at Davos, Bohemian Grove and Mosman.

GEN Y YOU HAVE NO MONEY

The obscene levels of wealth inequality that capitalism cooks up for us can be found within all generations. There are still plenty of Boomers who can't afford to eat, while some Millennials command more wealth than almost anyone else in human history. In 2022, the *AFR*'s 40th Annual Rich List boasted 'the widest gap between the nation's youngest and oldest entrepreneurs, proving age is no barrier to wealth creation' (cool!!!). At number eight on the list were thirty-something co-founders of the graphic design software business Canva, Melanie Perkins and Cliff Obrecht, and while these young things are enjoying their shared net

---

21 Bill Gates did this while continuing to be good friends with Jeffrey Epstein, who has done considerably less to improve the welfare of the world's children.

worth of $13.82 billion, the fastest-growing cohort of homeless people in this country is women over 55.

But if we zoom out from the individual exceptions, **we can clearly see a stark intergenerational wealth gap**. One would *expect* older people to be generally richer than the young, of course, because they've had more time to work and save and win Powerball and find loose change down the back of the couch. But this is different – **the gap is quickly growing wider.** Since 2003, people aged 55+ have grown their share of national household wealth by eight points to 56%, as the wealth of households headed by someone under 35 has barely moved. In fact, we've even gone backwards; the average net worth of Australians aged 25 to 34 in 2012 was $15k *less* than it was in 2004. The Millennials' slice of the national pie is getting thinner, as the Baby Boomers have gobbled up more and more.

This is overwhelmingly thanks to the naughty political economic system that we've been exploring throughout this book: **a system that is rigged to benefit people who own assets**. All the free-market restructuring that we've been subjected to since the 70s has combined ballooning asset prices with the proliferation of sweet tax breaks for capital-owners. The Boomers who were able to 'get in' before the housing boom took off have enjoyed a wealth bonanza, while more and more young people have been totally locked out. Seventy per cent of all housing wealth is now in the hands of the over-65s. Steady returns on shares and generous tax concessions on superannuation assets haven't hurt, either. The trickle-down mindset and capital's grip on our politics has created a society in which **the wealth that flows from assets and investments is taxed way more lightly than people's labour**, so younger, asset-poor working Australian households tend to pay much more tax than older, asset-rich households on the same income.

Add to this the rising cost of rents, student debt and having to deal with massive companies ripping us off all over the joint, and it's no surprise that **Australian Millennials simply can't 'get ahead' like our parents did back in their day, under their material conditions.** Indeed, across the board, **social mobility** in Australia has now been comprehensively kneecapped. Analysis from the OECD tells us that if you're born into a poor Australian family today, **it'll take an average of four generations before your descendants will be earning the average income**. By that time, you will be almost certainly dead, unless you and all your kids get to work early and start your families when you're in Year 9.

RICH MAN'S WORLD

As we've been told to wait for the trickle-down to get here, entire floods of wealth have been flowing upwards, enlarging a colossal super dam of riches that you and I are not allowed to swim in. In this highly financialised, radically unequal hell-world, there's never been more wealth sloshing around the place, and yet the greedy powerful rich pigs at the top are hoarding more and more of it, making them greedier and more powerful and more pig-like than ever before.

Things are now so blatantly and infuriatingly rigged for the rich, it regularly makes me want to punch a wall. First, there's the fact that **wealth begets wealth**. We hear that 'Hard work pays off!' and 'You've got to spend money to make money!', but really, when almost all forms of serious wealth redistribution have withered away, it's a lot easier to just *have* money, by being born. You can then use that money to increase your ownership over the means of production, and let that money make you more money. In his exhaustive 2014 work *Capital in the Twenty-First Century*, French economist Thomas Piketty spent 700 pages showing that globally, returns on wealth (owning real estate and financial investments like shares, etc.) have been growing at about 5% a year, while economic growth has been generally low and incomes have remained stagnant. In such a world, **inherited wealth will 'dominate wealth amassed from a lifetime's labour by a wide margin'**.[22]

According to Oxfam, **about a third of billionaire wealth today comes from inheritance**. The likes of Gina Rinehart and James Packer just happened to pick the right wombs to emerge from, and as such have been rewarded lives of luxury for their 'efforts'. Donald Trump inherited more than $400

---

22 This might give the impression that I have *read* Piketty's very long book. I have not read the book. Reading is for virgins.

million from his father Fred's real estate empire and proceeded to consistently fuck it all up (six of his companies have filed for bankruptcy protections), but he still managed to bravely fail upwards, eventually reaching billionaire status and the US presidency.

Plenty of the so-called 'self-made' billionaires weren't gifted with entire empires by birth, but they still had fairly decent head starts: Jeff Bezos' stepfather was a wealthy oil engineer who invested almost $250k in Amazon back in 1995; Bill Gates comes from a family of lawyers and bankers; Richard Branson's grandfather was a judge at Her Majesty's High Court of Justice in England; and Elon Musk's dad was an engineer, property developer and possibly part-owner of a Zambian emerald mine.[23] These men possess vast riches which are contingent on those fortunate beginnings, *as well as* their hard work, new ideas and risk-taking *and all the other factors over which they had little control*: education, infrastructure, law enforcement and industry subsidies (paid for with public money), private investment from other (very lucky) rich people, the labour of hundreds of thousands of (often less lucky) workers, and then heaps more luck along the way. Precisely *no one* makes a billion dollars in a vacuum, and yet we're all expected to just let them keep it all and carry on their day as if that's all perfectly fine.[24]

---

23 According to Erroll Musk, the family had so much money 'at times we couldn't even close our safe', which must have been a nightmare.

24 Some people seem to believe that Millennials' woes will be solved with the magic of inheritance. 'It'll all work out in the end!' they claim. 'Just wait for the Boomers to die and deliver that big fat intergenerational wealth transfer we've been hearing about!'

   This is wildly optimistic. For one thing, what with people living much longer these days (bit rude), chances are any kind of inheritance won't be coming your way until you reach your fifties and sixties, which is quite a long time to wait for some decent economic security.

   Moreover, as we can see, inherited wealth isn't exactly a great remedy for addressing inequality across society; rather, it entrenches it further. Without democratic redistribution, the biggest inheritances will be passed down by the richest people to their snotty-nosed fail-sons and -daughters, who'll be able to use that wealth to grow more wealth at the expense of the poorer kids, and we all go round and round again.

Secondly, **these uber-wealthy uber-cunts are consistently allowed to get away with murder.** In the wake of the GFC, for instance, everyone agreed that the banks and the speculators on Wall Street had been so extremely naughty that they were severely punished by having nothing bad happen to them at all. They were immediately rescued by the Obama administration with a gargantuan amount of public money. Under beautiful and righteous free-market capitalism, failed businesses are supposed to be left to go under, but banks and financial institutions like Goldman Sachs, Bank of America and JP Morgan were considered 'too big to fail' and simply had to be saved, no matter the cost. A paper from the Levy Institute of Economics at Bard's College has estimated that the US Federal Reserve's bailing out of the financial system with loans and asset purchases totalled about US**$29 trillion,** which is an absolute fuckload of donuts. Even though their criminal actions wrought economic and material misery upon literally millions of innocent people across the US and the globe – and even though dozens of bankers were prosecuted and imprisoned in Iceland, Spain and Ireland – the total number of Wall Street executives who have ever faced jail time for their role in the GFC is exactly **one:** former Credit Suisse investment banker Kareem Serageldin. He pleaded guilty to concealing hundreds of millions of dollars in losses to boost Suisse's position in 2013, and was sentenced to two-and-a-half years in prison.[25]

Indeed, many of the Wall Street bloodsuckers bounced back from the Crisis better than ever. Heaps of them chose to do some self-care by restoring their salary bonuses to normal levels within six months of the crash, and just a year after everything went belly up, Goldman Sachs paid out a company record of $16.9 billion in compensation to its

---

25 In 2010, an Oklahoma woman named Patricia Spottedcrow was arrested and imprisoned for selling US$31 worth of pot. She received a sentence of 12 years.

employees. After the bailout, global financial markets were able to recover thanks in large part to the magical practice of **Quantitative Easing (QE)**, in which central banks try to stimulate activity by buying up government bonds, thereby creating new, cheap money to be pumped into the economy. Following the GFC, central banks around the world have created something like US$30 trillion worth of new money like this, which worked out real real good for people who already owned stuff like property and shares (finally!), but not so much for the plebs. From 2009 to 2012, as the incomes of the bottom 99% of Americans crawled up by less than half of a percent, the top 1% saw their incomes grow by almost a third. The total number of billionaires in the world doubled, and between 2017 and 2018 a new billionaire was created every two days, like the little wet Gremlins they are.[26]

But worst of all, as the world's rich have become a thousand times richer, **it's always the poor and working class who pay the price.** As Reagan, Bush and Trump have demonstrated, supply-siders will happily argue that we can defs totes afford to cut taxes for the rich and for business at the same time that

---

26 For the record: **stock markets fucking suck and are bad.** I think we need a total and complete shutdown of all of them until we can figure out what is going on. In *theory*, they're supposed to allow successful firms to raise capital for innovation and productive reinvestment. In *reality*, they produce sweet fuck-all, and are lousy with speculation. Investors just buy stocks, and hope the price of that stock will go up, so they can sell it and make a profit. (Or maybe you'd like to buy/swap/sell/short future **derivatives**, which is basically just gambling on the prices of underlying assets, for shits'n'giggles.) As the economist Jim Stanford puts it in his book *Economics For Everyone*, stock markets are now basically just 'tax-subsidised casinos, whereby financial gamblers place bets on which way share prices will move in the next few hours or minutes'.

The size and influence of financial markets have been growing since the 1960s, but have become especially dominant and psychotically greedy in the wildly deregulated, post-70s decades. The financial sector has become almost totally divorced from the **real economy**; that is, the non-financial parts of the economy, where you and I live, and real things exist. This was never clearer than in 2020, when, after an initial crash, the global stock market absolutely BOOMED as economies were thrown into recession and millions of people lost their jobs. Only a *Wolf of Wall Street*-level coke-addled mind could look at such a state of things and think, 'Yep! Seems good!'

they're screaming about how the government is running out of money and we're in a 'BUDGET EMERGENCY!!!!!!!' and something simply must be done, *right now*.

That 'something' is never lifting the taxes on Mr Moneybags, of course. The ruling class much prefers pursuing **austerity**: the ruthless cutting of public expenditure to 'improve' a country's budget position after a crisis.[27] This is what was rolled out across the world following the 2008 crash, most notably in Greece and the UK. The GFC (which, lest we forget, was caused by the greed of evil rich lizards on Wall Street) devastated the Greek economy, but the private creditors who held most of its public debt didn't give a shit about that and still expected to get their repayments on time. The country eventually had to be bailed out several times with loans from the 'Troika' – a consortium of the European Commission, the European Central Bank and the IMF – on the condition that the Greek government balance its budget with slashed spending, increased consumption taxes and the privatisation of public assets. These harsh measures saw the Greek economy shrink dramatically; wages fell, unemployment reached 25% and at one point, one in three Greeks were living below the poverty line.[28]

In the UK, Gordon Brown's Labour Party responded to the Crisis (known over there as 'The Credit Crunch, Innit') by briefly nationalising the banks and unconditionally bailing out the financial system, then went to the 2010 election promising to make cuts to public spending that would be 'deeper and tougher' than those imposed by Thatcher. This wasn't enough to beat the Conservatives, who then took over

---

27 An 'austere' lifestyle is one with no comforts or luxuries, and in macroeconomic terms 'austerity' pretty much means doing away with the 'luxury' of a society that is able to function.

28 The IMF probably should have known that cutting public spending was going to backfire, seeing as its own research has found that **every dollar of public investment increases a country's economic output by $3**.

and initiated what Tory PM David Cameron called 'the age of austerity'. These upper-class nonces have since cut over £30 billion in social spending, decimating welfare benefits and social services, hobbling the National Health Service and presiding over a dramatic rise in unemployment and child poverty rates. By 2018, a United Nations report had found the years of austerity had been 'entrenching high levels of poverty and inflicting unnecessary misery in one of the richest countries in the world', while studies published by the British Medical Journal and the Institute for Public Policy Research have estimated that austerity is linked to something in the order of 100,000 preventable deaths. The UK now has more foodbanks than McDonalds, and yet the Royal Family (net worth US$88 billion) is still allowed to be a thing, its members looking down on their subjects as they sit on their golden thrones, drowning in jewellery and taking the occasional guilt-free holiday to Little St James.

Australians have copped a version of this raw deal over the years, too. After the stock market crash of 1929 (which, lest we forget, was caused by the greed of evil rich lizards on Wall Street) and the ensuing Great Depression, Labor PM James Scullin and his right-wing successor Joseph Lyons unleashed a brutal austerity program to achieve fiscal balance: they slashed government spending (including public sector wages and pensions), tightened credit and jacked up tariffs. This was supposed to help the country 'recover', but it saw the Australian economy contract by 17% in just three years. The country experienced one of the highest rates of unemployment in the developed world and millions of ordinary people were left to suffer harder lives for way longer than they should have.

Thankfully, in the aftermath of both World War II and 2008, we went the other way: Labor governments made huge interventions in the economy to try to ensure we didn't all end up living in tent cities and carrying our few worldly possessions around with us in a bag on a stick. As the shit was beginning to hit the fan in the US in 2008, the Rudd government moved quickly to maintain confidence in the economy by restraining stock speculation and by guaranteeing people's savings deposits and the banks' wholesale funds. By the end of 2009, around $53 billion worth of stimulus had been injected into the economy to keep the wheels turning, funding school and clean energy infrastructure projects and one-off stimulus cheques of up to $950 for more than 8 million people.[29]

This intervention is very good, but it requires the government to run a deficit budget, and borrow a fair bit of money.[30] Over the Rudd/Gillard/Rudd years, Australia's gross public debt grew to over 30% of GDP. **This was the third-lowest level of debt in the OECD at the time,** but the Coalition still proceeded to shit their pants about it every single day. In 2009, then-Liberal leader Malcolm Turnbull claimed that the country's debt was 'the biggest economic challenge facing Australia now', and at a media event in Perth he unveiled the Coalition's official 'debt truck', which was going to drive around to serve as 'a constant reminder that Mr Rudd has committed generations of Australians to crippling debts'.

---

29 I can't remember what I did with my stimulus money, but as it was 2009, I'm guessing I spent it on Black Eyed Peas merch, or maybe a copy of *Avatar* on Blu-Ray.

30 It does this by getting the Treasury selling **bonds** to local and foreign banks, super funds, and other institutional investors.

These bonds will eventually have to be repaid, plus interest, but the Australian government is able to lend on some pretty sweet terms, because *it's the Australian government*. When a couple take out a mortgage, for example, they're borrowing against the value of their home. But when the Commonwealth Government of Australia takes on debt by selling bonds, it's borrowing against *the productive capacity of the entire Australian economy*, which is a substantially less risky thing to do. Unlike human people, Australia will never go on the dole or call in sick because it's hungover, nor will it close, retire or die.

Despite what you might hear from the likes of Tony Abbott ('[I]f families have got to tighten their belt, it's only right and proper that government should be tightening its belt too') or Barack Obama ('Families across the country are tightening their belts and making tough decisions. The federal government should do the same.'), always remember that **a government is not like a household**: their respective budgets and their relationship to debt are fundamentally different.

A Rhodes Scholar in action.
(Photo: Marie Nirme / Newspix)

Turnbull claimed that Australia's debt would be heaps lower if the Coalition had been in power during the GFC because they would have been more fiscally prudent; an argument that was somewhat undermined by the fact the Liberal Party was spending about $4k a week on a fucking debt truck.[31]

By the time Tony Abbott came to power in 2013, his party had spent the past three years hysterically decrying Labor's 'debt and deficit disaster'. The Tories immediately tried to get the country back in the black by taking a huge austerity dump on us in the form of its 2014 budget. Treasurer Joe Hockey had proclaimed that '**the age of entitlement is over, and the age of personal responsibility has begun**', and handed down a fiscal vision for the country that proposed cuts to health, education, pensions, unemployment benefits, foreign aid, the public service (including the loss of thousands of jobs at the ATO), the CSIRO, renewable energy, public broadcasting, the arts and Indigenous services, as well as the introduction of a $7 co-payment to visit the GP and the raising of the retirement age to 70.

---

31 Labor responded to the truck stunt by making its own 'supporting jobs truck' and had it drive around Turnbull's Sydney electorate. We are a very stupid country.

Tony Abbott described this budget as 'an act of political courage'. Australians thought it was shithouse. It was the least popular budget in living memory, almost all of its major proposals were subsequently rejected by the Senate or dumped by the government, and it soon led to Abbott's tanking popularity and removal as PM, and his replacement by Ol' Debt Truck Turnbull.

Thankfully, the country managed to avoid the worst of the austerity pain that Abbott and Hockey had been dreaming of. But we still had to look on in disbelief as the same right-wing twats who had been whining constantly about Labor's mismanagement of the budget proceeded to double the debt and slash corporate and personal taxes all over the shop. In the age of personal responsibility, ripping more than $200 billion from the public purse to give millionaires a $9k tax cut is Superior Economic Management, but for anything else, the cupboard is bare.

'Would every politician love to increase [the unemployment benefit] Newstart? I think so,' Liberal Senator Eric Abetz told a *Q+A* audience in July 2019, with a heavy heart. '[But] you have to try to balance the budget . . . And if we didn't have that burden of debt, didn't have to pay that interest, chances are there'd be money around to, in fact, provide an increase for Newstart.'

Weirdly, Eric couldn't find any money to raise the rate of Newstart during the eleven years of the Howard government, either, even as his party was gleefully selling off public assets and reaping the benefits of the mining boom to reduce the country's net debt to zero.

It's almost as if these people only give a flying fuck about the Big Scary Debt when they can use it as a political weapon to beat back any calls for wealth redistribution to improve ordinary people's lives. Deficit hawks will somehow *always* find a way to cut taxes for the top and buy more submarines, fighter jets and drones, but when it comes to providing enough food or houses for the masses, then sorry, we'd love to, but you know – *The Debt*. Bank account says, 'No.'

YOU, ME & MMT

The debt hysteria becomes truly ridiculous when you consider that **it's literally fucking impossible for the Australian government to run out of money**.

This is the crux of a growing school of economic thought known as **Modern Monetary Theory (MMT)**, which holds that a 'monetary sovereign' country like Australia – a country with a central bank (the RBA) that issues, taxes and borrows in its own currency, with a floating dollar – can technically create as many Australian dollars as it damn well likes. There is actually no budgetary reason to limit public spending, because we *MAKE* the dollars, bitch. An MMTer would say that the government doesn't even need to issue bonds to raise money to cover a budget deficit; the RBA can simply *spend the money into existence*, like a goddamn genie.

Importantly, while the Theory tells us Australia *could* print an infinite amount of money, it also says that we definitely shouldn't, because at some point that will spark serious inflation. If a monetary sovereign government spends so much that demand in the economy outstrips supply – i.e. people want more stuff than the economy can produce with its real resources – then prices will shoot up, and the currency will be devalued. *But,* say MMT proponents, as long as there are so many underutilised resources in an economy – plenty of unemployed or under-employed people, plenty of work that needs doing (building public housing, providing care, helping the environment not die, etc.) and plenty of people who need stuff – we've got a fair bit of room to move before we run into that problem, so we should be prepared to run deficits in the near term in order to get to full employment and to create a better society yayyyy.

Perhaps one of the more mind-bending ideas embedded in MMT is that **taxes don't actually fund public spending**. We assume the federal government needs to collect taxes from us or borrow money before it can spend, but on the MMT view, it's the other way around: **the government creates new currency every time it spends into the economy**. That money is passed around for a while, then the government effectively destroys it through taxation. MMT still thinks taxes are *necessary*, just not because they raise revenue for government spending. Rather, taxes are important for controlling inflation, creating demand for our currency, changing behaviour (by discouraging you from buying cigarettes or delicious alcopops), and – my favourite! – **reducing inequality**.[32]

Modern Monetary Theory is grounded in an accurate description of how our monetary system works, but if you're waiting to see its policy prescriptions seriously implemented in the current Australian political landscape, you might be waiting for a long time. It's widely dismissed and despised by much of the political, economic and media establishment, which is firmly committed to the idea that budget surpluses are vital and deficits are evil and most importantly, better things aren't possible.

There are fun little moments, though, when MMT reality makes itself undeniable. Back in 2009, the Chair of the US Federal Reserve Ben Bernanke told CBS's *60 Minutes* that the US$1 trillion the Fed had used to bail out the American banking system following the GFC was not, in fact, 'taxpayers' money' – it was printed.

'It's not tax money,' he said. 'The banks have accounts with the Fed, much the same way that you have an account in a commercial bank. So, to lend to a bank, **we simply use the computer to mark up the size of the account** that they have with the Fed. It's much more akin to printing money than it is to borrowing.'

Perhaps like me, you'd assumed that working at a central bank was full of complex scary maths and charts and Excel and stuff, and I'm sure they do have all that, but apparently, at the end of the day, it's pretty much just like *bleep bloop blop* congrats you have a trillion dollars now.

So don't be fooled, people: **the elitist obsession with 'balancing the budget' is just another ruling-class con that helps the rich stay rich and the rest get screwed.** Even now, with the massive amounts of government spending during the COVID pandemic, Australia's gross debt is still only projected to reach 50% of GDP by 2025. That puts us about on par with the debt

---

32 I quite like the MMT notion that taxes don't really fund public spending, because it means that everybody who has ever said something mean on the internet about my ABC work being a 'waste of taxpayers' money' is objectively and categorically wrong.

levels of (super-economy) Germany, while the gross debts of the UK, Canada, France, the US and Japan all exceed 100% of GDP. Our national debt after World War II peaked in 1946 at 120% of GDP, and in the post-war boom times of full employ-ment and deficit spending, the economy grew and grew, and debt was reduced to pre-war levels in less than a decade.

'My hope is that moving forward, we focus on the deficits that matter,' Ed Miller told me on my podcast towards the end of 2020. At the time, Ed was the Economic Fairness Campaigns Director at GetUp!, and he clearly thinks the debt'n'deficit sideshow is anything but economically fair.

'I hope we focus on the deficit of jobs and income support above the poverty line; we focus on the deficit in affordable childcare or mental healthcare; we focus on the deficit in climate action on the scale and pace that we need it; and we prosecute an argument that says public investment in those things is good and will improve people's lives.'

TAX TIME, BITCHES

At this rate, **wealth inequality is only going to get worse.** Our future is set to be one in which democratic decisions will be almost totally dwarfed by the whims and preferences of our trillionaire overlords. Such a dramatically unequal world will inevitably squelch economic growth and worsen social mobility, and it'll be a real bummer of a place in which to live. Rates of mental illness are five times higher in the world's most unequal societies (low-tax, free-market AmeriKKKa) than in the more equal ones (high-taxing, social democratic Norway and Denmark), so an even more asymmetrically wealthy Planet Earth is sure to make us all the more miserable. It will also kill a shitload of people: Oxfam says that based on its 'conservative estimates', **global inequality is contributing to the deaths of at least 21,300 people every day.**

This spiralling inequality is, as Oxfam notes, straight up **economic violence.**

If you ask me, such radical inequality requires radical solutions. We have to liquify the rich and the world's corporate behemoths ASAP. They must be shackled and soaked and eaten and flipped upside down and shaken so that all the spare change falls out of their pockets and is redistributed to the masses, because – despite what you've heard – **taxing the rich is really good, actually.**

Supply-side economics has been unequivocally proven to be a failure and it has to die.[33] Even a cheerleader for free markets, free trade, smaller government, lower taxes and fiscal austerity like the IMF has had to change course on this; in 2017 the Fund said that income and wealth taxes for the 1% should be 'significantly higher', and that raising taxes on the oligarchs wouldn't damage growth. It recommended the same thing in its World Economic Outlook report for 2020, calling for progressive taxation, digital taxes and a crackdown on multinational tax avoidance.

Thomas Piketty has argued that billionaires should be taxed out of existence. He's called for a **graduated wealth tax** – a tax on all those unproductive assets that rich people love to hoard – of 5% on those worth €2 million or more, and up to 90% on those with more than €2 billion. Obama floated the **'Buffett Rule'** in 2011 (named after Warren Buffett, who'd publicly called for higher taxes on the wealthy when he realised that he was paying less in federal taxes as a proportion of his income than his secretary). The Rule is basically a deductions cap that would apply a **minimum amount of tax on high-income earners,** no matter what nonsense they wanted to claim to minimise their tax bill. The Republicans killed it in 2012, of

---

33 And we know it. In the 2019 *Australia Talks* survey, 59% of Australians thought that the statement 'When businesses make a lot of money, everyone benefits, even the poor' was bullshit.

course (because of freedom/socialism/Kenya etc.), but progressive think tank Per Capita's annual Tax Survey has consistently found broad public support for the introduction of a Buffett Rule in Australia, including from a majority of Coalition voters.

If you want to cut taxes for everyday workers, then absolutely don't increase the rate of the GST (as many on the Right are wont to do); lower it on essentials, cut income tax for everyone earning $60k or less and increase them for those making $300k and over. Blow the Stage 3 tax cuts up with dynamite. The fact that well-paid FIFO workers and Gina Rinehart are in the same tax bracket is insane, so whack a few more tax brackets in there while you're at it and let's get back to 80% marginal tax rates on the plutocrats.[34] We should scrap stamp duty (a tax on *buying* a house? Come on!) and impose property and land taxes instead. We should tax massive financial transactions and banks, end the use of super accounts as tax shelters and collect windfall taxes when energy companies make bajillions simply because Russia invades Ukraine. We should make the fossil fuel companies *actually pay their taxes*, and then we should tax them some more, just for fun.

Yes, we should have inheritance/estate/bequest taxes for the super-rich because they're efficient and righteous and help reduce inequality. Before 1979, Australian governments levied inheritance taxes for more than 60 years. We used them to help fund health, education and fighting the Nazis, before they were abolished in Queensland by the corrupt semi-fascist racist caricature Joh Bjelke-Petersen, and the

---

34 In fairness to Arthur Laffer, plenty of economists would argue that the Laffer Curve isn't incorrect *per se*; it's just that top tax rates in the developed world haven't been anywhere near the 'tipping point' at which they seriously affect people's incentives for decades. Therefore, cutting them even further is very stupid.

    A 2014 paper co-authored by Thomas Piketty found a 'socially optimal' top tax rate would be about 83%, which would cause Arthur Laffer and the rest of the ruling class to shit the bed and ruin their silk sheets.

rest of the country followed suit. When the Queensland tax was scrapped, it affected just 9% of deaths and most people paid a mere 3% of their estate's value, but now it's gone and we're one of the few OECD countries without any such levy. We should grow up for fuck's sake, dismiss the dumb little baby label of 'DEATH TAXES!!!' and rebrand them as something more accurate and cooler, like 'The Waterhouse/ Palmer/Cannon-Brookes/Murdoch/Rinehart Tax'. The children of this tiny group of objectionably wealthy people will still inherit more money than most of us will see in our lifetime. Trust me – they'll be fine.

Yes, all this will be painted as 'class war' – because that's precisely what it is, and what we need. We should heed the examples of Charles Foster Kane, Jay Gatsby, Lex Luthor, Montgomery Burns, Scrooge McDuck, Jabba the Hutt, Smaug the Dragon and every Bond villain ever: **under capitalism, where money is power, the super-rich become gods, and they will always use their excessive power to protect their riches.** They are our enemy, their interests do not align with ours, and the sooner we collectively recognise that and bring them to heel, the better.

As my mate and Australian *Jacobin* magazine contributing editor Daniel Lopez once tweeted: 'When the Left start talking about the rich the way Liberals talk about the unemployed, then we'll be getting somewhere.'

6

Nature Isn't Healing

BATMAN: What is it? Mankind's melting the polar
ice caps, destroying the ecosystem – they've got
it coming?
AQUAMAN: I don't mind if the oceans rise.
BATMAN: How about if they <u>boil?</u>

– *Justice League*, 2017[1]

In 1995, the Ballards hitched a camper trailer to the back
of our '85 Nissan Bluebird and set out from Warrnambool
on a three-month trip halfway around Australia. We went
straight up the guts via Alice Springs to Darwin, hooked
a right over to the Daintree, then headed home down the
east coast.

We drove for hours and hours and hours across the outback, cranking our Paul Kelly and John Williamson tape
cassettes, drinking in this seemingly endless country. For
weeks, I was surrounded by bucketloads of natural splendour: brutal deserts, luscious rainforests, perfect beaches

---

1   0 stars.

Our Priscilla.

and adorable animals. It all blew my tiny, five-year-old mind. Our little corner of Planet Earth was clearly magical, and I couldn't believe I got to live in it.

Gavin and me, getting sunburnt.

We even got to climb Uluru without getting cancelled because it was the 90s.

(Sorry.)

My parents encouraged me to keep a diary throughout the trip, and in its lined pages, I tried my best to capture the wondrous natural Australian beauty I was seeing all around me, every day.

> Saturday August 5th (MATARANKA)
> Or oley! we drove from Tarwin to MaTARAnKA. we went swimig in the theoow rool. it! was byotfoll! there was a wota rithen,

Translation: 'oley' = early, 'theoow' = thermal,
'byotfull' = beautiful, 'wota pithen' = water python.

I documented everything: our time kayaking through Katherine Gorge, watching camel races in Alice Springs and going to Hollywood (On The Gold Coast), and even the day when 'i went to hopsital becos my ear was sore and I vomitd in the trailer'.

But the part of Australia that Little Tom found to be the most byotfull of all was the Great Barrier Reef. In the last week of the trip, we set out on a catamaran from Airlie Beach to the waters around Daydream Island, and jumped onto a glass-bottomed sub to take in the stunning technicoloured corals and marine life below us:

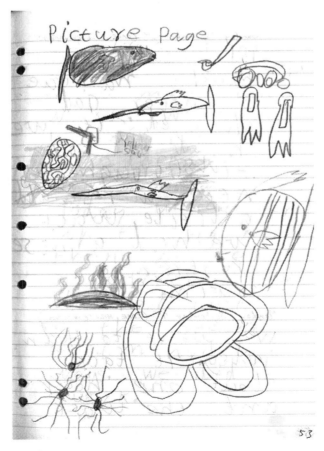

(Not to scale.)

In his diary, Gavin described the Reef as a 'world made by amazing architects – polyps', and delighted in the 'greens, browns, greys, purples and yellows, corals of all colours and sizes, <u>fish</u> of all colours and sizes, and plants' that he could see. I loved the 'spaghetti coral, plat coral [?] and bran coral [??]', and apparently I was stoked when we 'fed the fishe big and smol thay came etig there big dina'.

Almost thirty years later, I can still vividly remember snorkelling in the crystal-clear warm waters of the Whitsundays, hovering over mountain ranges of coral, surrounded by shimmering schools of bright yellow fish and, at one point, swimming alongside a motherfucking sea turtle. It was *dope.*

Back in '95, the planet's atmosphere had a carbon dioxide concentration level of around 360 molecule parts per million (ppm). Today, it's reached 420 ppm, and the Great Barrier Reef is getting bleached more regularly than an Instagram model's anus. As the planet cooks, much of the additional heat goes straight into the world's oceans, which causes more frequent marine heatwaves, which puts the world's corals under greater stress, and gives them less time to recover. Stressed corals discharge the algae that live inside them and give them most of their energy, which is what causes them to be 'bleached' white, placing them at a higher risk of dying completely and being unable to support the kind of vibrant ecosystem I was enchanted by as a child.

The Reef has experienced six mass bleaching events since 1998 – three of them since 2016 – and half of its coral has been lost. According to the UN's Intergovernmental Panel on Climate Change (IPCC), *even if* humanity is able to get its shit together and limit global heating to 1.5°C above pre-industrial levels, the world is still projected to lose 75% of its coral reefs. The Australian Academy of Science predicts the Reef will shrink by at least 70% in a 1.5°C warmer world, and if the warming reaches 2°C, then it's basically game over.

Just 1% of the Reef would (might?) survive, and almost all the coral would be bleached and the sea turtles and the Nemos and Dorys would die, and the underwater splendour of this Natural Wonder of The World would only live on in our hearts and minds, and in my drawings.

This is now the gigantic, all-encompassing elephant in every room. On top of everything else – the decimation of workers' power, a broken housing market, the commodification of everything from knowledge to water and rampant inequality – **the natural world that has been left to Millennials is on fire.**

My generation faces a big fat existential crisis not just of the prevailing political and economic order, but of ecological breakdown. Our time is running out, and it's becoming painfully clear that business as usual isn't going to save us, and neither will Batman, Aquaman, Captain Planet, Widget the World Watcher or Sir David Attenborough.

PROGNOSIS: NEGATIVE

Cards on the table: I don't really 'do' 'science'. I dropped out of all such subjects in Year 9 so that I could ignore *facts* and focus on my *feelings* in subjects like Theatre Studies and Philosophy. Ever since, I've done my best to avoid all numbers and words like 'hydrofluorocarbons' and 'megawatt hour', because they make me feel dumb and scared.

Why should I bother wading into the incredibly complex and controversial questions surrounding climate science? I'd often think to myself. *After all, these matters are already being considered and debated by some of the finest minds of our age.*

 **Britney Spears** ✔
@britneyspears   ...

Does anyone think global warming is a good thing? I love Lady Gaga. I think she's a really interesting artist.

5:31 AM · Feb 11, 2011 · Twitter Web Client

But by now, even a cucked little poet like me has had no choice but to get my head around the basics of this environmental crisis. I've watched the Al Gore movie and *Don't Look Up* and I follow the CSIRO on Twitter, and I've officially come to the conclusion that **it's looking real bad, folks.** Human activity is emitting unsustainable levels of greenhouse gases like carbon dioxide and methane, thereby trapping more of the sun's radiated heat that would otherwise escape the atmosphere, and warming the planet's average temperature.

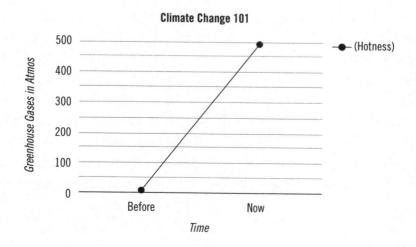

Basically, we are Dutch oven-ing ourselves to death.

This dramatic increase in hotness is, in geological terms, a very recent thing. In the 10,000 years prior to the 18th century – a period known as **The Holocene** – the earth's climate was remarkably stable: the naturally occurring greenhouse effect was doing its thing with a totally normal level of CO_2 in the atmosphere – around the 270 ppm mark – and all was fine and dandy. Then the steam engine came along in the 1700s, which eventually kicked off the Industrial Revolution, which heralded a new mode of mass production, featuring heaps of machines and factories, all of them powered by steam, which was produced by burning thermal coal. Industrialists started to burn the stuff for electricity in the late 1880s, then the internal combustion engine arrived in the early 20th century and so we needed to burn another fossil fuel – oil – to power our shiny new automobiles, and that craze eventually caught on and took off in a major way, and things have carried on like that for more than a century and it's been great fun and all but the entire time we've been unleashing more and more gas-blankets into the sky and boiling ourselves alive.

The IPCC estimates that between 1850 and 2019, humankind – particularly the humankind in the rich, developed Global North – has emitted about 2390 gigatonnes of CO_2 into the atmosphere.[2] **In that time, the earth's average temperate has warmed by 1.1°C.** The last time the earth's temperature changed this rapidly was back when an asteroid the size of a city slammed into Earth and wiped out the dinosaurs, which is widely considered to be a major L.

Now here we are, 66 million years later, living through what some have dubbed **The Anthropocene**: the period in Earth's history when human activity is significantly shaping the planet's climate and ecosystems. We've managed to cook

---

2   One gigatonne = one billion metric tonnes, so that's **2,390,000,000,000 metric tonnes of CO_2**. So a fair bit.

up an asteroid all by ourselves. Unless we stop doing that mighty fucking fast – in 2018, the IPCC told us we had just 12 years left before we exhausted our carbon budget – then life on this planet will eventually become unbearable, then impossible. Our extinction is just as assured as the dinosaurs' was, even if our apocalypse will be less wham/bam/dead, and more torturously gradual, playing out over decades and decades of rising sea levels, mass extinctions, hardcore natural disasters and general civilisational breakdown.

It's extremely dire, and I'm sorry about bringing it up, but – you know. It's quite important, and even though it feels like we're often endlessly talking about it all the time, we probably don't talk about it nearly *enough*.

In the interests of underlining just how grim our predicament is, below I've set out some of the most soul-crushing facts about humanity's crimes against nature and some chilling predictions of what might be coming. But to help soften the blow, I've put all that in a smaller font, and interspersed it with some delightful facts about the animal kingdom.

See how you go:

According to the World Wildlife Fund, humanity has wiped out 60% of mammals, birds, fish and reptiles since 1970.

Squirrels have been known to take in orphaned pups if the babies are closely related to the adoptive mother.

The world's oceans are now heating at the same rate as if five Hiroshima atomic bombs were being dropped into the water every second.

When playing with female puppies, male puppies will often let the females win.

Greenland's icesheets hold enough water to raise world sea levels by seven metres. The island is currently losing 283 gigatonnes of ice every year.

A pig's orgasm can last for 30 minutes.

The World Health Organization estimates that between 2030 and 2050, there will be around 250,000 excess deaths per year due to climate change, caused by heat stress, diarrhoea, malaria and childhood malnutrition.

A group of ferrets is called a 'business'.

BURNT COUNTRY

If that didn't blackpill you enough, remember that things are *uniquely* shitty for us here in Australia. There are now basically just two seasons in this country: 'on fire' and 'underwater'. These natural disasters are becoming so harsh and so frequent, Australia is starting to resemble the Bible, but with more swearing.[3] Our already-pretty-extreme climate, high fire risk, existing water supply pressures and our fondness for coastal living make us one of the most vulnerable countries in the developed world when it comes to the impact of climate change, and because warming doesn't impact the world in a uniform fashion, **we're actually experiencing 1.4°C of warming down here already.**

Millennials have been watching this reality play out in a brutal fashion over the course of our short lives: the Millennium Drought, the Queensland and Eastern Australia floods and the bushfires of Black Saturday and Black Summer. All of these devastating events were made more severe by our cooked climate, and in an even hotter world there'll be plenty more environmental dogshit where that came from.[4]

Plus, our country is not only highly vulnerable to the effects of climate change, it's also highly *culpable* for the

---

3   And fewer brown people.
       And – because we've privatised our vocational education system – fewer carpenters.

4   In the Australian government's latest State of the Environment Report, we learned that NSW's bushfire season now officially lasts for eight months.

crisis getting worse. Australia is a very naughty climate citizen: we make up less than 0.35% of the world's population, but domestically we emit about 1.2% of global emissions, making us **one of the biggest per-capita polluters on the globe.** We're also one of the world's top three fossil fuel exporters, and if you add in all the emissions embedded in our highly lucrative export industry, you'll find that almost **4% of the world's annual greenhouse gas emissions are Australian.**

Successive Australian governments have thwarted global climate action and actively expanded and subsidised the fossil fuel industry. They've used dodgy accounting tricks around changes to 'land use' so they can claim that we're massively reducing emissions, when in fact emissions have been steadily rising since 2014.[5] We're regularly ranked dead last in the developed world when it comes to climate action, and heaps of other countries like to call us 'climate laggards' who are 'dragging our feet' on this vital issue, and they laugh at us and look down their noses at us, even the fucking French.

So to summarise: we Millennials were born onto a planet that is being pushed to its absolute limits, and unless things change drastically ASAP, this heated Earth could visit untold misery upon billions of people in the coming decades. It could mean the end of all human civilisation, and at times it feels like the Xers and Boomers who run this country seem quite content for things to carry on as they always have, even as everyone with a lab coat is screeching at the top of their lungs, trying to shake us out of our stupor and into action, for the love of everything we hold sacred.

But try not to get too depressed about it. Look – here's another cute photo of me from that holiday:

---

5   The only major drop in national emissions we've seen recently was during the pandemic, which is cheating.

This is the last one of these, so make the most of it.

IT'S (POTENTIALLY) NOT THE END OF THE WORLD

Thinking about these realities and implications of the climate crisis is a major, constant, and inescapable bonerkiller.[6]

In recent years, it feels as though barely a week has gone by in which we haven't read an article about some new report from the scientific community pleading with us to stop ignoring the rapture that awaits us, or about some adorable animal that has now become endangered and been put onto Lexapro, thanks to our passion for environmental liquification. Our society generally tends to treat these warnings with the same level of attention and respect we give to telephone

---

6   When I was hosting *Tonightly* in 2018, I got to interview **Bill McKibben**: the renowned environmentalist and journalist, and the founder of the climate campaign group 350.org. When I bluntly asked him, 'Are we fucked?', he replied, 'It depends on the degree of fuck-edness you're worried about.

      'We raised the temperature of the Earth 1 degree so far: that's cost us half the ice in the Arctic, and half the Great Barrier Reef. We're headed for 2°C unless we take heroic measures. In fact, on the current business-as-usual, Paris Accord-kind-of-path, the planet will warm 3.5°C in the course of this century. That's warmer than it's been since before the beginning of primate evolution.

      'So – *yeah*. **We're not in a really good place.**'

contract terms and conditions, or to flight attendants giving the in-flight safety demonstration.

No wonder this torrent of bad news has triggered a widespread rise in **eco-anxiety**, especially amongst the young. Poll after poll has found Australians consistently naming the climate crisis as one of their top political concerns, and young people are increasingly losing hope that their future will involve a functioning planet. In an Australian Conservation Foundation survey of more than six thousand women in 2019, for example, 78% of respondents said they or their friends and family had experienced worry or anxiety about our climate future, and one in three women under 30 were 'reconsidering having children or having more children because I am increasingly worried they will face an unsafe future from climate change'.[7]

Plenty of youngsters have already gone full doomer. In one global survey of nearly 23,000 Millennials and Zoomers, more than 40% of respondents said they believed the world has 'already hit the point of no return when it comes to the environment and that it's too late to repair the damage', presumably before cranking up Billie Eilish and Post Malone's 'Happier Than Ever' and livestreaming their Tide Pod-overdose suicides to TikTok.

And fair enough. It's perfectly logical to be so bleak. Considering everything we know about the way the climate crisis is melting the planet, and considering the paltry efforts of the world's political leaders to do anything to stop that melting, it's understandable that kids today would see no choice but to adopt a blunt pessimism about it all, and will just morosely try to accept the fact that their future is going to look like some combination of *Waterworld* and *Floor Is Lava*. I mean, even on the most optimistic view, we still

---

7   This is seriously messed up. Of *course* people should continue to have babies in the face of the looming climate crisis! Just think of the organs.

have to acknowledge the basic reality **that climate change is already very much here with us right now**, shaping our world in a million ways, and there's a certain amount of heating already locked in that is definitely going to change what life on Earth is like over the rest of this century. No matter what we manage to do in terms of climate action over the next couple of decades, we're going to have to, in some ways, adapt to and mitigate the damage from our busted atmosphere. That's just #facts.[8]

BUT – at least for now, on a technicality, almost certainly (I'm pretty sure) – **it is still totally possible for us to avoid the absolute worst-case scenario.**[9] The best available science tells us that our collective climate demise is not yet a foregone conclusion: we still have a window in which our actions can make a serious difference in just how much damage and suffering is inflicted on the babies of today over the decades to come. Yes, 1.5°C of warming is certainly going to be, er, *challenging*, but it's going to be shitloads better than a 2°C warmer world; the IPCC predicts that just half a degree could mean the difference of 10 million or so more climate refugees escaping rising sea levels by 2100, the extinction of twice as many species, and the death of *all* the world's coral. Every decimal of a degree of warming that we manage to avoid is a very good and very important win, and we really need to start winning, and we need to start yesterday.

Thankfully, we have all the knowledge and the technology to allow us to do this. Yay team. But the seismic effort required involves **changing pretty much everything**. It looks something like this:

---

8   According to the Tory politician and demographer Lord David Willetts, keeping warming to 1.5°C will require the typical European Millennial to produce less than two-thirds of the CO_2 that European Boomers have pumped out over the course of their lifetimes.

9   (Probably.)

⇒ DECARBONISE LIKE A MF

Humanity needs to decarbonise, quick sticks. We need to return the level of CO_2 in our atmosphere to a safe level of 350 ppm. According to the Climate Council, in order to limit warming to 1.5°C, Australia must cut its greenhouse gas emissions by 75% on 2005 levels by 2030, and reach net zero emissions by 2035 at the latest.[10]

⇒ FOSSIL FUELS? YOU'RE CANCELLED

We have to stop the burning of coal, oil and gas entirely. Existing fossil fuels need to be rapidly phased out over the next decade, the squillions of dollars in fossil fuel subsidies our government hands out need to be nixed and **we can't afford to have any new fossil fuel projects,** thank you very much. At least 95% of Australia's coal needs to stay in the ground and we can't be having any new oil or gas fields. Zero. None. Zilch. Nada.

'Not even just a couple more fossil fuel projects, Tom?' you ask.

I shake my head, frowning sternly.

'Not even the really big ones that will make, like, *billions of dollars?'*

---

10 In 2011, Labor PM Julia Gillard established the **Australian Climate Commission** to provide independent, expert, scientifically rigorous advice to government on climate change, which was a super lovely idea. But when Tony Abbott got elected in 2013, his government abolished the Commission because it cost money that could have been better spent on shiny medals for Prince Philip or on forcing drag queens to read the Bible.

In response, the former Climate Commissioners – led by former Australian of the Year, Professor Tim Flannery – organised a mass crowd-funding campaign to establish a new, independent and community-funded organisation called the **Climate Council** to keep doing the original Commission's important work, which is exactly what they've been doing ever since.

Unfortunately, even though the Council is the legacy of a great decision made by a former Labor government, today's ALP seems perfectly happy to ignore the body's authoritative advice when it comes to the climate crisis and the action required to seriously confront it. Throughout the 2022 election, the Labor Party carried on advocating for unsatisfactory emissions reductions targets that will send us into a 2°C warmer hellworld, all while crowing about how their election would mean 'the Climate Wars are over!!!', presumably because they're happy to let the climate lose.

'I'm afraid not, little fella. Hey – I don't make the rules. Take it up with the International Energy Agency, the UN, and physics.'

'But wha–'

'No.'

⇒ GO-GO RENEWABLES

Electricity generation is our country's largest source of emissions, so we need to move to 100% renewable energy, ASAP. (And make as much of it publicly owned as possible, please.) We can absolutely achieve this in the very near future, what with the costs of switching to renewables plummeting so quickly in recent years that it is now the cheapest form of energy available, and what with us living on the sunniest and windiest continent on Earth.

About a quarter of Australia's total energy now comes from renewables. There are already more than three million Australian homes with rooftop solar installed, the Australian Capital Territory is already at 100% net renewable energy, South Australia is on its way there too and Tasmania has a legislated renewable energy target of 200% by 2040, which either means they're terrible at maths down there, or they're planning on becoming a renewable energy *exporter*, which is a thing.

Plus, while we're saving all the money on the cheapness of renewables, we can afford to invest in lots of storage technologies like big-ass batteries and pumped hydro to ensure that all that yummy renewable energy becomes dispatchable power that we can use whenever we goddamn please, and even start creating hundreds of thousands of good new jobs by exporting renewable energy overseas.

And 100% renewable energy will deliver us clean and meaningful 'energy independence'; a country can't really be held hostage by another over its access to the sun or to wind, so a world free of fossil fuels will mean far fewer chaotic energy crises and resource-based conflicts, and if you hate wind and solar farms you're basically admitting that you want Putin to win, which is very uncool.

⇒ ELECTRIFY EVERYTHING

We're talking **everything**: electric vehicles replacing petrol cars and buses and (high-speed rail) trains; induction stoves replacing gas cookers; reverse-cycle air conditioning replacing gas heaters and those shitty, inefficient oil column heaters that you always burn yourself on when you're living in a shitty Melbourne sharehouse in your early twenties.

This cunt.
(Photo: iStock.com/Grassetto)

Through the mighty power of incentives, mandates, rebates, subsidies, regulations and royal decrees, we need to whack a power cord onto everything that's currently fossil fuel-y and plug it into our shiny new green electricity grid. This will be better for the planet, and better for humans; the World Health Organization estimates about 7 million people die from air pollution every single year.

⇒ **SWALLOW CARBON**

As well as not pumping *more* CO_2 into the atmosphere, we've got to draw down as much of the gunk that's already up there as possible. Fortunately, a great way to do this is by doing something that we should be doing anyway: **restoring nature**. Australia has one of the highest land-clearing rates in the developed world, so we really need to end that immediately, and do everything we can to convince Brazil to stop turning the Amazon into Chernobyl. Then, by planting shitloads of trees and mangroves, preserving wilderness in existing national parks and wetlands (and making new ones), and by funding and empowering First Nations rangers to use their ancient knowledge systems to care for country, we can create massive natural carbon sinks that can draw down and store emissions.[11]

☢☢ WARNING ☢☢ Be careful of pricks in the fossil fuel industry and conservative governments getting *very excited* about the idea of sequestering

---

11 This sort of thing can even happen underwater, by growing more seaweed and even using marine life. Whales store huge amounts of carbon in their big blubbery bodies, for example, and research from 2021 suggests that if global whale populations were restored to their pre-whaling levels, they could sequester 1.7 billion tonnes of carbon every year and ensure it's all trapped way down in the deep sea, which would be them really doing us a tremendous solid, especially after we've been spending the past couple of centuries killing the shit out of them and subjecting them to the horrors of Sea World.

carbon IF it allows them to spruik their pet science project, **Carbon Capture & Storage (CCS)** technology. This is the magical idea that we can make the burning of (dirty) fossil fuels 'clean' by capturing its emissions before they float up into the sky and permanently bury them deep underground, like a teenage boy stuffing desecrated tissues under his mattress. If CCS can be proven to work, then companies like Chevron and Shell can happily carry on making billions of dollars and claim to be emissions-free because they're storing their rotten farts under the carpet.

It's a wonderful notion, except that it sucks and it doesn't work. Since 1999, Australian governments have sunk more than $4 billion of public money into CCS research and development, only $60 million of which has ever made it to a commercial-scale project: Chevron's massive Gorgon gas project off the north coast of WA, which went way over budget and emitted 7 million more tons of CO_2 than it was supposed to. CCS has consistently been shown to be crazy-expensive and completely ineffective at meeting its emissions-reduction targets, and has been exposed for what it is: a way for corporations and governments to put off the important work that needs to be done now based on the hope of some future sci-fi fix.

'Clean coal' is an oxymoron, used by morons and hucksters who are just trying to keep their dying industry alive, even if that means killing the planet. Give me more whales over fossil fuel fat cats any day.

⇒ TRANSITION JUSTLY

This radical shift away from burning old shit to power everything and the complete transformation of what the Australian economy looks like is going to be quite the to-do. For the communities that have relied on the mining or the burning of fossil fuels for aeons – like Gladstone in Central Queensland, the Hunter Valley in NSW or Collie in WA – a rapid transition to a renewable economy could understandably look terrifying and uncertain. The only tenable way forward for any of this to work is to ensure that our transition to a zero-carbon future is a just one, in which not a single worker or community is left behind.

We know this, because it's been done. Governments in Germany, France and Spain have managed the closing down of their black and brown coal industries in recent times without sacking a single worker. After the French company that owned the Hazelwood power station in Gippsland suddenly announced its closure in 2016 – leaving its workers just five months' notice to rethink the rest of their lives – a community campaign to save the Latrobe Valley pushed the Victorian state government to establish the Latrobe Valley Authority, which has centred community involvement and decision-making in its efforts to help workers to retrain with new skills or build new industries. These transitions have varied from community to community, but the successful ones have all involved the same ingredients: long-term, orderly economic planning that places people before profits, and gives locals a real say over how their community's green transition will work. Thanks to this kind of planning, some Australian mining towns are already planning to switch to mining other rare minerals needed for green technology like lithium and nickel, while others are reforging their economies around renewables, tourism, agriculture or mine rehabilitation. It takes a lot of time and hard work – and it *must* be informed and guided by what climate science is telling us, even when it's telling us pretty brutal truths – but it can totally be done.

The alternative, of course, is to leave the fate of such communities in the hands of The Market, which really couldn't give a flying fuck about them. Fossil fuel bosses have never had the best interest of workers at heart; over the years, they've been happy to subject coal miners to brutal working conditions and Black Lung, crush them when they go on strike, isolate them in FIFO ghost towns, replace them with robots wherever possible and immediately leave them in the lurch as soon as production becomes unprofitable. Private fossil fuel capital's version of transition will be painful and chaotic for ordinary people on the ground; democratic intervention and investment by non-market forces has to be the way to go, even if that means using all that fossil fuel subsidy money to pay out every single one of Australia's 38,000 coal miners their full wage until death, and ensuring they have awesome retirements by showering them with jet skis and piña coladas and the very best in haemorrhoid pillow technology.

⇒ AND HEY, LET'S GET NUTTY WITH IT

If we can get all that done and we're *still* staring into the face of some serious climate shitfuckery, we should be open to the possibility of trying out some weird stuff, just for fun. Recently, various scientific outfits have proposed tackling the climate crisis by employing **geoengineering**: using large-scale interventions in the planet's climate system to halt or reduce global heating. Examples include getting planes to spray millions of tonnes of sulphur into the atmosphere to dim the sunlight hitting the Earth, building a 500,000 sq km 'space shade' to protect us like a gigantic legionnaires hat, and even slightly pushing the Earth's axis a fraction away from the sun.

I am not at all qualified to say whether any of this is at all possible, useful or moral, but it is very funny to think about, and it makes me feel like I'm in an episode of *Futurama*, which is a nice distraction from the reality that things are quickly getting worse and we're living on borrowed time.

. . . YES, IT'S A LOT

Like, a *lot*. This transformation clearly requires a huge amount of work and effort and planning, and a fuckload of investment. In his 2006 UK government-commissioned Review on the Economics of Climate Change, leading economist Nicholas Stern estimated that cutting emissions to a safe level would cost the world about 1% of global GDP per year, which today would be something in the order of US$1 trillion.

That seems very pricey, until you start to consider the costs of everything being on fire all the time. Stern projected that ignoring climate change would cause economic damage in the order of up to 20% of global GDP (US$20 trillion) every year, while Deloitte Access Economics has put the price tag of unchecked climate change in Australia at about $3.4 trillion in lost economic opportunities, and has suggested we'll be copping an economic hit on par with COVID-19 every single year by 2050 if we don't get our shit together.[12]

---

12 This recognition that there really are **no jobs on a dead planet** is a far cry from the Australian government's approach to climate change back in the 90s. Faced with international pressure to do more, the Keating government desperately clung onto its '**no regrets**' policy, under which Australia would only consider measures that involved cutting emissions without any adverse impact on the economy or trade competitiveness. This meant no taxing carbon or phasing out fossil fuels.

So – heaps of regrets, then.

The size of the challenge and the timeline of action and the consequences of it all can be nightmarishly overwhelming. But it's important to reiterate that **achieving meaningful climate action is still within our reach.** Collective human action can do extraordinary, world-changing things, like winning a world war or going to the goddamn moon or splitting the atom or coordinating global cooperation and regulation to fix the hole in the ozone layer, so we do know that it's possible for humans to pull off something on this scale. And really, everyone *should* be totally on board with doing what's required to address the climate crisis, because it's about saving Planet Earth, which is the place – and I cannot stress this enough – where we all live.

So surely – *surely* – we can all unite as one nation and one species for the common good, and work together to fix this massive challenge now, right? *RIGHT, EVERYONE??*

crickets

Well . . . no. Even though the continuing existence of life on Earth is at stake here, it seems that our society is currently quite shithouse at 'coming together' to form a green/rainbow/kumbaya coalition to implement anything like the vital actions outlined above. Instead, ever since we Australian Millennials began watching the news, we've seen the climate 'issue' play out as a grinding, endless, toxic debate that's brought us nothing but partisan screaming, lies, political executions and inertia. Emissions are up, our dogshit energy system has prolapsed, and we've been treated to a steady stream of droughts, floods and fires. As the world's been burning and our window to change things has been shrinking, Australia has seemed happy to continually shoot itself in the foot and punch itself in the face.

For a Serious Centrist Commentator from Australia's media class, the correct diagnosis of this state of affairs is simply *Too Much Ideology!!!* 'The extremists on the Right are denying science,' they might say, 'while the extremists on the Green/Left are being overly alarmist and unreasonable, and they're just as bad as each other and really, why can't everyone just stop squabbling and being so polarised and sit down to work out some *pragmatic solutions* in The Sensible Centre? *Why can't we all just get along?!*'

This, I hope you will recognise by now, is 😀 😂 thinking. It's what a baby might think about the nature of the climate debate in Australia, if that baby were to turn its soft and silly baby brain to the subject, because a baby can only deal with simple concepts (like liberalism), and hasn't yet figured out how our country actually, materially works.

The bitter division surrounding the environmental crisis we face and what to do about it isn't simply rooted in good-faith disagreement between some losers in Canberra. Rather, it is rooted in and churned around by old mate **Capitalism.** Our fossil fuel economy has funnelled enormous amounts of wealth into the hands of a tiny class of very powerful corporations and individuals, and for these vampires, **saving the planet is bad for business.** These guys are not going quietly; they're extremely keen on maintaining the massive profits they make from turbocharging the climate crisis, and so for more than half a century they've been using all that wealth and power to wage a war on science, the truth, all forms of serious climate action and, by extension, us.

They have waged this war with the power of **The Three Major Ds:**

1) DENIAL

If you're worried about the government disrupting your multi-billion dollar grift by implementing serious action to address the climate crisis, why not simply deny that 'climate change' isn't even happening, and also you suck so there?

The major issue with this novel approach is the extensive, overwhelming scientific evidence that shows that it is stupid and wrong. Climate change is definitely happening, and it's definitely being caused by us. Our understanding of certain gases' role in exacerbating the greenhouse effect stretches all the way back to 1856, when American scientist Eunice Newton Foote conducted an experiment with an air pump, gas cylinders and thermometers to successfully demonstrate just how good CO_2 is at trapping heat. Following the results, she wrote her paper *Circumstances affecting the heat of the sun's rays*, in which she theorised that changes in CO_2 in the Earth's temperature might affect global temperatures.[13]

Over the next 160 years, heaps of smart virgins in lab coats have done lots and lots of science to flesh this theory out. Physical chemists started drawing the link between the greenhouse effect and the combustion of fossil fuels in the 1890s, and by the early 1910s, news reports like this were appearing in the print media without causing too much of a ruckus:

COAL CONSUMPTION AFFECT-ING CLIMATE.

The furnaces of the world are now burning about 2,000,000,000 tons of coal a year. When this is burned, uniting with oxygen, it adds about 7,000,000,000 tons of carbon dioxide to the atmosphere yearly. This tends to make the air a more effective blanket for the earth and to raise its temperature. The effect may be considerable in a few centuries.

From the 'Science Notes and News' section of
New Zealand's Rodney & Otamatea Times, *August 1912.*

---

13 Foote would later be praised for her discoveries in an edition of *Scientific American* magazine entitled 'Scientific Ladies', which was like the 1850s equivalent of a major broadsheet doing an 'Are Women Funny??' feature in 2022.

We already knew things were getting spicy by 1965, when President Lyndon Johnson's Science Advisory Committee issued a report that stated that 'pollutants have altered on a global scale the carbon dioxide content of the air' and the effects of all this 'could be deleterious from the point of view of human beings'. The world held its first ever world climate conference in 1979; by the 80s, the CSIRO was warning that unchecked climate change could mean that 'by the middle of next century, every year would be a potential "Ash Wednesday" year of extreme bushfire danger'; and before you know it the UN and the World Meteorological Organisation had set up the IPCC and it was drawing on the work of thousands of peer-reviewed scientific papers and pumping out a report in 1990 with a big clear bit at the start that says:

We are certain that emissions resulting from human activities are substantially increasing the atmospheric concentrations of the greenhouse gases carbon dioxide, methane, chlorofluorocarbons (CFCs) and nitrous oxide. These increases will enhance the greenhouse effect, resulting on average in an additional warming of the Earth's surface.

So really, this shit has been Case Closed for as long as I've been alive. In case you needed any more convincing, by the time we hit the 2010s, multiple peer-reviewed papers make it abundantly clear that the scientific consensus on human-induced global warming had reached the 99% mark, and the reality of what we're doing to our planet has been accepted and endorsed by everyone from the Bureau of Meteorology to NASA to The Australian Academy of Science to Leonardo DiCaprio. There is no longer any meaningful debate about the validity of this science, and if you're someone who is actively engaged with this stuff and *still* insisting on being a climate denier in the 2020s, I'm very sorry to say it but you are unequivocally a moron.[14]

But hey, perhaps you're just a humble mining executive who doesn't really *want* any of this to be true, and so you're willing to spend buckets of cash to purchase some 'science' that's more amenable to your bottom line. That's certainly been Big Fossil Fuel's strategic response ever since the eggheads handed LBJ that report back in the 60s: **to fund the production and propagation of climate doubt and denial wherever possible.**

Just as Big Tobacco used its resources to try to convince the public there was no link between smoking and cancer, the coal, oil and gas industries have poured squillions into funding 'independent' scientists and think tanks, and on mounting scary advertising campaigns to tell us all to calm down because the climate science is 'unsettled' or 'inconclusive'. As climate change became an increasingly mainstream political issue throughout the 90s, the big polluters like Exxon, BP, Chevron and the auto industry organised into lobby groups like the 'Global Climate Coalition' and the 'Information Council for the Environment' (ICE lol), whose explicit aim was to 'reposition global warming as theory (not fact)'. They've used their collective power to unleash a public relations assault on the idea that we should do anything to reduce emissions (especially moving away from fossil fuels), on the US's ratification of the UN's Kyoto Protocol, and on any four-eyed so-called expert who dared to speak the climate truth in public.

This was a deliberate mission to sow doubt and confusion, for the sake of advancing fossil fuel interests; in a 1998

---

14 'Come on, Tom – nobody who's an *actual* climate denier will have purchased a book written by *you*, a well-known bleeding-heart left-wing ABC homosexual!' I hear you say.

   To which I say, 'Who knows? These people are not exactly known for their research skills.'

strategy memo, the American Petroleum Institute's 'Global Climate Science Communications Team' noted that they'd be able to declare 'victory' when 'average citizens "understand" (recognise) uncertainties in climate science' and when 'those promoting the Kyoto treaty on the basis of extant science appear to be out of touch with reality'.[15]

The same war has been waged here in Australia, where we've been #blessed with our own corporate-funded pseudo-scientific whackjob propaganda outfits, including:

- **The Lavoisier Group**: a pressure group named in honour of the French chemist Antoine-Laurent Lavoisier, who went against the scientific orthodoxy of his day (and was put to the guillotine during the French Revolution for his trouble).

    The Group was founded in 2000 by Ray Evans (a very energetic reactionary neocon and former engineer at the Western Mining Corporation), Peter Walsh (a former Labor Finance Minister) and a board stacked with executives and engineers from Santos, Shell, BP and the mining industry. All of these men share both a fierce animosity towards all evidence of human-caused climate change, and a profound lack of scientific qualifications.

---

15 The case of Exxon is particularly enraging, because these motherfuckers *really knew*. They were publicly denying climate science and expanding their filthy operations at the same time as they were spending millions of dollars on their own ground-breaking research that was unequivocally telling them the climate crisis was very real – research which they then buried from public view for years.

   Even when Exxon's in-house scientists were advising them that the world had to quickly phase out of coal, and even as they were taking the time to *climate-proof their oil rigs from rising sea-levels*, the company was happily forking out pocket money for right-wing climate disinformation factories like The Heartland Institute and the American Enterprise Institute and probably the Jesus Freedom Eagle Deregulation Academy or whatever.

   The American writer and activist Upton Sinclair once famously observed that 'it is difficult to get a man to understand something when his salary depends upon his not understanding it'. Exxon executives might have understood what the climate science was saying, but they also understood that *their* salaries depended on policy makers and the public not understanding what was really going on at all.

- **The Galileo 'Movement'**: a now-defunct activist organisation founded in 2011 by two retired engineers in Noosa to campaign relentlessly against the Gillard government's carbon price legislation, on the basis that climate change is a hoax being pulled on us by a shadowy (((global elite))). Its ranks include the former coal executive (now One Nation Senator) Malcolm Roberts, while its patron is legendary talkback radio host and hate speech enthusiast Alan Jones, who has described the notion of global warming as 'witchcraft'.

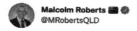

Malcolm Roberts 🇦🇺 ✔   ...
@MRobertsQLD

They want to remove carbon dioxide. You breathe out carbon dioxide. They want to get rid of you!

11:44 AM · May 5, 2022 · Twitter Web App

Checkmate

Prior to beginning the Movement, the two co-founders had previously organised an Australian speaking tour for the British toff and ~~Lord~~ Christopher Monckton, who is extremely hot:

(Photo: James Croucher / Newspix)

Not that it's at all relevant or anything, but according to *Scientific American* this speaking tour was underwritten by mining magnate Gina Rinehart to the tune of $100,000.

- And our mates at the right-wing think tank, the **Institute of Public Affairs.** For years the IPA has been accepting millions of dollars in donations from Gina and her company Hancock Prospecting; dollars which allow them to continue their vital work of spewing bankrupt denialist tosh across Sky News and the ABC, and producing articles and 'research' papers with titles like 'The Life-Saving Potential of Coal', 'Net Zero Means Heaters Off', 'A Law Unto Themselves: The Australian Bureau of Meteorology' and 'The Case Against the Four Bin System'.

Flush with their pocket money from their corporate masters, these prophets of denial have worked diligently for years to preach as much misinformation as they can, and to corrupt the public's understanding of the threat of climate change: 'The climate is *always* changing'; 'The planet's actually *cooling*, you know'; 'It's all because of sunspots!'; 'What would "scientists" know, anyway?'; 'How DARE you insult sweet, defenceless carbon dioxide – it is the bringer of life!!!', etc.

They've been ably assisted along the way by a corporate media that's willing to uncritically platform and amplify these talking points; a corporate media that also happens to receive bucketloads of advertising money from fossil fuel companies and industry lobby groups. This is especially true of the biggest and grossest chunk of Australian media which belongs to billionaire Rupert 'Climate-change-has-been-going-on-as-long-as-the-planet-is-here' Murdoch. A 2020 analysis of more than

8600 pieces of news and opinion in News Corp papers over a 12-month period by GetUp! found that 45% of the company's climate coverage expressed climate scepticism, and just 6% of all sources cited in these climate pieces were scientists.

The company's Sky News channel – home to prominent non-scientist troglodytes Andrew 'This-global-warming-hysteria-is-totally-off-the-dial' Bolt and Rowan 'Climate-change-is-a-fraudulent-cult' Dean – has been identified and condemned as a popular global hub for climate disinformation, and an inclusive safe space where capitalists won't feel triggered by facts that don't care about your fossil fuel feelings.[16]

By *pure coincidence*, the only time the Murdoch Death Star has made any effort to try and change its tune on this stuff was in 2021, when the Morrison Coalition government was in desperate need of some political cover as it was trying to pivot towards a (vague) commitment for Australia to reach Net Zero by 2050 ahead of the UN climate summit in Glasgow. It was then that the Australian Murdoch tabloids launched their shameless **missionzero2050** campaign, which was all about putting 'Australia on a path to a Net Zero future', emphasising the economic opportunities of decarbonisation and creating 'a clean future while having fun and feeling good

---

16 The quintessential Sky News denialist moment came on the *Outsiders* program in May 2019, when hosts Dean, Rita Panahi and James Morrow gave a very friendly interview to the 'astrometeorologist' David Burton.

Burton claims to have previously used Hindu astrology to predict the outcome of horse races, and he says he can predict weather events up to a thousand years in the future by looking at the position of the planets. He believes that the idea of human-induced climate change is 'all just rubbish', and in fact all our droughts and floods are caused by sunspots and Mercury being in retrograde or whatever. When Morrow asked Burton, 'What exactly is the science behind planets affecting droughts and rainfall?', Burton replied, 'Well, it's energy points that line up at certain degrees. And Jupiter is the biggest planet, has the greatest magnetic pull. So when other planets get in between the earth and the sun, and – it's quite complex, actually.'

Except it's not. It's actually very simple, David: **Sky News is a child's drawing of a news channel come to life.**

at the same time'. Unfortunately, this new campaign did not involve firing staunch denialists like Andrew Bolt (either from his job or out of a cannon), and it didn't change anything about the media company's willingness to accept advertising dollars from climate-sceptic organisations like the Climate Study Group or United Australia Party leader and future Prime Minister Craig 'Do-Your-Own-Research' Kelly.

Big Denial has even got to work brainwashing the younger generations by inserting itself into the education system. Fossil fuel companies like Woodside, Chevron, BP, BHP and Shell are major sponsors of various science education programs across Australia, and they design educational materials to be presented in classrooms and can exert considerable sway over how climate-related content is presented and framed to the kiddies. Rinehart has openly admitted that she once arranged for Monckton and climate-sceptical geologist Professor Ian Plimer to speak at her former school in Perth, and she encourages the young ladies there to 'do their own independent research' on 'which comes first – global warming, or an increase in carbon?'[17]

❤ ❤ MY CLIMATE CRACKPOT FAVES ❤ ❤

The insistence of many political and media elites on denying scientific reality is deeply infuriating. But you've got to hand it to these weird units: they're extremely committed to the bit, and they're not afraid to publicly engage in some of the worst cringe you've ever seen as they try to argue their case, and it's often quite funny.

So for all the laughs, let's send some big love and shout outs to:

---

17 This is bullshit. I don't send my kids to school to be indoctrinated by the fossil fuel lobby; they are SUPPOSED to be getting indoctrinated by genderfluid Marxist critical race theorists, and this is NOT the last you'll hear from me on this, I can assure you.

⇒ **DENNIS JENSEN:** the ultra-conversative Liberal MP for the WA seat of Tangney, who warned in his first speech to parliament in November 2004 that global warming would 'probably go the way of the flat earth theory: restricted to a few adherents who have become totally divorced from reality'.

Ironically, 'a few adherents who have become totally divorced from reality' is now a pretty decent summary of the Liberal Party. Jensen left the Liberals in 2017 to join Cory Bernardi's ill-fated Australian Conservatives party, which was so divorced from reality that it wanted to outlaw divorce.

⇒ **JAMES INHOFE:** the Republican senator from Oklahoma who in 2015 brought a snowball onto the US Senate floor to disprove the ridiculous claim that the previous year had been the hottest on record. (He did this in February, which is in wintertime, which is when it is colder than other times.)

According to the political transparency project OpenSecrets.org, since Inhofe was elected in 1994, he's received more than $2.3 million in political contributions from the oil and gas industry.

⇒ **PRUE MACSWEEN:** a PR consultant who is one of the Australian media's many 'social commentators' for some reason. Prue refuses to let her lack of expertise or ability to construct sentences stop her from opinion-ating as frequently and as hard as possible, and when she isn't threatening to run over young brown women with her car over a tweet or calling for the implementation of a second Stolen Generation, she loves nothing more than telling people who are worried about climate breakdown to stop being so hysterical. Prue flat out refuses to accept there is a climate emergency – 'There is no emergency. The only emergency is in your heads!' – and has decried the fact that Australians are 'paying these exorbitant energy bills because we've got this feel-good climate change wank', which is a very rude way to refer to Adam Bandt.

⇒ **ISRAEL FOLAU:** in a 2019 social media video, the former Wallaby suggested that the Black Summer bushfires were God's punishment for Australia's legalisation of same-sex marriage and abortion. He cited a passage from the Book of Isaiah as his evidence: 'The earth is defiled by its people; they have disobeyed the laws, violated the statutes and broken the everlasting covenant . . . Therefore earth's inhabitants are burned up, and very few are left.'

This is moronic and offensive, but it doesn't change the fact that I find Folau to be extremely attractive in a dumb-hot-guy kind of way, and I would like nothing more than to smooch him as I patiently explain to him that dinosaurs are real and that anal sex is fine.

⇒ **PAULINE HANSON:** the proud founder of One Nation, the 'only political party to question climate science', who has claimed 'the climate is changing pure to nature itself and our relation to the sun' (??) and once argued that police should be allowed to use cattle prods to move along climate protestor 'pests'.

Personally, I think the only way to get Pauline to change her tune on this stuff is to somehow convince her that the climate crisis is connected to Islam, and hopefully her racism will fuel a new-found concern about the fate of the planet. I have no doubt that if Pauline thought that emitting CO_2 was halal, she'd be calling for us to invade Iraq again just to put the oil *back.*

⇒ **DONALD TRUMP:** the former US President who once tweeted 'The concept of global warming was created by and for the Chinese in order to make U.S. manufacturing non-competitive'.

This guy hates renewable energy, loves coal, and is still pissed off that hairspray is 'not like it used to be' because the world phased out ozone-depleting chlorofluorocarbons in the 1990s. Perhaps he will have evolved and matured and will hold a different view during his second term as President, which is definitely going to happen in 2024.

2) DISTRACT

If your flat-out climate denialism fails, you can always try the time-honoured technique of yelling *'HEY LOOK OVER THERE!'* and hope that will buy you some time. Carbon polluters would rather we didn't spend any time blaming *them* for the problem they've caused; they'd rather lay the blame on ordinary rubes like you and me. Don't engage in mass movements or collective action to save the climate, we're told; no, the only way we little people can try to fight the global existential threat of climate change is by using our 'power' as *individual consumers*. Think global – act local, be the change you want to see in the world, start with the man in the mirror, etc. The oceans are rising, and gigantic deadly bushfires are creating their own weather – so please make sure you turn off your lights when you leave a room and use a KeepCup.

This malicious distraction tactic has been around for quite a while now. The whole concept of an individual 'carbon footprint' was popularised in the mid-2000s thanks to BP's $300 million award-winning 'Beyond Petroleum' marketing campaign. Members of the public were to 'learn how to lower your carbon footprint' by going to the footprint calculator on BP's website, because 'It's a start'. Sure, BP is a humungous, multi-billion-dollar oil company with more than 18,000 petrol stations all over the world and you're just one tiny person reading a book, but, according to the campaign, 'We can **all** do more to emit less'.

While making more environmentally conscious choices at an individual level isn't a bad thing at all (provided you can afford to make them), the positive impact of our little tofu-based lifestyle changes is hilariously dwarfed by the colossal footprints of fossil fuel giants and other carbon-intensive industries. A major report from investor disclosure charity CDP and the Climate Accountability Institute in 2017 found that **71% of all greenhouse gas emissions since 1988 can be traced back to just 100 fossil fuel producers** – a list that includes the likes of ExxonMobil, Shell and yes, BP. Any attempt to shift the lion's share of blame for this crisis from these corporate criminals onto the diets and lightbulbs of regular people is gross and misleading, and can only be described as **oil-and-gaslighting**.[18]

Some have claimed that the real villain in all this is not the *manner* in which human beings interact with nature, but rather human beings *themselves*, and their very annoying habit of being born and existing. Fears of the destructive impacts of human 'overpopulation' have been buzzing around ever since the 18th-century English cleric and economist Thomas Malthus argued in his *Essay on the Principle of Population* that using welfare to help the poor was bad because it led to the survival of an unsustainable number of mouths to feed. Since the late 1960s, some elements of the global environmental movement have made similar arguments in relation to population numbers and our ongoing ecological crisis; most famously, academics Paul and Anne Ehrlich contended in their 1968 bestseller *The Population Bomb* that humanity had to face a choice between 'population control, or a race to oblivion'. Various scientific institutions have released reports giving the same dire warnings, and groups like Zero Population Growth and the 'Voluntary Human Extinction Movement' have sprung up

---

18 Reducing the scope of climate politics to the level of the individual is also very handy if you want to diminish and undermine certain individuals who are calling for more serious climate action. Sneering conservatives love to paint any climate activist as a hypocrite because they once drove a car or ate a hamburger or were born in a hospital that uses electricity. Rather than acknowledge the obvious truth – that none of us have *chosen* to be born into a world in which pollutant fossil fuels are embedded into almost every aspect of our lives, but we were, and now we all have a responsibility to work to change that as quickly as possible so as to mitigate the worst impacts of climate breakdown – the Sky News losers prefer to yell 'NO YOU FLEW ON A PLANE ONCE IPSO FACTO YOU ARE WRONG'.

Of course, if any climate activist actually *does* make drastic green changes in their personal life – like going vegan, living entirely off the grid or, like Greta Thunberg, choosing to travel internationally by boat rather than plane – the right-wing press doesn't take them any more seriously; they just dismiss them as weirdo hippies who love rainbows and twigs. Honestly, you can't win with these pricks.

to try and convince the rest of their species to stop selfishly fucking and reproducing themselves.[19]

Even beloved environmental figures like Jane Goodall and Sir David Attenborough have expressed some Malthusian sentiments lately, suggesting the world is just getting too crowded and if we could just cut back on our numbers by a couple of billion, we'd be fine. Of course, at the very extreme and terrifying end of this argument are nutjob racist ecofascists like the mass shooters of El Paso and Christchurch in 2019, who partly justified their murder sprees by pointing to ecological concerns about an 'overpopulated' Earth.

(See also: Thanos.)

This is yet another sideshow. Yes, the world's population has certainly been booming of late; since the first Millennials started showing up, humanity has grown from 4.4 billion to just over 8 billion people today. And global consumption – measured as a percentage of Earth's capacity to regenerate itself – has ballooned too, from 73% in 1960 to more than 170% now. But this growth isn't exponential. The *rate* of the world's population growth has been falling ever since the 70s, as people have become more and more urbanised, and as more women have had greater access to education, work and family planning autonomy, leading to a fall in fertility rates. The UN's latest projections suggest the world's population will slowly grow to a peak of about 10.4 billion people during the 2080s and pretty much stay there until the end of the century. Some developed countries – including Japan, Italy, Spain and South Korea – are even predicted to see their

---

19 At the start of 2020, one of the founders of the Voluntary Human Extinction Movement, Les Knight, told the *Guardian*, 'Fifty years ago, I concluded that the best thing for the planet would be a peaceful phase-out of human existence . . . With us gone, I believe ecosystems will be restored and there will be enough of everything.

'The idea wasn't as well received as I had hoped.'

Full credit to Les – even though he's a bit nuts, he can at least appreciate that the cause he's dedicated his entire life to is a very tough sell.

populations more than halve. The population 'bomb' looks like it'll be more of a fizzle.

But perhaps more importantly, the overpopulation distraction misses the main game: **the consumption of the world's population is not evenly distributed.** According to Oxfam, in our topsy turvy, unequal world, the wealthiest 1% are responsible for twice as much carbon pollution as the poorest half.[20] Under our current organisation of affairs, millions of people are starving even though there's plenty of food, and a tiny elite get to guzzle everything they like and whizz around the globe in toxic private jets, while some of the most destitute folks around are forced to suffer through the consequent heatwaves and worry about rising sea levels lapping at their door.

At this point, you'll know that I consider this to be an extremely shitty situation. But we should really be taking it up with the greedy, super-rich adult arseholes who are already here, rather than blame it on the adorable babies coming down the pipeline.

My niece Cecilia isn't cooking the planet – she's too busy being perfect. Leave her alone!

---

20 So if you *really* want to make a climate impact in your personal life, don't go vegan – eat the rich.

Some other classic climate distractions that the wealthy and powerful like to use include:

- 中国

  Many on the Right argue we shouldn't worry about Australia's crappy climate performance or decarbonise any time soon **because China.** Our emissions are tiny compared to theirs, and they're doing heaps of massively bad carbon stuff, so – you know. Fuck it.

  Certainly, China's carbon impact is huge. It's become a massive economic superpower extremely quickly, and sometimes it's hard for us to get our heads around the sheer scale of that growth; between 2011 and 2013, for example, China's construction industry used more cement than the US did during the entire 20th century. The country overtook the US as the world's biggest emitter of CO_2 in 2007, it's now responsible for about 30% of the world's emissions, it's built almost 600 coal-fired power plants since 1992, and in 2021 it announced its (very annoying) plans to build 40 more.

  But this doesn't tell the full story. It should be noted that *it makes total sense* that China is responsible for a very large number of emissions, what with it being the world's leading manufacturer – accounting for almost 30% of global output, including your phone and heaps of your furniture and all the cheap tat we buy every Christmas – and being home to *1.4 billion fucking people.* On a per capita basis, Evil China actually has a *lower* carbon footprint than the US, Canada, Germany and yes, Australia, so perhaps it might be nice if we *all* recognise that we all have heaps of room for improvement and we should be prepared to Do The Work.

  Sinophobic critics also like to conveniently ignore the fact that in many ways, China is *very much* Doing

The Work. China has very quickly become something of a turbocharged renewable energy superpower; the country was responsible for 50% of the world's growth in renewable energy capacity in 2020. It has more domestic solar capacity and hydropower than the US and the EU combined; it's been the world's biggest producer of wind power since 2015; and since 2010, it's increased its nuclear power capacity by 500%. It's also replacing domestic air travel within its borders by building tens of thousands of kilometres of high-speed rail and pumping out heaps of electric cars. Plus, it's reforesting its landmass like crazy; in 2019, NASA found that the tree-planting efforts of China and India were the principal reason why the Earth is now greener than it was twenty years ago.

None of that (under-reported) effort changes the reality of climate science, or the fact that China's current decarbonisation ambitions aren't enough for our species to avoid devastating heating. But if we Australians and the rest of the global community want to have *any* chance of being able to make a convincing case to China that they should do more so that future generations – the Chinese, Australian, American, *human* generations – can enjoy a habitable planet, we'll probably want to be doing everything we can to get *our* house in order first, and to get our emissions as low as possible as quickly as we can.

After all, if China jumped off a bridge/into climate hell, would you do it, too?

- **'WE CAN HAS GAS?'**
As it becomes ever clearer that the game's over for coal and oil, the captains of industry have tried to pivot our attention to a shiny new *cleaner* fossil fuel for us to fall in

love with: **natural gas.** According to the likes of Santos, Origin and Woodside, gas is supposedly the greener 'bridge' fuel that's the 'natural partner' for renewables; a partner that can help us avoid climate doom and transition to a cleaner tomorrow. In recent years Australia has become one of the world's largest producers of natural gas, and the industry has managed to capture the enthusiastic backing of both major Australian political parties, at both the state and federal level.[21]

The problem is that being 'not as dirty as coal' is kind of like being 'not as annoying as Ben Fordham'. That bar is too low. While the burning of natural gas produces about half as much CO_2 as coal, it's still a filthy fossil fuel that will do its darnedest to heat our atmosphere and bugger up the climate. Throughout gas exploration, extraction, transport, processing and combustion, gas emits plenty of carbon and heaps of methane, and depending on efficiency levels – which vary widely across the country – there are gas-fired power stations that are actually dirtier than some of those powered by coal.

Plus, no matter how much 'cleaner' gas might be, that doesn't really count for much if we end up burning *heaps* of it. The natural gas industry is now the fastest growing source of carbon dioxide pollution; in 2019, a UN-backed team of researchers found the world was on track to produce 70% more natural gas in 2030 than would be consistent with keeping global heating to 1.5°C.

This is why any suggestion that *gas will save us* has to be rejected, and why we **must** insist that Australia

---

21 In 2020, Prime Minister Scott Morrison declared the country would bounce back from the COVID-19 pandemic with the power of a multi-billion dollar 'gas-led recovery', after receiving advice that that would be a good idea from his National COVID-19 Commission, which was chaired by a bunch of plutocrats with links to gassy outfits like Strike Energy, EnergyAustralia and Saudi Aramco.

can't expand its production of natural gas any further. Woodside's $16 billion Scarborough Gas Field in Western Australia, for example, is set to emit an extra 1.6 billion extra tonnes of carbon into the atmosphere over the next 25 years, which is the equivalent of building 15 new coal-fired power plants. It just really, really can't happen, please and thank you.[22]

- **'WE MUST GO NUCLEAR!'**
Some claim that if we're really serious about lowering emissions, we shouldn't be pussyfooting around with dainty little wind and solar (which is for girls). Instead, we should crank up our uranium mining operations, end Australia's existing moratorium on nuclear power, start building heaps of plants and get that green, glowing low-emissions shit into our electricity grid right now.

This is both a distraction, and kind of a troll. Australian nuclear advocates are fully aware that nuclear power is the most expensive energy technology that takes the longest time to recoup from invest- ment and hasn't benefited from the same economies of scale experienced in solar and wind energy. Plus, nuclear energy requires the mining of a non-renewable resource, produces heaps of radioactive waste, and there have been some quite famous instances of nuclear plants having very messy meltdowns; in some extreme cases, nuclear radiation has been known to produce dangerous Hulks (both regular and She-), and even Dr Manhattans.

22 In 2021, Scott Morrison told the Business Council of Australia that when he heard that the Scarborough project had been approved, he 'could not be more thrilled' about it and was so happy that he 'did a bit of a jig'.

For no other reason than to ensure that Morrison never dances with joy again, please do what you can to stop this ecological disaster from going ahead: **saynotoscarborough.com.au**

All of the time, money and effort that would be required to set up an Australian nuclear industry from scratch would be infinitely better spent scaling up the zero-emissions renewable energy options that already exist and work, here and now.

- **'FOSSIL FUEL COMPANIES ARE OUR FRIENDS!'**
If you're losing the scientific argument and the public's trust and you can feel your social licence to pollute slipping through your fingers, you can always try to buy people's love and approval by shamelessly **greenwashing** yourself. As the climate crisis has only gotten worse, fossil fuel companies and major corporates have poured hundreds of millions of dollars into rebranding and marketing campaigns to reassure us all that they care deeply about Mother Gaia. Big banks and hedge funds produce shiny slide decks and annual reports with heaps of trees and smiling faces, while mining companies trumpet their Net Zero plans and their fancy ESG commitments and tell us they're *super excited* about getting to a carbon-free world (at some point). The green future is going to be great and we're going to get there *as a family*.

     If you're still sceptical, then just check out all this culture and sport that we've slapped our big dirty names on. Santos is a major sponsor of the Wallabies, the Australian Open and Darwin Festival; Fortescue Metals Group supports Perth's Black Swan Theatre Company; and Woodside Energy sponsors everything from the 'Woodside Nippers' swimming program to the Western Australian Ballet. In perhaps the most perfect encapsulation of just how captured this country has become by the big fat slimy tentacles of Big Fossil, even the Australian of the Year Awards are now brought to you by fucking Chevron.

3) DELAY

When all the lying and distractions fail, dirty corporate forces can simply rely on deploying their massive resources and power to delay, undermine or just straight up sabotage green innovations and climate action. If it looks like some democratic environmental progress is going to come along and affect their margins, fossil executives enjoy nothing more than getting their Looten Plunder on and shooting that progress in the head.

They're very good at doing this, because they've had heaps of practice. Ever since there's been an automobile industry, for example, car and oil barons have been working to shape our society and brainwash us all for their benefit. When combustion-engine cars first arrived on the scene in early 20th-century America, ordinary people tended to hate them, because they were luxury items owned by the rich that took up public space and were noisy, polluting and tended to kill people. The car companies soon went about combating this bad PR by using media campaigns to invent the figure of the 'jaywalker', so that the deaths of pedestrians could be blamed on pedestrians, as opposed to the vehicles that had run into them. The motor industry happily promoted their products as symbols of individual 'freedom' (you can go ANYWHERE in a car [provided you stick to the publicly-funded road infrastructure]), lobbied city officials to prioritise cars above everything else on public streets, and actively sabotaged cleaner, cheaper and public-ly-owned transport alternatives; during the 1930s, General Motors and various players in the oil and rubber industries formed a consortium to buy and shut down streetcar systems throughout California.

These oily bastards have also used their corporate power to stifle the development of electric vehicles (EVs); they've bought up patents for electric batteries and shelved them, and they've funded massive lobbying campaigns against the building of public car-charging stations. In the 90s, after the California Air Resources Board passed its Zero Emissions Vehicle mandate requiring car companies in the state to offer EVs in their product range, General Motors leased out thousands of its GM EV1s to customers, then erroneously claimed there was insufficient customer demand for the things, and took them all back from the lessees (despite the lessees' protests) and had them crushed, just as they crushed all of our dreams of a cleaner future.

So much for the wonders of free-market capitalist competition and innovation, I guess.[23]

The same tools of delay and obstruction are being rolled out today, even as the reality and severity of the climate crisis grows ever clearer. Big oil companies have created fake 'grass-roots' groups to campaign against the construction of wind farms, while energy companies have tried to hobble the rollout of rooftop solar and the gas industry has lobbied hard against the electrification of buildings. These players make their case publicly, and behind closed doors; according to the UK-based climate-focussed think tank InfluenceMap, in the three years following the UN Paris Climate Agreement, the five biggest oil and gas majors invested more than US$1 billion on climate misinformation and political lobbying. When the think tank had a look at the situation in Australia, it found that almost all of the climate-focussed political lobbying that goes on around here is dominated by the resources sector and energy

---

23 Thanks to all this sterling effort by American big business, there are now over 290 million cars in the US, transport is the country's single largest source of greenhouse gas emissions (mainly because of all the cars), and motor vehicles are still the leading cause of death for Americans aged between 4 and 34.

Planet Earth is now home to a total of 1.4 billion cars and our societies have become almost entirely fossil fuel-powered-car-centric, when a different timeline – one filled with high-speed rail, high-quality public transport and affordable, mass-produced EVs – was entirely possible.

companies trying to stop, delay or limit government action as much as possible.

If you'd rather not have to *talk* to our political leaders (and really – who does?), one can simply just buy them. A 2021 report from the independent Centre for Public Integrity found that in the two decades to 2019, the resources sector was far and away the biggest donor in Australian politics, dishing out a grand total of **more than $136 million** to the political class. A whopping $83 million of that total was accounted for by Clive Palmer's Mineralogy company donating to Clive Palmer's United Australia Party, while more than $15 million went to the Coalition and almost $5 million went to Labor.[24]

More recently, the amount of cash the fossil fuel industry – in particular the likes of Woodside Energy, Adani and lobby group the Australian Petroleum Production and Exploration Association (APPEA) – has been handing out to the major parties has grown roughly even, ensuring that no matter which way those pesky little elections might turn out, our corporate overlords will be listened to by whoever's in power and they'll be able to enjoy all the benefits of **state capture**. This is working out to be an extremely good investment, as Australian governments of both political persuasions have been awesome at delaying and watering down serious climate action and have happily handed out millions of dollars of public money to help fund private companies' coal and gas projects, turned a blind eye to the fact that those same companies are paying sweet fuck-all in taxes, and committed dog acts like this:

---

24 Keep in mind that all this money in the donations data is *just the shit we know about*. The Centre estimates that in that same 20-year period, Australia's useless political donation disclosure laws have allowed almost $1 billion in **dark money** – that is, money from unknown sources – to wash through our politics.

A balding child partakes in Show and Tell.
(Photo: Kym Smith / Newspix)

---

bUt ThE gReEnS VoTeD aGaiNsT tHe CprS

For the perfect example of the kind of shitshow that can arise when climate reality clashes with the interests of fossil fuel capital and a fossil fuel-captured 'democratic' political system, look no further than The Unholy Carbon-Pricing Wars that were waged during the Rudd/Gillard/Rudd governments: a time of much rancour, division, betrayal, and boring acronyms.

Here's what happened, in a (large) nutshell: in 2007, the Rudd Labor government was elected with a massive mandate to act on climate change, which Kevin07 referred to as **'the great moral challenge of our generation'**. His government immediately did what the Howard government had refused to do and ratified the Kyoto Protocol; at a UN climate conference in Bali, Rudd's government acknowledged the IPCC's conclusion that in order to keep warming to 2°C, developed countries would have to reduce their emissions by 25 to 40% below 1990 levels by 2020; and he asked respected economist Professor Ross Garnaut to write a big smart wide-ranging report to outline the best way for Australia to do its climate duty.

When Garnaut eventually handed down his Climate Change Review in 2008, he recommended the government implement an **Emissions Trading Scheme (ETS):** a market-based system designed to impose a cost on carbon pollution. Under an

ETS, the government puts a cap on the total level of emissions, creates a certain number of **carbon permits** (also known as 'carbon credits' – units that allow you to emit a certain amount of a greenhouse gas) and then emitters buy and sell those permits in a regulated market. Heavy polluters will need to pay for extra credits if they want to keep polluting, while businesses that can cut back on their emissions can profit from selling their surplus permits to others. The general idea is the system creates incentives for everyone to reduce their emissions and to decarbonise the economy in a timely and efficient manner, and so we can all live happily ever after.

Garnaut recommended that the ETS be robust. He believed it should apply to all sectors of the economy, that it shouldn't involve the handing out of free permits to businesses, and it should have a very limited reliance on (often quite dodgy) international carbon offsets. Labor's response to this expert opinion was to say, 'yeah ok cool thx but probs not gonna do that'. Unsurprisingly, carbon-intensive industries were quite accustomed to being able to do cost-free pollution, and they weren't too stoked about the idea that they'd now have to pay for it, so they proceeded to have a massive sook and demand that Labor give them heaps of treats and loopholes. The ALP government – which included Minister for Resources and Energy, Martin Ferguson, who would later leave politics and immediately join the advisory board for APPEA and take up the position of head of natural resources for Seven Group Holdings – obliged, and soon Garnaut's vision became more watered down than a Lismore swimming pool in flood season.

The policy that the Rudd government eventually presented to parliament – the **Carbon Pollution Reduction Scheme (CPRS)** – included a temporary exemption for agriculture, a complete exemption for forestry, the handing out of free permits and huge compensation payouts to polluting companies, the cutting of the fuel tax to offset the impact of the scheme on transport fuels, a reliance on the magic bunkum of 'clean coal' technology and the imposition of a price cap for five years to make sure that paying to pollute (which is the whole point of the scheme) wouldn't be too expensive. This put it in the awkward position of being a 'carbon pollution reduction scheme' that wasn't going to be very good at reducing the country's overall carbon pollution. By the government's own Treasury modelling, the CPRS wasn't going to do anything to move us away from fossil fuel extraction or coal-fired power for ages, it would actually *increase* the costs of running electric public transport and **it wouldn't have led to a reduction in Australia's emissions for 25 years.**[25]

So – the legislation was real bad. And it was friendless. The Australian Greens, the broader environmental movement and even Ross Garnaut himself didn't like it (because it was bad), while the LNP opposition – led by climate-luvvie Malcolm Turnbull, but populated with various climate sceptic fruitcakes and IPA fans like Tony Abbott, Nick Minchin and Dennis Jensen – thought it was all way too much, way too soon.

The Greens approached Rudd and the Minister for Climate Change, Penny Wong, to push for changes so they could support the bill in the Senate – like increasing the emissions reduction target to a minimum of 25%, in line with the climate science and the base international ambitions – but the ALP said 'Piss off, hippies!' and barrelled on. After the CPRS was voted down by the upper house in August 2009, the government then decided to negotiate with the Coalition to secure its support, which meant the bill was hollowed out even further to please the demands of industry and the kinds of people who donate to the Liberal and National parties. Soon the legislation included even *bigger* handouts to polluters and the agriculture sector was exempted from the ETS entirely. Not even this was enough to placate the likes of Abbott, who by now was telling members of the Liberal Party faithful that 'the so-called "settled science" of climate change is absolute crap'. Just before the new bill was about to be brought back to parliament, Tony – with some help from the busy bees in the Lavoisier Group – successfully staged a leadership coup against Turnbull, and promptly announced the Coalition's opposition to Rudd's 'great big new tax on everything'.

In the wake of this catastrophe, the Labor government followed the ingenious strategy of simply presenting the version of the CPRS they'd negotiated *with right-wing nutjobs* to the Senate, refusing to enter into any serious negotiations with the Greens or other crossbenchers to make it less horrible, and then getting extremely angry at the Greens for voting against a worse version of a bill they'd

---

25 *Even if* the Scheme was somehow able to do what it said it would, its stated emissions reduction target was a pathetic 5 to 15% below 2000 levels – a target that was inconsistent with the Australian government's own goals when it came to avoiding catastrophic heating. It also had the potential to 'lock in' failure; under the CPRS, polluting industries might have been able to successfully sue any future government that wanted to raise its climate ambitions to the tune of billions of dollars in compensation.

already clearly said they opposed – a principled position that was supported by the likes of Greenpeace, the Australian Youth Climate Coalition, Friends of the Earth, the Wilderness Society and GetUp!. With all but two Coalition senators, the Greens and the crossbench opposed to the bill, the CPRS was defeated again. Rudd then headed off to the UN's Climate Change summit in Copenhagen – where nations failed to commit to any concrete action to reduce emissions and, according to comments reportedly made by the very diplomatic Rudd in private, 'those Chinese fuckers' tried 'to rat-fuck us' – then he came home very sad, once again refused to reach any kind of compromise with the Greens to get something passed, and in 2010 his government finally made the call to shelve the Scheme for three years.

This was a move which didn't exactly scream 'WE ARE TAKING THE GREATEST MORAL CHALLENGE OF OUR GENERATION THING SERIOUSLY'. His public approval ratings immediately took a nosedive, and in just a couple of months – following that mining tax debacle – he faced a political coup of his own. His party replaced him with Julia Gillard (for reasons that weren't exactly made *crystal clear* to the public), who then went to the 2010 election with a policy of establishing a 'Citizens' Assembly' on climate change to 'build community consensus' around the issue, which was a very funny joke that made everyone laugh.

Ever since those crazy days, this chaotic episode in #auspol history has been relitigated and decried in countless political memoirs and vicious Twitter exchanges. The CPRS debate is constantly held up by Labor hacks and centrist pundits as a tragic example of the intransigent Greens 'letting the perfect be the enemy of the good'. Some even claim that the party's decision to vote against the CPRS is *the reason* why the country suffered the ensuing so-called 'Climate Wars' throughout the 2010s, and why we've lagged so far behind when it comes to achieving climate progress.

Not only does this rewriting of history completely ignore how lacking, compromised and unpopular the original CPRS was, it also ignores what happened next: the Greens enjoyed what was then their best ever election result in 2010, and used its new position in the balance of power with the Gillard minority government to dump the silly Assembly policy and help facilitate the passage of the **Clean Energy Package (CEP)**: a world-leading, still-definitely-not-'perfect'-but-heaps-better piece of legislation that included a price on carbon, more ambitious reduction targets, a quicker transition out of fossil fuels, (slightly) reduced assistance for polluters, and billions of dollars of investment in renewable energy and carbon farming. The CEP came into effect only a year after the CPRS was supposed to begin, and it did have an impact: during the two-year period in which the carbon price was in place, Australia's emissions fell by about 2%.

'If Labor had been willing to negotiate on the CPRS, it would have been passed,' Tim Hollo told me on my podcast in June 2021. Tim was a senior advisor to Greens senator Christine Milne at the time of the CPRS fun and games.

'The Greens' knocking it down was *part* of a negotiation process. The way you negotiate is by showing you have the strength to say "No" to something that you don't want.

'The only reason we were able to get the Clean Energy Finance Corporation (CEFC) and the Australian Renewable Energy Agency (ARENA) is because the Greens had the guts in 2010 to stand up and say, "This policy isn't good enough; we're willing to go to an election saying this policy isn't good enough; we *did* go to an election saying this policy wasn't good enough; we got to balance of power, and we luckily then had a Prime Minister in Julia Gillard who actually *could* negotiate — as opposed to Kevin Rudd, who couldn't negotiate with his own left foot — and managed to get fantastic policies into place.'

It's important to note that **Gillard's Clean Energy Act did not introduce a 'carbon tax'**. A carbon tax slaps a fixed level of tax to be paid by emitters per metric tonne of CO_2 they produce; emitters can either choose to reduce their emissions or pay the tax. The CEP introduced a *fixed price* on carbon for three years, before transitioning to a *floating price* under an ETS. Ahead of the 2010 election, Julia Gillard said 'There'll be no carbon tax under the government I lead', and she was correct, although she would later kind of concede that it basically *was* like a carbon tax (even though it wasn't?), and she would then later concede that in making that concession she 'made the wrong choice and, politically, it hurt me terribly'. Goblin Tony and his Coalition relentlessly misrepresented the ETS as a 'carbon tax' (even though they knew — as Abbott's former chief of staff Peta Credlin would publicly admit in 2017 — that it wasn't a carbon tax at all), and accused Gillard of breaking her promise of never introducing a carbon tax (which she didn't), and called her 'Ju-Liar', and did deranged things like speak at 'No Carbon Tax' rallies and agree with Alan Jones.

By the time the 2013 election came around, the parliamentary Labor Party, in its eternal wisdom, had replaced Julia Gillard with Kevin Rudd (who was the guy they got rid of before because he was so terrible?) and they got absolutely rinsed by the Coalition. Abbott quickly went about repealing the demonised carbon price and abolishing the Climate Commission, and tried (but failed) to nix the CEFC, ARENA and the Climate Change Authority. **Almost immediately, Australia's emissions began to rise.**

Obviously, all of this — the fossil fuel industry's dominating influence over our politics; Labor's toxic in-fighting and poor political judgement; the Coalition's internal machinations, climate denialism and vicious political campaign tactics; the existence of physics and the implications of climate science, etc. — is the fault of the Greens. The minor party that's been banging on about the environment forever and that doesn't accept political donations from fossil fuel corporations is the main villain in this saga, and we should blame them for that and ignore all other relevant points of fact and history.

And yes, the Greens' voting against the CPRS in 2009 is also responsible for your eczema, COVID, triple j not being as good as it used to be, and NFTs.

... AND NOW WE'RE HERE

The result of all this ruling class-funded Denial, Distraction and Delay is the climate clusterfuck we find ourselves in today. Australia's vital and inevitable transition away from our lethal fossil fuel economy was started far too late, has been way slower and more painful than it needed to be, and its future is still not assured. Our country still has one of the highest rates of climate denial in the developed world; a 2020 YouGov poll found that 5% of Australians believe the climate isn't changing, and 9% believe that it *is* changing, but it's not caused by humans. Climate deniers and sceptics can still be found in both of our major political parties and across our state and federal parliaments, and while our current ALP overlords love to talk a big game on 'ending the Climate

Wars' and 'listening to the science', their willingness to keep playing footsie with their fossil fuel donors and their often anti-scientific climate agenda mean they are, at best, weak sauce, and at their worst, they're as guilty of climate crimes as the next Tory dinosaur.

Worst of all, as we look on in despair as our political class treads water and fails to meet this existential challenge, we still have to listen to climate cranks gasbagging and being taken seriously throughout the Australian media landscape; not just in Murdoch-land, but in Nine/Fairfax outlets, Channel Ten, all over morning television and even on our public broadcasters.[26] The voices almost never express any outrage or despair at the predicament that massive, greedy, lying, evil fossil fuel corporations have landed us all in, of course; they'd rather reserve all that bile for anyone who might try to do something about it, by having the gall to protest or engage in civil disobedience or be a Greens MP or suggest that things might need to change.

AND YET . . .

Despite it all – **hope persists.** The hope of a climate reckoning lives on, and it can be found in the hearts of The People.

Back in 2013, John 'Finger-On-The-Pulse' Howard confidently predicted that 'the high level of public support for overzealous action on global warming has now passed. My suspicion is that most people in countries like ours have settled into a state of sustained agnosticism.'

---

26 In April 2022, the ABC invited Gideon Rozner – the climate-denying Director of Policy at the climate-denying, Rinehart-funded IPA – on its *Q&A* program to discuss whether he thought it was a good idea for Australia to try to reach net zero emissions by 2050. You'll never believe this, but he said, 'No'.

    When host Virginia Trioli challenged Rozner about the impact of his 'think' tank's coffers being filled with Rinehart's coin, he responded by saying '[F]rankly, I think it's very sad that people have a problem with a successful woman in this country', which is just yet another example of the IPA doing toxic woke identity politics.

He was – to put it mildly – fucking way off. The Australia Institute's Climate of the Nation report found that the proportion of Australians who believed that man-made climate change was happening and was of serious concern had grown from just 20% in the year of Howard's speech to almost 80% by 2020. The same poll showed supermajority support for the idea of Australia becoming a world leader on climate action and for closing down coal-fired power stations, while the Lowy Institute's 2021 Climate Poll found that most Australians support a ban on new coal mines and a reduction of our coal exports (63%), believe that the benefit of taking further climate action will outweigh the costs (74%) and they're very much behind the idea of the federal government subsidising renewables (91%). At the 2022 federal election, Australians turfed out the fossil-fucking Coalition government that had robbed us all of so much precious time, voted for a more ambitious (but still C+) ALP government, and voted in record numbers for the Greens and climate-focussed independent MPs, in an unequivocal cry for something better.

Despite the multi-decade onslaught of misinformation and bastardry from those at the top, **the overwhelming majority of Australians get it**. We trust scientists and we see through Big Business' bullshit. We recognise the severity of the climate crisis, and we want serious action *now;* for our own sake, for the sake of our kids, and for the sake of this ☆ ☆ ☆ ☆ ☆ planet to which we've become quite attached.

At the same time, it's become bleedingly obvious that there are powerful forces arrayed against us; Millennials, Boomers, Xers, Zoomers and little Alphas alike. These forces simply cannot countenance a world in which their profits and power are subservient to ecology and democracy, and they're fully prepared to stand between us and the safe climate future we need and deserve. All because, at the end of the day, *say it with me now . . .*

THE 'CLIMATE WAR' IS CLASS WAR

Just like all the other shit I've been banging on about throughout these pages, **the crux of our environmental predicament comes back to the political economic system under which we live, and the class society it gives rise to.**

This thing is class war all the way down:

1. the Industrial Revolution turbocharged both wealth inequality and humanity's destruction of nature in the eternal pursuit of profit;

2. that pursuit demands that everything which *can* be commodified *must* be commodified, and as such the natural world – our collective commons – has been turned into private property, to be owned exclusively by a wealthy few;

3. that wealthy few – a handful of plutocrats and corporations – have privatised the massive profits that come from exploiting those natural resources and socialised the costs (environmental destruction and climate breakdown) onto the rest of us;

4. as we've seen, they've actively used their money and outsized power to fuck over working people's efforts to change any of this;

5. *and* – most brutally of all – as the consequences of our warming planet are made manifest, the world's poor and working classes – those who are *the least responsible* for

the crisis – will be hit the hardest, while the ruling rich will be able to insulate themselves from the worst of the damage for the longest time.[27]

Now, you'd probably reckon that any sort of rational society might look at all this and think something like, 'Gee, hitching our wagon to this monstrous and unjust system for two centuries appears to be steering us towards environmental and civilisational oblivion – *I don't suppose we could look at some other options?*'

But you'd be sorely disappointed.

'The key to meeting our climate change ambitions is commercialisation of low emissions technology,' then-PM Scott Morrison told a Business Council of Australia dinner in April 2021. 'We are going to meet our ambitions with the smartest minds, the best technology and the animal spirits of capitalism.'

'If the [climate and energy] policy certainty is there, the market will drive the solutions,' Anthony Albanese told a press conference back in 2020. 'The market will drive the right solutions, which will lead to lower prices as well as lower emissions and lead to more job creation.

'Labor believes that the best allocator of resources is markets.'

Yes, as the world floods and burns around us and the calls for action grow louder, the political establishment consensus appears to be '**The only possible solution is to just capitalism harder**.' The Market will solve the very disaster that The

---

27 Some weirdos like to dismiss climate change as some kind of elitist, post-materialist 'luxury issue' that's completely removed from the day-to-day reality of working people's lives.

    They might like to run this perspective by the tradies and gig economy workers sweltering in Penrith in 48.9°C heat, or the millions of ordinary people who can't afford to get insurance for their homes or move out of bushfire zones and flood plains, or the more than 120 million people across the world the UN estimates could be pushed into poverty as a result of the crisis.

Market has created, and we must trust in the 'green' faction of finance capital to rescue us from the fossil fuel faction of finance capital. Elon Musk and Michael Cannon-Brookes will save us, even though under Green Capitalism, the green billionaires will still be billionaires, and will continue to amass huge amounts of wealth and resources, avoid paying their taxes and exert an excessive, anti-democratic level of control over what our world and our futures look like.

This, apparently, is the best we can do. We've outsourced the task of avoiding the end of the world to market-based logic: a logic which forbids any profitable industry from being closed down before the market says so, even if that industry has the 'negative externality' of cooking the fucking planet and threatening the ongoing survival of the species. Our sense of *what is required* to address the problem is limited by ideas of *what is profitable,* and even though the climate crisis is the most radical challenge humanity has ever faced, we're not allowed to consider radically reorganising the way things work, because anything that looks like a **Green New Deal** or a **Green Industrial Revolution** – a democratic, State-led reimaging of society that combines big public investment and industrial planning to help us rapidly decarbonise and deliver economic justice to all – would simply be too radical. That'd be heavy-handed regulation, and would look too much like **central economic planning**, which is simply not the done thing these days. Better to leave it all to the suicidal chaos of the Free Market, then, and just cross our fingers.[28]

---

28 The great irony of the whole Labor vs. Greens/CPRS/ETS/'carbon tax' debacle is that if we look back on it now, knowing all that we know, it's abundantly clear that by 2009, any version of a technocratic, market-based mechanism was going to be woefully inadequate anyway. It would have been great to have had carbon pricing and emissions markets up and running in the 90s, but of course that didn't happen, and now it's simply too late for such half-measures and tinkering around the edges. Our response now has to be *drastic*. As the Oxford University climate scientist and 2018 IPCC report author Myles Allen told the *New York Times*, '[W]e need to reverse emissions trends and turn the world economy on a dime.'

BOILING MAD

It's really no wonder that people are getting extremely pissed off. Millions across the world are desperately trying to do whatever they can to shake those at the top and their fellow citizens out of their stupor and **wake the fuck up**. Greta Thunberg is swearing, Extinction Rebellion weirdos are dressing up in elaborate costumes and making giant puppets, Blockade Australia activists are locking themselves to steering wheels and millions of kids across the globe continue to hit the streets in the School Strike 4 Climate movement.

As the crisis worsens and those in power refuse to act, it's not hard to imagine things getting considerably spicier. The suffragettes were prepared to throw themselves under race-horses for their right to vote; what can we imagine people will be prepared to do for their right to a liveable planet? Blow up a pipeline? Occupy a gas plant? Stage a hostile corporate takeover of Sky News and imprison Rowan Dean in an abandoned coal mine for the rest of his life??[29]

Frankly, I get it. Whenever I really take the time to consider the sheer magnitude of the climate injustice that me and all the other young people across the globe have inherited from this fucked-up system, I feel a profound and deep Millennial rage vibrating in my bones.

How the fuck could they let this happen? I find myself thinking, fists beginning to clench. *Greta's right – how **DARE** they?*

I was able to channel a slice of this rage into screaming out that old Baby Boomer comedy routine of mine, which finished like this:

Thanks for climate change too, Boomers – thank you so much. *You've left us with a fucked economy and a dying*

---

29 I'm just spit-balling here. Slide into my DMs to discuss further.

planet; we're headed for a post-apocalyptic, Waterworld *scenario and Millennials like me –* we're not going to be able to afford a BOAT!

In 2050, when the world's flooded, it's just going to be me and a bunch of other 60-year-olds, living in a share dinghy.

You'll be dead by then, won't you Boomers? *You've timed it all very nicely – climate change kicks in, you're like,* 'Ok, see you bitch! Byeeee!'

Then you'll go up to the Great Big Caravan In The Sky. Meanwhile I'm down here, working 15-hour shifts for fucking Uber-Swim, trying to save up a deposit for a fucking KAYAK!

It was cathartic, if nothing else.

This rage was much more succinctly expressed a few years ago by my fellow Millennial, Chlöe Swarbrick. Swarbrick was elected to the Aotearoa New Zealand parliament as a Green Party MP in 2017, aged just 23. Two years into her first term, she rose in the parliamentary chamber to speak in support of the decent-but-still-insufficient 'Zero Carbon Bill' – which commits New Zealand to Net Zero by 2050 – and delivered an impassioned condemnation of the failure of the political status quo to meet this existential moment:

We are in a climate crisis. If we don't get this right, nothing else matters . . .

Our current political institutions have proven themselves incompetent at thinking outside of a short political term. Change is so regularly sacrificed for power. Slogans are easy, but this stuff, this action, *is hard.* **Climate action cannot be sacrificed anymore for political convenience.** *Climate change is a deeply inconvenient truth, and Mr Speaker, if climate action is indeed our 'nuclear-free' moment, it should be – and it* must be – **transformational**.

It was great stuff. But things got particularly lively when Swarbrick began to frame the debate in terms of intergenerational justice:

Mr Speaker, how many world leaders, for how many decades, have seen and known what is coming but have decided that it is more politically expedient to keep it behind closed doors? My generation and the generations after me do not have that luxury.

In the year 2050, I will be 56 years old. Yet, right now, the average age of this 22nd parliament is 49 years old –

Here, Swarbrick was heckled from across the chamber by Todd Muller, the 51-year-old conservative opposition's spokesperson for climate change. (We don't know exactly what he said, but we can guess, and it was probably exactly the kind of thing a 51-year-old conservative politician would shout out at a young Leftist woman talking about how runaway climate change will trash our future.)

Chlöe Swarbrick responded to the interruption with a simple phrase; a snappy retort that has been birthed in the fires of Millennial and Zoomer online culture in recent years, and which manages to succinctly encapsulate my generation's fury at the raw deal we've been told to accept, and our collective exhaustion with the ossified institutions and ideologies that continue to dominate us and misunderstand us and condescend to us, and which simply refuse to die and to stop holding us all down and back.

With a small smile, a roll of the eye and a flick of the hand, Swarbrick spoke for all of us as she breezily shot back at her heckler just two little words:

'OK Boomer.'

Epilogue

TLDR: This Sucks We Need Something Else

Welp – there you go. That's the book, folks.

I'm sorry. I know there was a lot of dry information and memes and swearing in there. Hopefully it wasn't as painful to read as it has been to write. Who knows? Maybe my incredible prose and great points have absolutely blown your mind, or maybe you knew all that stuff already and now you're feeling ripped off.[1]

It doesn't matter. The publication of this book is the realisation of a dream I've had since my early, chubby childhood, so that's the main thing.

Before it's all over – and before I die and am forever remembered as one of Australia's greatest authors – we should review. Just like the bit at the end of an episode of *Play School,* let us reflect on What We've Learned Today, what it means – and what might come next.

---

1   No refunds.

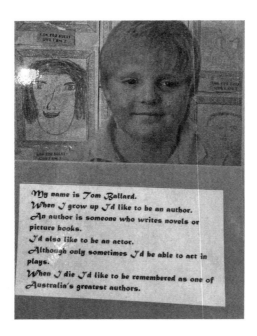

My name is Tom Ballard.
When I grow up I'd like to be an author.
An author is someone who writes novels or picture books.
I'd also like to be an actor.
Although only sometimes I'd be able to act in plays.
When I die I'd like to be remembered as one of Australia's greatest authors.

A GENERATION DENIED

Broadly speaking, **the Millennial generation has been uniquely screwed over by the radical, vicious class war that's been raging in this country and across the world over the past five decades of global capitalism.**

This war has smashed organised labour (which is why **work sucks** more than ever and we lack the power to seriously change it) and resulted in the **commodification and financialisation** of basic social goods like **housing** and **education** – goods that have now become so expensive that trying to attain them either drives young people into debt slavery or becomes straight-up impossible. It's seen our society **privatise** everything: we've sold off and outsourced infrastructure, utilities, and giant chunks of the welfare state to the market, thereby turning almost every facet of life into a profit-making exercise and robbing us of democratic ownership and control over our own bloody country. All this marketisation has overwhelmingly made life harder and shittier and way more expensive than it needs to be – especially for young people and the poor – and has taken a chainsaw to collectivist notions of social solidarity and community.

At the same time, our **class society** has worked hard to transform Australia into what is increasingly an **asset economy**, in which your security and ability to enjoy a decent life is determined less by your labour, and more by how much stuff you own (often due to the sheer good luck of inheritance). The ruling class has used its wealth and influence to further enrich itself and to inflict **economic violence** on ordinary people, courtesy of that fucking drawing on that fucking napkin and the trickle-down lie, the widespread deregulation of corporate power, and brutal austerity politics. The upshot: more and more wealth has been concentrated in the hands of (Xer and Boomer) asset-owners and the super-rich, and that's just given them even *more* power – power which they can then wield to bend society to their will.

Oh, and this same political economic system has **put us on a course towards ecological collapse.** The forces of fossil fuel capital have captured much of our politics and will do everything they can to protect their profits from democratic action to avert the worst impacts of the climate crisis, and the ramifications of how humanity has failed to act in response to this existential threat has already shaped, and will *continue* to shape, the lives of Millennials and Zoomers and our kids and all the generations to come.

So no, my fellow Millennials – you are not crazy, or stupid. You are not 'entitled', 'spoiled', or excessively snowflake-y. We really have been massively short-changed here, and it fucking sucks. Yes, we were lucky enough to be born at all, but we were unlucky enough to be born at a time when the world was being reshaped by these hostile forces in extremely dodgy ways. It's sad and it's scary, but you should know – just like in *Good Will Hunting* – **it's not your fault.**

LUCK O' THE BOOMERS

Nor is this really the fault of the Baby Boomers.

'It's funny yeah but do you ever wonder if the intergenerational banter thing is a big distraction?' wrote an account named 'Shmebecca Shmeeler' on the ABC TV Facebook page underneath my anti-Boomer comedy routine. 'Like everyone would have done pretty much the same thing under the same economic circumstances so isn't it the economic system we're waiting for to die? **crunches into a nice big piece of avocado toast**'.

Schmebecca is exactly right. We didn't choose the timing of our births, and neither did the Boomers. It just so happens that our parents were born into an extraordinary time of relative peace, stability, rising living standards and social progress; indeed, the Baby Boomers really are **the single luckiest generation in all of human history.**

The historical sweet spot of the Long Boom 'Golden Age' in the mid-20th century followed the devastation of the Great Depression and World War II, both of which had fucked up society so much that they effectively reset the entire economic order. A traumatised nation rejected the prevailing wisdom of classical 'let it rip' economics, because everyone could see that approach was shithouse at creating a decent society. The combination of visionary Labor governments, a powerful (and often radical) trade union movement and the almost hegemonic Keynesian consensus delivered **a far more 'tamed' version of capitalism** during this time, in which a begrudging compromise between capital and labour meant that ordinary working people were more empowered than ever before. As a result, throughout their childhoods and early adulthood, the massive Boomers cohort were living in an increasingly prosperous and egalitarian Australia that was blessed with high growth, rising wages, low unemployment, cheap housing, low private debt, and meaningful social solidarity. At the height of the Whitlam years, this country came the closest it ever has to transforming into something like a **social democracy**.[2]

Unfortunately, the economic crises of the 1970s, and the free-market revolution that ensued (more on this in a sec) made sure that the post-war boom was an anomaly; **a limited, one-time-only offer**. This revolution changed everything, overwhelmingly for the worse, and while millions of lucky Boomers have come out of it with enough assets and security to preserve their good luck for decades to come, their Xer and Millennial kids simply have not been able to enjoy the same favourable material conditions, and that's why that whole **intergenerational bargain** thing has broken down.

So no – blaming individual Boomers for the way massive macroeconomic forces played out isn't fair at all.[3] This does *not* mean that I shall refrain from making jokes at Boomers' expense, of course, because they're very fun jokes to do and some Boomers do get super defensive about them and that makes me

---

2　That is, a country with substantial government intervention – a strong welfare state, public ownership of lots of things, lots of regulations and wealth redistribution, etc. – but which is still oriented around a capitalist economy, with private ownership of the means of production. The Nordic countries – particularly Norway, Denmark, Finland and Sweden – are widely viewed as the most successful examples of social democracy today.

　　Notions of social democracy originated in Germany in the 19th century, growing out of the radical socialist political tradition across the Western world at the time. Social democrats thought they could achieve a 'peaceful transition' from capitalism to socialism through incrementalist reforms (and not so much with the hassle of violent revolution); its critics attacked it as either being way too much like actual socialism (from the Right), or nowhere near enough like socialism (from the Left).

　　In a real bummer move, the economic transformation of the Western world over the past 50 years has warped the political terrain and our imaginations so much that now the bog-standard social democratic policies of the likes of Bernie Sanders, Jeremy Corbyn or the Australian Greens are decried by our political establishment as insane, radical, impossible and immoral, even though they're not.

3　Indeed, pretty much all the main antagonists we've touched on in this book hail from either the Greatest (Friedman, Reagan, Thatcher) or the Silent (Fraser, Hawke, Keating, Howard, Laffer, Murdoch) Generations.

　　Yes, Costello, Rudd, Gillard, Abbott, Turnbull and Albanese are all Boomers – while Morrison, Hockey and Frydenberg are fresh-faced Xers – but really, they've just been the cover bands, playing the hits of their ideological forebears.

laugh and that feels like some kind of small victory because let's face it, at the moment it's pretty much all my generation has.

I mean, when Boomer conservative talkback radio hosts sincerely tweet out shit like this, what the hell are we supposed to do? *Not* laugh in their wrinkly faces??

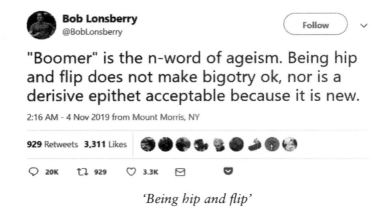

'Being hip and flip'

In their defence, plenty of Baby Boomers are self-aware enough to *actually get it*.

'We were just so blessed,' 68-year-old self-funded retiree John Feehan told the ABC when he was interviewed for a story on intergenerational inequality in 2022. 'We even had the best music, I think!

'The Baby Boomers just landed on their feet, and we've been so rapacious, we've been just terrible.'[4]

One of the more poignant reflections on this generational injustice came from one of my all-time favourite Boomers, comedy genius Shaun Micallef. In July 2020, when the pandemic was still all-consuming and scary and we were all asking big existential questions about everything, Shaun appeared on Wil Anderson's podcast *Wilosophy*, and discussed the contrast between his happy Boomer life and the prospects ahead for his Zoomer sons.

---

4   His (accurate) words, not mine.

'All three of them share the view that the world's pretty shit and the prospects for enjoying that world are pretty limited,' Shaun said, sadly. 'Whatever joys it may hold, they're going to be very few and far between and it's going to be very difficult to access them.

'Which really disappointed me. I guess I'd never really looked at it from their point of view. I've got a little less road out ahead of me than I've already covered so for me, life's been great. I've loved it enormously and continue to do so. I literally said to them when they were children, "*You can do anything you want . . .*"

'But as was explained to me by the 22-year-old, he said, "You don't realise – you were born in 1962. You were far enough away from the end of the Second World War not to have dealt with the War itself, or the austerity that came from the War. You've lived your childhood and most of your adulthood life in the most prosperous and safe times that have existed in history. And that's finished now. It's looking a little bleak. The fuse on this bomb is almost up."'

THE 'N' WORD

The radical and dogshit revolution that brought the Boomers' Golden Age to an end does actually have a name. It's a name that I've deliberately avoided using until now, because it can be a bloody slippery and loaded term, and I figured it was easier for you to actually see it in action first.

I'm talking about

NEOLIBERALISM

Perhaps you've heard this word before, perhaps not. Maybe you've heard it a bunch of times and you've never really got a clear read on what it means, but, like me, you haven't let that stop you referring to anyone or anything that annoys you as either a 'neoliberal shill' or evidence of our 'neoliberal hell-world', because it makes you sound smart and cool.

So what the fuck is it? Well, that's a very big and annoying question that's been swirling around academic circles for decades now, and chances are this book isn't going to be the one to put it all to bed. Some people will claim that 'neo-liberalism' as a term is too fuzzy and all-encompassing to be of any use, others will say it's not even a thing, or if it *is* a thing, it exclusively refers to bad stuff that bad people do, case closed.

Although it may have many various names and faces and caveats, **neoliberalism really *is* a definite 'thing' that exists and happened.** We can identify and observe and critique it in our politics and in our daily lives, and we really *should,* because it's a tricksy little fucker that's infected almost everything in the world around us.

I think we can understand neoliberalism in **three important ways:**

1) AS AN IDEOLOGY

In his seminal 2005 book *A Brief History of Neoliberalism,* the British academic David Harvey gives a basic summary of the set of *ideas* that make up the ideology, defining it as:

> *a theory of political economic practices that proposes that human well-being can best be advanced by liberating individual entrepreneurial freedoms and skills within an institutional framework characterised by strong private property rights, free markets, and free trade.*

Basically, it's a worldview that believes that **human society should primarily be shaped by market forces.**

We've seen how this political theory has been used to inform and justify what's happened to Australian society and the capitalist West since the 1970s. Neoliberal ruling elites – feverishly claiming that The Market is more efficient and superior at doing stuff than government – have pursued a policy of **economic liberalisation**, 'freeing' existing markets (by deregulating everything from industrial relations to the finance industry to environmental protections) and extending market competition and market logics to as many areas of social life as possible (including the provision of housing, education, pensions, and essential services, via privatisation). Trade barriers have been torn down in the name of open, globalised markets, while taxes – generally viewed by neolibs as an annoying infringement on an individual's private property rights – have been slashed, all under the cover of magical supply-side/trickle-down economics.

Ideologically speaking, neoliberalism is basically a new ('neo') version of **Classical Liberalism**, revived for the 20th century.[5] The term 'neoliberal' was first coined in the

---

5   Classical Liberalism is the centuries-old political tradition associated with thinkers like John Locke, Adam Smith, and David Ricardo, and it **generally prioritises individual liberty above all else.** Classical Liberals love their civil liberties and property rights, a supposedly 'impartial' rule of law, and they have big boners for very limited government and unencumbered, 'self-regulating' free markets, which they sincerely believe produce wonderful and meritocratic outcomes. Robert Menzies is the quintessential Classical Liberal: virulently opposed to any kind of anti-capitalist politics, but tolerant of government intervention in the economy (to a degree) and open to (certain kinds of) social progress.

During the Great Depression, a more progressive branch of liberalism – known by various names such as **New/Social/Modern/Welfare/New Deal Liberalism** – began to emerge, advocated by people who still prioritised individual freedoms and were on board with capitalism and everything, but felt bad about the inevitable inequalities it creates, and called for more State intervention to address things like poverty and discrimination. (John Maynard Keynes was a lifelong liberal, to the point where being a 'Keynesian liberal' is synonymous with this sort of position.)

It's because of these divergent ideological branches and various political historical developments that in Australia, the term 'liberal' is associated with the Classical/centre-right tradition, while in the US it's more commonly associated with the Social/centre-left one (e.g. 'Hey let's go eat at Chick-fil-A and watch a Dave Chappelle special to trigger the Libs.').

late 30s, but it wasn't until the post-war years that this philosophy really started to cement itself in the crusty hearts and minds of Classical Liberal thinkers who were extremely worried about the dominance of Keynesianism and all the collectivist, freedom-killing central economic planning that was still going on across the West. In 1947, the Austrian-British Classical Liberal economist Friedrich A. Hayek secured some funding from wealthy backers to host a conference of 39 economists, historians and philosophers – including a spry Milton Friedman – at a spa resort in the Swiss village of Mont Pèlerin, where attendees discussed how free enterprise might be restored.[6] Over ten days, the gathering would debate the best economic medicine for (what they saw as) the West's current sickness, and while they totally condemned anything approaching socialist-ish central planning, they would also reject a completely *laissez-faire* approach. The Society generally accepted that the State should play a limited role in the economy, mainly by protecting property rights, enforcing legal contracts, regulating the money supply, doing nice things to 'incentivise' free enterprise, and maintaining a (minimalist) welfare state, I guess to make sure that not everyone starved to death, because that can be pretty bad for business.[7]

For almost everything *outside* of all that, though, **private individuals and The Market should be left to sort things out.**

These godfathers of neoliberal thought were sketching out their vision of the good society, and a new global order: a world of capitalist market economies with protected private

---

6   This was the first meeting of what would become **The Mont Pelerin Society:** a now international organisation/think tank dedicated to celebrating and preserving neoliberal ideology and ensuring it continues to be inflicted upon humanity.

   The Society would later be joined in the cause of advancing the neoliberal political project by a plethora of (oligarch-funded) Foundations and Institutes and Centres all over the joint.

7   This acceptance of the State's role differentiates the neoliberals from the 19th century *laissez-faire* Classic Liberals and modern loony libertarians, who hate government regulations so much they consider seatbelts or gun control to be Stalinist impositions.

property and almost no trade barriers and shitloads of competitive markets that would be always twirling, twirling towards freedom. This vision would be developed, expanded, and championed by Hayek's disciples in popular culture and academia in the decades to come, and would eventually burrow its way into the brains of some of its biggest champions: John Howard, Margaret Thatcher, Ronald Reagan and yes, even Bob Hawke and Paul Keating.

2) AS AN ACTUAL THING THAT HAPPENED IN TIME & SPACE

It's one thing to have such horrific ideas in your head about how things should be, but they still need to be actually *implemented* in the real, messy world via political action. To pull *that* off, you need to wait for material conditions to be just right.

That's what happened with neoliberalism. The neolibs bided their time and built up an army of zealots across the globe (no doubt helped by all the Cold War anti-communist hysteria in the air at the time), then when the Long Boom ended and various economic crises hit in the early 1970s, they were ready to pounce with their radical policy prescriptions. The CIA, Friedman and the Chicago Boys went hog-wild in turning Chile into a laboratory for the neoliberal doctrine, and when New York City was hit with a budgetary crisis a few years later, its bankers demanded the city implement a program of union-busting, slashed welfare spending and reduced public services. By the end of the decade, as the impacts of the oil shocks and the stagflation crisis continued to bedevil Western economies, the neoliberals' diagnosis – *Keynesianism's failed! Government intervention sucks! Unleash the market forces!* – was ready to be given a fair hearing. Thatcher and Reagan were swept to power with their popular promises of something *new* (and would both stay there for pretty much the entire 80s), and Fraser and his Treasurer Howard were able to keep deregulating and privatising and breaking the Australian labour movement. Later, Hawke would win office, in part by promising to discipline the power of the trade unions and by reassuring capital that his ALP would help to restore profitability, while over in New Zealand a Labour government was selling off almost the entire farm to private hands under **Rogernomics** – the neoliberal policy prescriptions of the Minister for Finance, Roger Douglas.[8]

By the time we reached the 1990s, neoliberalism – this market-oriented counter-revolution to the post-war economic order of Keynesian semi-social democracy and full employment – was 🔥. Western governments were slashing taxes, shrinking union power, privatising public assets, and signing up to free trade deals that would massively accelerate the process of **de-industrialisation**, in which local firms would move – or threaten to move – manufacturing offshore to China, Vietnam, Taiwan and Mexico, where they could more easily exploit the local (un-unionised, less-regulated) workforce and further maximise profits.

To be clear: this ideology was implemented in different places at different times in different ways, with varied results. Neoliberals certainly didn't get everything they wanted, always and everywhere. But broadly speaking, they enjoyed a colossal political victory; the deference to markets had won out, it was the End of History, ideology itself was 'over', and any mainstream

---

8   Neoliberalism was spread all over the shop throughout the 80s, whether people wanted it or not. It was brutally imposed upon debt-laden Latin American countries that were forced to turn to the IMF and the World Bank for financial help. These bodies offered these nations **structural adjustment loans**: loans that were given on the condition that the borrowing governments implement an agenda of privatisation, deregulation, trade liberalisation and austerity – an agenda that would later be labelled **The Washington Consensus**.

   Yes, this economic exploitation worked out to be extremely profitable for global capital, and no, it hasn't worked out brilliantly for the peoples of Latin America, many of whom have since enthusiastically turned to Leftist political leaders who've tried to abandon Consensus policies and bring natural resources back into public ownership.

dreams of seriously challenging capitalism – especially after the collapse of the communist Soviet Union – were abandoned.

Indeed, the defeat was so comprehensive that parties of the broader Left would swallow the tenets of the neoliberal bullshit. We've seen how this began to play out under Hawke and Keating in the 80s and early 90s, but a more 'progressive' version of neoliberalism really hit the big time with the **'Third Way' politics** of US Democratic President and sex pest Bill Clinton, and New Labour war criminal Tony Blair (who was inspired by the Hawke–Keating example). The Third Way is not quite Right, not quite Left – but *por qué no los dos?* We can have deregulated, competitive markets and free trade *AND* 'social justice', the Third Wayers argued; we can hang out in the Sensible Centre and do nice capitalism now – the kind that looks after people and says please and thank you.

While the Clinton and Blair administrations undoubtedly did some progressive things – and yes, they were (slightly) less evil and bonkers than the Republican and Tory alternatives – they still both accepted the doctrine of privatisation and deregulation, enthusiastically joined the demonisation of 'big government', preferred to manage and *limit* the welfare state (rather than expand it) and sucked off corporate donors and economic elites. These Third Way Wankers killed off any hope that the Left might provide an alternative to the fundamentals of neoliberal economics, and pretty soon the ideology had become so powerful and ubiquitous, it was just regarded as *common sense*. Both sides of the political aisle – which were traditionally thought to represent the competing interests of capital vs. labour – now basically agreed on the **neoliberal consensus**.

This really was a massive shift in the make-up of what Western politics was *about,* and what was and wasn't up for debate. Famously, when she was asked to name her greatest achievement, Thatcher would reply, 'Tony Blair and New

Labour'. For his part, Blair agreed; in his 2010 memoir, he wrote that 'Britain needed the industrial and economic reforms of the Thatcher period' and he acknowledged that 'the credibility of the whole New Labour project rested on accepting that much of what she [Thatcher] wanted to do in the 1980s was inevitable, a consequence not of ideology but of social and economic change'.[9]

3) AS A DELIBERATE CLASS PROJECT

Finally, while 'neoliberalism' can refer to a certain set of ideas about markets and the State or to a certain economic program that's been implemented by various governments across the world over the past five decades, it's crucial that we keep our eye on the big picture here – on **what this thing is actually** *for.*

'Neoliberalism,' writes Elizabeth Humphrys in *How Labour Built Neoliberalism: Australia's Accord, the Labour Movement and the Neoliberal Project*, 'is **a project intended to restore stable capital accumulation after the global economic crisis of the 1970s.**' David Harvey says he's 'always treated neoliberalism as a political project carried out by the corporate capitalist class as they felt intensely threatened both

---

9   One passionate Third Wayer in Australia in the 1990s was the future Labor PM Kevin Rudd. In his first speech to parliament in 1998, Rudd explicitly rejected Thatcherism but described what he saw as the big challenge facing 'Parties of the Centre Left around the world': how to achieve 'the creation of a competitive economy while advancing the overriding imperative of a just society'. A decade later, Rudd would write a big fat essay in which he argued that the 2008 GFC exposed the ultimate failure of neoliberal economic orthodoxy (correct), but insisted that the only tenable response to it was moderate, social democratic regulation of markets, so that we could all eschew 'the extremism of both the Left and the Right' and 'save capitalism from itself'. (This did not happen.)

In March 2021, Rudd wrote another essay calling for the Australian Labor Party to now pursue what he called 'a fourth way' – 'Neither conservative, nor neoliberal, nor embracing the blind socialism of the utopians'.

But hey what about this, Kev: a *Fifth* Way? Or maybe a Sixth Way, or perhaps a Sixth Way + infinity + 1?

politically and economically toward the end of the 1960s into the 1970s', while the French sociologist Pierre Bourdieu has summed it up as 'a program for **destroying collective structures** which may impede the pure market logic'.

Neoliberalism, then, **is a *doing word*.** It's not merely a benign set of prescriptions held by people in good faith; what Scott Morrison or Arthur Laffer might tell us is just 'fundamental economics 101'. Rather, it's a **political strategy**, actively deployed to redirect wealth and power upwards, into the hands of the ruling class. It's just the modern version of capitalist class war, baby, and to its credit, it's done a great job at achieving its goal; economic elites and private capital have totally been able to wrench back control over the economy and society since the post-war compromise collapsed.

When we keep this in mind – that **neoliberalism's primary concern is the use of State power to help out the rich** – it's a lot easier to understand why neoliberal governments are so often caught up in hypocrisies and contradictions with their ideological faith. The neolibs claim to be about 'shrinking the size of government', but in fact the State has never been bigger, especially when it comes to military/police/surveillance/border security/carceral spending, not to mention all the regulatory bodies and expensive outsourced public sector work that's required to maintain all the private markets neoliberals love to create. The budget deficit is an absolute outrage and we have to slash public spending as much as possible *RIGHT NOW*, but oh yes we definitely *can* afford to give gargantuan tax cuts to the rich and to big business, that's fine. These fuckers say they love nothing more than 'free' markets and competition, but are happy to hand out billions in subsidies and sign anti-competitive contracts with private (friendly) corporations, or suddenly demand the government build a coal-fired power station if the market won't do it, or step in to bail out the neoliberalised, deregulated finance sector when it's about to collapse.[10]

It doesn't *matter* if pursuing these actions mean the neoliberals are committing ideological heresy; as long as you're doing the job of keeping capitalism stable and protecting the interests of the rich and powerful, you're good as gold.

WELCOME TO OUR WORLD

So by the time the 21st century arrives, this counter-revolution has fundamentally changed the political economic landscape across the West. The power of governments and organised labour was dissolving, levels of inequality were surging, and no one in charge really cared. We'd been brought into a new, distinct phase of capitalism: since the 1970s, we've been living in **The Neoliberal Era.**

Millennials are the first generation to be born, come of age and be fully immersed in this brave new world. By the time Australian Millennials were entering early adulthood at the dawning of the new millennium – living as we were under the legacy of Hawke-and-Keating-ism and the yoke of Howard-and-Costello-ism – **neoliberalism was the air we breathed.** It was the status quo, the hegemonic ideology of our now market-dominated politics and culture, and as we grew up, we found it perfectly natural to view everything – products, services, labour, art, information, experiences, relationships, nature, other people, ourselves, *everything* – as something to be commodified and valued in market terms.

This era has also indoctrinated my generation with a mindset of **hyper-individualism.** Liberalism has always prioritised the individual over the collective, but while liberals of

---

10 It's pretty funny how neoliberalism was sold on the promise that it would prevent economic crises like those in the 1970s from ever happening again – only to then produce the biggest economic crisis since the Great Depression in 2008 😔 😔 😔

the past conceived of the individual as a **citizen** with political rights, freedoms and responsibilities, neoliberalism has transformed those citizens into **consumers**. We don't 'live in a society'; we *consume and compete in a market*, where our whole thing is about buying and selling shit and accumulating capital, because that's what's supposed to make us feel happy and fulfilled.

Thatcher fucking loved this stuff. In an interview from the late 80s, she decried the fact that generous welfare states had caused people to abandon the holy virtue of individual 'personal responsibility', telling a journalist:

> *I think we have gone through a period when too many children and people have been given to understand 'I have a problem, it is the Government's job to cope with it!' or 'I have a problem, I will go and get a grant to cope with it!' 'I am homeless, the Government must house me!' and so they are casting their problems on society and who is society?* **There is no such thing!** *There are individual men and women and there are families and no government can do anything except through people and people look to themselves first.*

Truly, she was a cold-hearted scumbag. But she was a cold-hearted scumbag who was quite good at succinctly expressing the neoliberal position: there's no such thing as 'society', we're all just individuals competing in the marketplace for resources and happiness, and when it comes to being afforded 'luxuries' like basic welfare or housing, you're on your own, champ. Don't expect diddly squat. If you want to 'get ahead', you should compete in the 'meritocratic' market like everybody else, and the wonders of capitalism will meet your needs. If you're fucked over by that process at all, I'm afraid *that's on you*.

Haven't you heard? Collectivist ideas about social solidarity and notions that the public sector should redistribute wealth to guarantee universal welfare have now expired, and any support the State does provide to you will be stringently means-tested, underfunded, and provided on a one-to-one, user-pays basis, ya dirty little leech.[11]

This reduction of everything to the level of The Individual is very good at discouraging people from applying any kind of structural or class-based analysis of our society (which doesn't exist!). As they waged their legislative assaults on the power of trade unions and lauded the liberatory power of the market, neoliberals successfully removed the 'class question' and anti-capitalist critiques from mainstream political discourse entirely, and put all that silliness to bed. You weren't a 'worker' anymore; you were now an *employee*, and you shouldn't worry about getting organised with all the other *individual employees* working alongside you and getting exploited in a similar fashion – that'd be too close to *class warfare*, and we don't do that anymore.[12]

---

11 I mean, Thatcher and the other neolibs didn't exactly sell it like this. They were much more positive. Maggie talked about how it was time to 'put people's destinies back into their own hands'; Reagan celebrated the myth of American 'rugged individualism'; and Milton Friedman always dressed up his theories in the language of freedom, 'choice' and aspiration.

   And fair enough. It's understandable why so many people might find the *promise* of neoliberalism so appealing; the ability to have control over one's life and enjoy the freedom to achieve one's dreams are awesome things, and living under any kind of authoritarian regime in which all your individual rights are subsumed for the sake of the 'collective good' would be annoying and bad.

   Unfortunately, as we've seen over the course of this book, this view of the political economy completely ignores all the ways in which people can be dominated and controlled and made extremely *unfree* not by governments, **but by the power of private capital, our class society and poverty.** It's hard to see how anyone is meaningfully 'free' or can be said to have their destiny 'in their own hands' when their boss exercises huge control over their daily lives, or when they can't afford healthcare or to make any consumer choices at all.

12 In his super-wrong essay back in '89, our friend Francis Fukuyama boldly declared that 'the class issue has actually been successfully resolved in the west' and 'the egalitarianism of modern America represents the essential achievement of the classless society envisioned by Marx', which is . . . a take.

In fact, 'we' don't really do anything anymore. In our neoliberal wonderland, the institutions that tended to bring people together and build the power of collective action, are gone. Forget 'we'; **it's all about *you*.**

THAT FUNNY FEELING

'[I]t isn't that I set out on economic policies,' Thatcher explained to *The Sunday Times* in the early 80s, 'it's that I set out really to change the approach [of collectivism], and changing the economics is the means of changing that approach. If you change the approach you really are after the heart and soul of the nation. Economics are the method; **the object is to change the heart and soul.**'

Mission accomplished, Maggie. Thatcherism made sure that Britain's heart was dramatically hardened, and its soul was sucked out of its body. Across the West, neoliberalism changed the very *nature* of what it means to be the average person trying to survive under capitalism and live a decent life, and it's given rise to what can only be described as **extremely bad vibes**.

For me, this is a defining aspect of the Western Millennial experience: along with all the economic insecurity we're saddled with, we live with this nagging, hard-to-pinpoint-but-definitely-there sense that there's something *off* about things. It's a feeling that's difficult to put into precise words, but you know it when you see it: it's the Uber-fication of everything; it's 'prayer apps' like 'Instapray' which allow corporations to data-mine people's conversations with God; it's that fucking Kendall Jenner/Black Lives Matter/Pepsi ad; it's the Virgin Australia entertainment system telling you that now you're connected to the in-flight wifi, there's 'no need to talk to the stranger beside you!'. It's the fact that we're able to 'connect' with everyone, and yet we feel ever more atomised and isolated from those around us. It's knowing that there's something fundamentally NQR about the presence of profiteering private companies in every single area of our lives (in our homes, our schools, our bedrooms, our conversations with loved ones on social media), about a nihilistic, postmodernist culture that seems to have run out of new ideas (and just keeps pumping out reboots, sequels and nostalgia), and about a political establishment that has become so weak that it seems unwilling or unable to seriously change *anything,* or even just to tell a different story about what the future might look like.

This weird *ennui,* one suspects, is the kind of thing that comes from living under a totalising political and economic system that's solely concerned with free markets and the liberation of **The Self:** self-improvement, self-expression, self-care, self-employment, self-help, self-reliance, self-interest. When we're all reduced to 'free' individuals focussed solely on ourselves, with no real ties or obligations to one another, any sense of the common/collective/national interest – of *community* – fades away. We're left with nothing more than our relationship to the market, and all the crap we've bought to try and fill our spiritual holes.

As the British documentarian Adam Curtis puts it in *Can't Get You Out of My Head* – his sprawling 2021 series on the rise of individualism – the neoliberal age has created a world in which '**you are free, but you are alone**'.

Now sure, humans have been feeling lost and alone in various ways for millennia, long before neoliberalism arrived. Yearning for a sense of *meaning* is a fundamental part of the human experience, and that existential angst will probably always be with us, no matter what. And yes, I understand that the experience of *feeling weird and bad* is something of a 'First World Problem', and pales in comparison to the economic devastation and misery that global neoliberalism has wrought upon working class people across the Global South for decades and decades.

But I think it's really important to underscore **just how severely neoliberal hyper-individualism has alienated my generation from political life**, and how *disempowering* that can be when it comes to the matter of trying to make anything better. In the post-war era, Boomers could join trade unions, churches, political parties (with much bigger memberships than they have now) and mass social movements to try to change things. Now, all that collectivism's out the window, and young people have been brainwashed into thinking that the way to change the world's (structural) problems is solely through our (individual) actions. We may not have any real class power, but we do have personal Instagram accounts, so we'll be *the change we want to see in the world* by posting a black square to end racism and getting lots of likes. We'll add a social justice filter to our profile picture, tweet to *raise awareness* about #idpol stuff, we'll cancel problematic individuals, police language, decry micro-aggressions, and make all the correct consumer choices.[13] The phrase **'The personal is political!'** was popularised in the 1960s to highlight the way that women and minority groups can see larger social and political structures manifest in their daily lives, and as a call for collective, feminist *action* – but in the neoliberal era, it's come to be a slogan for something quite different. Now we view the political as almost *exclusively* reduced to the personal sphere: your politics is about what *you personally* think/do/eat/say/buy/post, so just focus on that, and nothing more.

I think most people my age have come to recognise by now that this kind of politics does sweet fuck-all to really change power relations or material reality or pretty much anything, really. But we can't imagine a serious alternative, so we just get sad again, and we kind of check out, and feel even more *free-but-alone* than before.

THE STRAYAN EXPERIENCE

So now we have the catch-all term for the thing that I've been trying to describe throughout these chapters: **the neoliberal transformation** of the Australian political and economic landscape over the past half a century. Locally, all this economic reforming was referred to by another name, **'economic rationalism'**, but it was all the same shit: liberalise the economy, discipline labour, unleash and introduce competitive markets everywhere, and privatise/deregulate/individualise what you can. This neoliberal turn was started under Whitlam and Fraser, embraced under Hawke and Keating, and intensified under Howard, and would eventually form the bedrock of the bipartisan political consensus we're still being subjected to today.

And I put it to you, dear reader, that **it is this particular phase of capitalism that is responsible for the raw deal that Australian Millennials have inherited.**

---

13 I once saw an ad for a toilet paper company that screamed 'WIPERS OF THE WORLD UNITE – YOUR BUM COULD CHANGE THE WORLD!'

This story of things is a contested one, especially by passionate defenders of the Australian Labor Party and its legacy – most notably, Paul Keating himself. When Greens leader Adam Bandt pointed out that '[s]ince Keating and Hawke, Labor has adopted neoliberalism, which has privatised public services, cut taxes for the wealthy and adopted more and more austerity' at the National Press Club in August 2022, PK was seriously triggered.

'This is both a lie and a slur,' he told the *Sydney Morning Herald*. He dismissed Bandt as 'a bounder and a distorter of political truth' and listed a range of what he views as his super-cool achievements (like universal Medicare, superannuation, and the enterprise bargaining system) as clear evidence that he's innocent of the neoliberal charge.

'How could any reasonable person describe these mammoth changes as "neoliberalism",' he asked, 'a word associated with the likes of Margaret Thatcher and Ronald Reagan?'

'Someone published a book recently claiming the Hawke–Keating years were neoliberal which is just *rubbish*,' former Labor Treasurer and ALP President Wayne Swan told me on my podcast in September 2020. 'We're a laborist party with unions affiliated with us and I find it offensive, some of that analysis, which somehow suggests that the union movement of the country and Labor politicians of enormous stature . . . were somehow neoliberals.'[14]

Elsewhere, Swan has acknowledged that while *some* of Labor's policies of the period fit the neoliberal label, Hawke and Keating still couldn't possibly be described as 'simple merchants of neoliberalism' because they did things like Medicare, taxed capital gains, and collaborated with the

---

14 He was referring to Elizabeth Humphrys' aforementioned book on the Accord era. When I asked Swan if he'd actually *read* the book so that he might be able to fully appreciate its nuanced arguments and detailed history, he replied, 'I've read summaries of the book, yeah absolutely'.

union movement to expand the social wage. Swan believes this should instead be described as **'Australian Laborism'**, which he considers distinct from and superior to neoliberalism, because it led to lots of economic growth and rising living standards and has meant that wealth inequality isn't quite as bad here in Australia as it is in the US or the UK.

Certainly, it's a *mixed* legacy. Yes, Bob Hawke and Paul Keating and the ALP can be credited with a bunch of non-neoliberal achievements and their governments did a bunch of cool things that the Tories would never do in a million years (passing environmental protection laws, recognising native title and increasing university funding, for example). Their political agenda was a response to global conditions and trends, but it was also informed and developed by their centre-left dispositions, Australian labour history, and domestic political realities of the day – none of which played into how the neoliberal counter-revolution was rolled out elsewhere.

But I'm sorry, **a party of the Left doesn't deserve a bunch of cookies for simply not being as fucked as Margaret Thatcher.** The ALP's nicer 'Laborist' reforms of the period don't negate all the other stuff they did; the stuff that was clearly informed by a neoliberal desire to discipline labour and expand the scope of the market, all in an effort to stabilise Australian capitalism. Hawke and Keating might not have been 'simple merchants' of the neoliberal craze, but it's fair to say they weren't exactly *hostile* to it, either, and they were perfectly happy to embrace and impose parts of the agenda on our society, even though it weakened workers' power and helped the rich get richer.

'The defeats of the 80s and 90s were a global phenomenon – in the Global North, anyway,' Jim Casey summed it up to me on *Like I'm A Six-Year-Old* in March 2022. Casey is a long-time trade unionist, firefighter and Leftist hunk who's previously run as a Greens candidate against Anthony Albanese in Grayndler.

'So you look at, say, Britain, America and Australia, and you'll see different experiences of that. In America and Britain, you actually saw the Right with their hobnail boots on, literally dismantling the labour movement, kicking the Labour Party apart.

'In Australia it was a little bit different: **Labor oversaw the process**, and we got an improved welfare state out of it. But we have a demobilised labour movement, a *corporatised* labour movement, a shift to the Right within the ALP, and – here we are now.

'So if you had the choice between the two, you'd take the Australian experience, because we got Medicare. But having said that, the defining feature of all three examples is that the other side – capital – successfully mobilised and successfully got a bigger share of the national cake; they successfully made us work harder, successfully shifted some of the costs of the welfare state off them and back onto us.

'So *that's* the defining feature. It's not that Labor's a bunch of bastards; it's that our side's been losing, and social democratic parties like Labor had two choices: they can either try to actually mobilise and turn against it, or they can try to adapt to the new circumstances – **and we've seen the latter.**'

Plenty of Labor hacks and Stans and drips will tell you that Hawke and Keating had no choice in enacting their reforms at all. All this 'modernising' was *inevitable*; there was, as Thatcher liked to put it, **'no alternative'**.

'We don't know what would have happened had there not been an Accord,' Elizabeth Humphrys tells me. 'Had there been a massive fight by the unions, maybe we would have ended up somewhere similar to some of the European countries, where things *didn't* neoliberalise in the 80s; actually, it took some time for that to happen into the 90s.

Even Finland's really only going through it now. Who knows what would have happened?'

Nobody does. And in a way, it's moot, because what happened *did* happen, and we can't change any of it now. We can, however, try to clearly see and evaluate this history – both the good, and the terrible – so that we might reckon with it, and we might know how to do something about all of its shitty consequences that still plague our lives today.

Unfortunately, the modern Labor Party seems very reluctant to do this. After Keating lost to Howard in 1996, an internal party review identified Labor's neoliberal-ness as the primary reason why working-class voters had become disillusioned with them. It read:

> *Labor's record on Qantas and the Commonwealth Bank raised questions about our candor and ideological commitment to public ownership. Selling off national icons was deeply unpopular and **raised questions about what Labor stood for**. Many of our own people didn't believe us when we said we wouldn't sell off Telstra.*

The general response to this finding from party apparatchiks was not to reconsider their pro-market, anti-worker, pro-inequality outlook, but rather to just get better at *explaining* to voters why privatisation and free trade deals and unleashing capital were actually really good. The Labor faithful (especially the parliamentary party and the internal bureaucracy) would laud Hawke and Keating as political and economic geniuses, and 'neoliberalism' would come to mean all the terrible stuff that was enacted exclusively by the likes of Thatcher, Reagan and Howard.

In reality, the neoliberal/Third Way brain disease has been ingrained in Labor politics ever since.

'Governments make choices between different models when they want to introduce social welfare schemes,' says Humphrys, 'and the Australian Labor Party, in the neoliberal era, has consistently chosen to introduce neoliberalised versions. The health system is private-subsidy-based, superannuation is highly exposed to the market, the NDIS is a privatised insurance scheme, rather than the government providing services directly, and people even said the same thing about the Gonski school reforms ... [Rudd and Gillard] did nothing to wind back funding for private schools, which is absolutely undermining racial diversity, equality and quality in the public system.'

Again, this doesn't mean that Labor governments haven't done and won't continue to do some good things; even some things that go against the neoliberal grain (maybe). As hollowed out and as cosy with the forces of capital as the ALP has become, you'd still have to take a Labor government over the malignant Coalition any day of the week.

But it's also true that, thanks to the bipartisan adoption of the neoliberal consensus and Labor's significant shift to the Right since the Whitlam years, **it really is getting harder and harder to tell Australia's two major political parties apart.** They're both of the view that capitalism can't be challenged, and they agree on giving tax cuts to the rich, the efficiency and supremacy of markets, privatising assets and services (even education), punishing people on welfare, 'balanced budgets', locking up refugees, keeping workers' power in check, and dumb culture war shit like the absolute vital importance of celebrating our national day on 26 January, for fuck's sake.

'Hawke got in, and it was very exciting,' my mum, Judy, told me during a special post-Trump, parent-interview episode of my podcast back in November 2016. 'We thought the whole world would shift – and it didn't.

'He did some good things, and it was a reasonable time. I had much more faith that Labor could make positive changes than the Liberal Party.

'But then, in recent years, I just think the Labor Party – it's just not achieving any of the things that we had hoped that they might. Particularly their position on asylum seekers – it's just inhumane and it's just so frustrating that they can come out with all this talk justifying their position and the bottom line is it's . . . it's *shocking*, what's happening.'

I asked what she thought the Labor Party should really be about.

'Well . . . the Labor Party is for the ordinary person,' she replied. 'It's for the everyday man; it's for equality, justice – not big money, capitalism.

'But it's changed. It's changed *remarkably*, and those basic human values seem to have gone.'

IS IT OVER YET?

I know this is all quite tragic and depressing, and perhaps a bit overwhelming. Again, sorry about that; I feel like throughout these pages I may have come across as something of a fully black-pilled Debbie Downer/Negative Nelly/NegaTory Amos, and that's not really the full picture.

I know that **modern Millennial life is not a total misery.** Australian Millennials aren't the hardest-hit victims of neoliberalism; **as bad as things are for us, they could be heaps worse** – and for billions of our fellow human beings on this planet, they are. There are plenty of reasons to love and cherish living in a country like Australia, neoliberalised though it may be, and I'd be remiss if I didn't acknowledge all the nice things that Boomers missed out on that are now commonly enjoyed by my generation: cheap international air travel, low crime rates, a vast array of consumer goods, and super-convenient technological advances, most notably the motherfuckin' internet.

Thanks to the blood, sweat and struggle of millions of ordinary people of all ages continuing to organise mass social movements throughout the neoliberal years, there's undeniably been a bunch of cool social progress on matters of race, gender, and sexuality. I for one am very glad that I live in a country in which I won't be conscripted and shipped off to fight in some stupid war against my will, and I'm very grateful that I can live a free and happy life as a big ol' poofta without going to jail or being completely ostracised from polite society.

(And yes, as we've touched on, **the neoliberal revolution *did* result in a dramatic increase in the world's *overall* level of wealth and prosperity,** and some [crumbs] of that have occasionally 'trickled down' to benefit ordinary working people, once in a while. It's nothing like what was promised, of course, and it's come at far too high a cost – but even the lizards in the ruling class know that you've got to throw the proles some scraps every now and again, if only to discourage them from whipping out the pitchforks.)

But Millennial outrage is not rooted in a belief that we live in the *worst of all possible worlds*. Rather, we are worn down and infuriated by how hard and unfair the status quo is, **when it could so clearly be so much fucking better.** We know only too well that things could be a lot easier and fairer, because for the bulk of our parents' generation, they were. A more empowered, better housed, less debt-ridden and more secure experience of Australian life totally existed, in living memory. While it'd be naïve to think that we can simply press a button and instantly replicate the post-war settlement today, it has become bleedingly obvious to millions of people – Millennials and Boomers alike – **that what we have now is cooked, and it cannot last.** Especially since 2008, the polycrisis we've been living through – spiralling inequality, low growth, the failures of privatisation, crumbling services and looming climate breakdown – has shown that neoliberal capitalism has failed, and has no answers when it comes to solving the big problems we face, or imagining a better future. After all, if the system is working so brilliantly, why are so many people turning away from the West's centrist major parties and institutions, and instead finding something in political outsiders (Trump, Farage, Hanson, Le Pen, Sanders, Corbyn) who explicitly campaign against the neoliberal status quo?

This is not to say that it's going to go quietly. People have been declaring The Death of Neoliberalism for quite some time now; Kevin Rudd thought it couldn't survive the GFC, the Occupy Movement wanted to dance on its grave, ACTU Secretary Sally McManus claimed 'the experiment has run its course' in 2017, and Jacinda Ardern declared modern capitalism to be a 'blatant failure' when she was elected as New Zealand's PM in 2019.[15] When the pandemic hit, folks got a little bit carried away about how everything was going to radically and permanently change; the *New York Times* even ran a piece in April 2020 under the title 'It's the End of the World Economy as We Know It', while the stockbroking arm of Macquarie Group warned that 'conventional capitalism is dying' and claimed that the world was headed for 'something that will be closer to a version of communism'.

It now seems these rumours may have been greatly exaggerated. Our neoliberal political class isn't ready to fully

---

15 Even Paul Keating has acknowledged that 'liberal economics has run into a dead end', although he thinks that its decline only started in the wake of 2008, so I guess none of it has anything to do with him.

break from this orthodoxy just yet. While there was a sudden and unprecedented level of State intervention during the COVID crisis (a necessary step to, once again, save capitalism), much of that didn't last, and in the end the billionaires got heaps fatter, while workers got screwed. During the pandemic, Treasurer Josh Frydenberg named Reagan and Thatcher as 'an inspiration' and Morrison was always hoping we'd quickly 'snap back' to the neoliberal norm once it was all over. Even coming in to the 2022 election – after Australians had suffered through two long years in which the brutal inequalities of our neoliberal society were on show for everyone to see – the Australian Labor Party deliberately shifted its vision even further to the Right, and eked out a win. They appear to have convinced themselves this is the *only* way for them to take power, even if it makes it even harder to figure out what the hell they're really *about*. Now they're in government, Labor have been amenable to tax cuts for the rich, committed to starving the poor, and are happily dangling the threat of austerity over our heads.

Meanwhile, as I'm writing this, the new Tory PM Liz Truss is trying to roll out 'Trussonomics', featuring some reheated Thatcherite trickle-down tax cuts for the rich, and everyone seems to think that Trump – who campaigned as a right-wing populist, but basically governed as a trickle-down neolib – will run (and win) in 2024.

OKAY, JESUS CHRIST, SO WHAT THE ACTUAL FUCK CAN WE ACTUALLY EVEN DO ABOUT IT ALL THEN, TOM? *HUH?!?!*

Great question. Full disclosure: **I have no fucking idea.**

Not *really*. I mean, I'm just a dumb uni drop-out comedian who somehow managed to land a book deal, and I've really only been able to fully get my head around most of this extremely recently, so you know, to quote Joe Biden, gimme a break. If I knew all the big smart political answers that were definitely going to work, I'd probably keep them on the DL, move to Canberra and make millions by joining the political consultancy industrial complex.

What I *can* share with you is where I've ended up. All of this – this thinking, re-thinking, feeling, crying, reading history, talking with people, arguing online, and book-writing during these strange and scary neoliberal times – has turned me on to **anti-capitalist, class-based politics,** and has pushed me into the loving arms of

DEMOCRATIC SOCIALISM

Yes, I'm one of those filthy **Millennial Socialists** you may have heard about. The kind of young person that came to find something inspiring and meaningful in the politics of Bernie Sanders and Jeremy Corbyn: old-school universal Leftists who meant what they said and said what they meant, and who told an inspiring, collectivist story about what a fairer world might look like. Leftists who proposed bold, universal, social democratic policies like Medicare For All, free tertiary education, free public transport, nationalised key industries and a Green New Deal/Industrial Revolution – all of it paid for by taxing the wealthy – which would make working people's lives materially better; and who, unlike other polit-ical actors, weren't afraid to **identify and challenge the clear enemy**: the billionaires, massive corporations and capitalist media that make up the ruling class.[16]

---

16 Contrast this with the thinking of neoliberals like former Wal-Mart board member Hillary Clinton ('If we broke up the big banks tomorrow . . . would that end racism?') or Joe Biden ('I don't think 500 billionaires are the reason why we're in trouble').

Omar Essam Lhc
@OmarEssamLhc

10:05 PM · Aug 19, 2017 · Twitter for Android

25.5K Retweets   **867** Quote Tweets   **79.3K** Likes

As my anxious generation was wondering why the world wasn't living up to all the shiny neoliberal promises we'd been sold, the End of History thesis collapsed, and political ideology came roaring back. These slightly awkward self-identified socialist grandpas came into the spotlight, and Millennials found something in what they were saying, and we decided to find out more. 'Socialism' was the most looked-up word on Merriam-Webster's website in 2015, and soon – as debates about Trump and Brexit and the mysterious 'white working class' and identity politics and economic stagnation raged in the culture – multiple opinion polls across the West confirmed that for Millennials, the 's' word wasn't a dirty one. One survey commissioned by the Centre for Independent Studies (CIS) in 2018 found that **58% of Australian Millennials had a favourable view of socialism,** and **59% agreed that 'capitalism has failed and government should exercise more control of the economy'** – findings that the CIS, a neoliberal, right-wing think tank, did not like at all.

'Australian Millennials' limited exposure to the horrors of socialism may be causing them to romanticize the ideology,' read the CIS report outlining the results. It called for cooler capitalist heads to combat this new trend; to set these naïve kids straight and 'educate them on socialism's role in some of the greatest catastrophes in human history'.

That's one response, I guess. Another one might be to try actually *listening* to young people, and reflecting on why millions of us are so thoroughly unimpressed by the current way of doing things, and are desperately looking for something better. I've climbed aboard the socialist train because I can now recognise that it is capitalism – this political economic system of production and exploitation – that's been screwing over billions of people for hundreds of years now, and quite frankly, **I think it stinks**. It is anti-human, suicidal and unjust. It is, as the American socialist Eugene Debs (the OG Bernie) once put it, 'a social order in which it is possible for one man who does absolutely nothing that is useful to amass a fortune of hundreds of millions of dollars, while millions of men and women who work all the days of their lives secure barely enough for a wretched existence.'

I can now see that **our capitalist class society is fundamentally anti-democratic**. As long as the means of production are in private hands, the capitalist class will be able to disproportionately set the terms over our lives, our politics and our happiness, and that's just profoundly unfair. To me, **democratic socialism is the idea that *everyone* should be in power**; that a just society is one with deep, meaningful political *and economic* democracy where the means of production are owned collectively, and where people can make decisions together about how things are run and how resources are shared. It's about organising our communities and our country around *meeting human needs,* not profits. It's about redistributing both wealth *and power,* about actually guaranteeing the principle of 'One Person, One Vote' (not what we have now, which is more like 'One Dollar, One Vote'). It is a vision of the world for the many, not the few; and it is about a fuller, more meaningful conception of **freedom and liberty:** one in which everyone in society is free to live a good, decent life, where all their basic material needs – food, shelter, healthcare, education, meaningful work and a social life – are fulfilled, no matter what.

I've also come to realise that being what it is, **our beloved liberal 'democracy' is not capable of delivering a world that looks anything like that.** Even in its nicest form, liberalism's celebration of free markets and its blinkered focus on The Individual means that it can really only try to win a better society by guaranteeing *individual rights and freedoms;* liberties that are very nice to have *in theory*, but are often rendered meaningless when you try to assert them in a class society full of vast inequalities in property and power. We're all supposed to have 'freedom of speech', but only some of us can afford to be sued for defamation. We all have 'the right to vote', but only oligarchs and massive corporations can afford to fork out hundreds of thousands of dollars in political donations.

Plus, **people can't eat freedom, nor find shelter in liberal rights.** Everyone needs and deserves *actual material resources* in order to live with dignity and be truly free, and guaranteeing those resources to all takes more than liberal platitudes and a reliance on the market. Political actors from across the political spectrum will *say* that they care about 'equality' and 'social justice' and 'fairness' etc., but very few will acknowledge that **liberal capitalism actually makes all that impossible;** instead, it leads to a society rigged for the rich. A society that seems perfectly fine with the fact that here, in one of the wealthiest countries in a world of abundance, people are sleeping on the street while mining barons fly over them in private jets.

Fuck that shit. It's not right, I tells ya. Any political movement that's serious about making life better in this country for ordinary people has to first and foremost be about wrenching power *away* from capital and *towards* labour, and doing everything possible to tame, erode, and finally smash this system, so that it might be replaced with something better, for everyone.

. . . HOPE? MAYBE?

I regret to inform you that Jeremy Corbyn is not currently the Prime Minister of the United Kingdom, nor is Bernie Sanders in the White House. Both political projects were brutally defeated in their shots at power, and for little baby socialists like me, it was pretty soul-crushing to watch, particularly when they both came so goddamn fucking close.[17]

The only serious federal electoral project that's close to socialism/social democracy in Australia right now is **The Greens**; a party which in recent years has come to adopt a grassroots organising strategy around an explicitly anti-neoliberal, left-wing populist platform, that tells a story about redistributing wealth from the super-rich and using democratic State power to deliver climate and economic justice. It's this agenda that finally made me pull my finger out and become a member of the party during the pandemic, and I must say that the 2022 election night – in which the Right was

---

17 These men are not saints, and (clearly) their campaigns were far from perfect. They made mistakes, and Leftists everywhere can and should learn from that.

But it's also true that **both of these dudes were brutally fucked over and betrayed by the centrist, neoliberal political establishment.** We know that the top brass of the Democratic Party worked to sabotage the Sanders campaign in 2016; Barack Obama intervened directly in the 2020 primaries to back Biden; and right-wing members of the UK Labour Party were constantly working to undermine Corbyn's leadership and slag him off in the (extremely hostile) media. These treacherous arseholes simply could not tolerate the political success of people who said they were socialists *and actually meant it,* and they organised their black little hearts out to make sure the movements around them were crushed. Fuck those people; Corbyn rules, and yes, #BernieWouldHaveWon.

trounced, and the Greens broke through with their best ever results, winning a record number of senators and three new seats in Queens(Greens)land – was one of the most joyous nights of my life, filled as it was with laughter and relief and whiskey.

Yet, as great as it was, that night can only be considered to be one small shift in the right direction. The Greens are not yet a mass party that's able to wield serious national power, and even the most spirited optimist would have to acknowledge that we have a very long way to go.

So in many ways, **it's all a bit bleak.** Some argue that with Sanders and Corbyn out of the picture and a generally sidelined Left, the Millennial socialism moment is over. It was a wild and crazy fad, but it's done, and now we can all go back to doing Sensible Politics again, in which the centrist grown-ups carry on doing what they do, changing nothing, while everything gets worse.

I'm not so sure. (And not just because if that *is* true, I will have been seriously owned.) I think there's still life in this movement yet, because while Jezza and the Bern might have been defeated, **the failures of neoliberalism that they railed against are still with us, and people still fucking hate it.** The *Australia Talks* surveys have found that **half of all Australians agree that 'capitalism as it exists today does more harm than good', and a whopping 76% agree that the gap between the rich and the poor is too big.** As we've seen throughout this book, issue polling consistently shows that the Australian people are well to the Left of our political and media classes on so many big issues: from workers' rights to public ownership, from strengthening the welfare state to big democratic interventions in the economy for the sake of serious climate action. Working people are overwhelmingly and increasingly dissatisfied with the ways in which our capitalist liberal democracy is failing them, and as long as that's the case, anti-capitalist politics will have a chance of breaking through.[18]

This **is what gives me hope; hope for Millennials, for Zoomers, for Australia, for the future.** Even with all the economic and social power backing it in, most ordinary people can still see through capitalism's bullshit, and they know the extreme inequality that it produces is not 'the natural order of things'. Yes, we *do* live in a society, goddammit; neoliberalism is based on a dirty fucking lie, and collectivism isn't dead. We can make a society in which we can be human beings with a stake in something bigger than ourselves, as opposed to just alienated consuming automatons brutalised by our exciting perma-flexi lifestyle brought to us by UberLife. **Things do not have to be as they are;** there *is* an alternative to this – there has to be, otherwise we're fucked.

For me – and for millions of Millennials all over the world – these strange times have delivered us this massive, intense and liberatory revelation. Getting socialist-pilled and learning that so much of what we've been told about our society and the world is total bullshit can be very disorienting, and sometimes quite scary.

But it's also amazing, because it feels like you're able to see the world clearly for the first time. You can begin to understand the giant forces that have been shaping human history on an epic scale and have led to the creation and organisation of everything around us today.

---

18 It's got to the point that even Francis Fukuyama has had a major rethink. These days, Fukuyama has abandoned his neoconservatism, views the neoliberal revolution as 'self-defeating' and is a strong critic of the US's Cold War crimes, the deregulation of financial markets, the failures of privatisation, and runaway inequality.

'Over time I've become something of a social democrat,' he told Novara Media's Aaron Bastani in an interview in March 2022, 'in the sense that I actually think that that kind of redistribution and provision of universal services to people is necessary to sustain a liberal society.'

You really are hearing it more and more: **neoliberalism sucks, and we need something else.**

*(Source: https://memezila.com/History-book-Wait-its-all-
class-struggle-Always-has-been-meme-5081)*

Once that lightbulb goes on, you soon realise that you're getting at the same truth that millions of your fellow human beings have come to see over the past few centuries, too. The End of History and the voices of the ruling class might insist that socialism has been a universal failure, and that calling yourself a 'socialist' is ridiculous and dangerous and majorly cringe – but read enough history and you'll learn that an anti-capitalist/socialist politics has been found in the heads and hearts of everyone from Albert Einstein ('The economic anarchy of capitalist society as it exists today is, in my opinion, the real source of the evil') to Dr Martin Luther King Jr ('Call it democracy, or call it democratic socialism, but there must be a better distribution of wealth within this country for all God's children').

Helen Keller, Nelson Mandela and Malcolm X were all Leftist radicals. Great writers like Oscar Wilde, H. G. Wells, Ursula K. Le Guin, James Baldwin, James Joyce, Ernest Hemingway, Dorothy Hewett, Kurt Vonnegut, Arthur Miller and George Orwell were all socialists, as was Nina Simone, Richard Pryor, astronomer Carl Sagan and George freakin' Michael. Modern celebrity socialists include the likes of

2Pac, Jane Fonda, Danny Glover, *Anchorman* director Adam McKay, Danny DeVito, Susan Sarandon, Roger Waters, Rage Against the Machine, Serj Tankian from System of a Down, Wallace Shawn (aka Vizzini from *The Princess Bride*) and, based on all the nice stuff he says, Pope Francis.[19]

And yes, **socialist/communist/Leftist ideas have played a huge part in shaping the Australia we know and love.** Gallipoli hero John Simpson Kirkpatrick (of 'Simpson and His Donkey' fame) was a unionist organiser and socialist; while the humanitarian ophthalmologist Fred Hollows, native title rights hero Eddie Mabo and the beloved *Gardening Australia* host Peter Cundall were all peace-loving commies. The 'International Women's Day' that we celebrate every March was established by explicitly socialist working-class women as part of their fight for suffrage and against capitalist exploitation, while the Sydney Gay and Lesbian Mardi Gras originated with the brave struggle of anti-capitalist queers.

It's been a socialist vision that has guided the Australian Labor Party when it's been at its best, from Curtin and Chifley to Whitlam and his Treasurer, Jim Cairns. It is the promise of a world beyond capitalism that's inspired ordinary Australians to organise, strike, campaign, scream, sweat, bleed and even die in the fight to win a better tomorrow.

This same fight rages today. And as far as this entitled little snowflake sees it, we really have no choice but to join that fight, and *that* requires us to see ourselves and each other as what we truly are, first and foremost: not strangers, not consumers, not competitors in some brutal war of all against all, not Millennials or Zoomers or Alphas or Xers or Boomers, but as something else:

---

19 In one exhortation, the Pope argued that trickle-down economics 'expresses a crude and naïve trust in the goodness of those wielding economic power and in the sacralized workings of the prevailing economic system'.

He then went back to live in his city made of gold.

comrades.

(End Bits)

DO YOUR OWN RESEARCH

All the major facts and figures in this book have come from upstanding, reliable sources and the lamestream media, and are all pretty easily Google-able, if you don't believe me. I've included the sources for all the major claims, but I couldn't be bothered doing a full list of references for everything because that felt too much like writing an actual book.[1]

If you're interested in going further down the revolution-ary rabbit hole, here are some titles and sources that I drew on/plagarised and might be useful:

⇒ **For Australian political history:** Dr Elizabeth Humphrys' *How Labour Built Neoliberalism: Australia's Accord, the Labour Movement and the Neoliberal Project* is dense, but fascinating and important. Dominic Kelly's *Political Troglodytes and Economic Lunatics: The Hard Right in Australia* is a brilliant, funny, and much-needed history of the small group of right-wing demons behind the H. R. Nicholls Society, the Samuel Griffith Society,

---

1 Again, if you have any issues with anything at all, please don't hesitate to reach me on avi.yemini@idftraining.com.au.

the Bennelong Society and the Lavoisier Group, which have all done a fair bit of damage to our political landscape. I'd also recommend Shaun Crowe's *Whitlam's Children: Labor and the Greens in Australia*, Paddy Manning's *Inside the Greens*, Bernard Keane's *The Mess We're In*, as well as labourhistory.org.au and the blog pipingshrike.com. The ANU's *Australian Dictionary of Biography* is a fantastic (free!) resource, too.

⇒ **For some Big Fat Socialism/anti-capitalism (and some laffs)**: check out Helen Razer's *Total Propaganda*, Bhaskar Sunkara's *The Socialist Manifesto* and *The Chapo Guide to Revolution: A Manifesto Against Logic, Facts, and Reason*. While you're at it, have a squiz at (and, if you can, support) the likes of *Jacobin* magazine (especially its Australian articles), *Current Affairs, Overland, Red Flag, Green Left*, Independent Australia, *Marxist Left Review,* Flood Media, New Matilda and Michael West Media. For funny and righteous analysis of the horrors of late capitalism and empire, you can't go past Caitlin Johnstone (her blog can be found at caitlinjohnstone.com).

⇒ **On climate:** Jeff Sparrow's *Crimes Against Nature: Capitalism and Global Heating* is a brilliant examination of why our relationship to the natural world has become so broken. I'd also suggest Tim Hollo's recent *Living Democracy: An ecological manifesto for the End of the World As We Know It,* and pretty much everything that climate and energy communicator Ketan Joshi puts out into the world (@ketanj0, ketanjoshi.co).

⇒ If you hate **privatisation** as much as I do, check out publicfutures.org and the work of Professor John

Quiggin (@JohnQuiggin). If you want to get angry about how many goddamn **political donations** our major parties accept and the various industries they come from, head to DemocracyForSale.net, then please join the Australian Greens.

⇒ Lastly, as you know, **listening to podcasts is the greatest praxis anyone can ever do, ever.** Apart from my pods, I recommend having a listen to *Chapo Trap House,* everything on Novara Media, *Bad Faith, Well May We Say, Boonta Vista, Floodcast,* The Australia Institute's *Follow the Money,* the sporadically released *Living the Dream, People's History of Australia,* and, of course, the IPA's *Australia's Heartland with Tony Abbott.*

SHOUT OUTS, MAD LOVE & RESPECT

This book simply wouldn't exist without the continuing love and support of my family, friends, and colleagues, so please blame them.

My editor Ben Ball is a saint whose brain should be studied in a lab so that we can discover the secret to eternal patience, good humour and understanding. Thank you for all the thoughts and the laughs, and for putting up with me, especially during the trickier times. Seriously, mate – I can't thank you enough.

I am deeply grateful to copyeditor Rosie Outred for helping whip this messy nonsense into shape. She was even nice enough to highlight the bits that made her laugh, which is positive attention, which is all I've ever wanted. Thank you very much, Rosie, and sorry about the rush. Indeed, thanks to everyone at Simon & Schuster for letting me spew all this out into the world, and thank you to Barney for the brilliant design.

I'm indebted to everyone who's been kind enough to talk to me for this book both on and off the record; in particular Dr Elizabeth Humphreys, Emma Dawson, Andrew Norton,

Van Badham, Alison Pennington, Russell Marks, Daniel Lopez, Jen Rayner, Gian and Sam from twinkrev, Tim Hollo, David Richardson, Tom Switzer, Josh Bornstein, Stephen Koukoulas, Richard Cooke, Josh Thomas, Mark Davis, Melanie Raymond, Michael Janda, Will 'Egg Boy' Connolly, Anne Knappett and Guan, and Terry Burke from AHURI.

Thanks to all the guests who've given me their time for podcasted conversations over the years, even all the right-wing nutjobs lol. I'm especially thankful to the smart and funny people who have helped me see the light and think gooder, especially Helen Razer, Osman Faruqi, Erik Jensen, Jeff Sparrow and my *Serious Danger* comrades Emerald and The Griff.

To Dioni, Kevin, and everyone at Token – my life would be a mess without youse. Thanks for dedicating your lives to the business of comedy, even though it's a very stupid use of everyone's time. Cheers.

To Peter Warsaw and Jeff Kiev – wow. What can I say? You've both done it again, and you both continue to do it, every day. I feel lucky to know you.

To Mum and Dad, Gavin, Victoria, and Cecilia – I love you all so much, and I can't believe I get to have you in my corner during a project like this, and in life. Thank you, and sorry about the swearing.

To Harley – you're everything. Thanks for loving/looking after/putting up with/not breaking up with me. I love you. Remember to respect your elders.

Finally, I wrote a lot of this book in various public libraries across Australia, and fucking hell they're great. What brilliant, joyous institutions they are, and how lucky we are to have them. Free knowledge and learning and space to think for everyone, all the time. Please go kiss/hug/thank your local librarian today – they are heroes, all.

* * *

This book was primarily written in Naarm, on the lands of the Wurundjeri Woi Wurrung and Bunurong/Boonwurrung peoples of the Kulin nation, where I am lucky enough to live. I grew up in Gunditjmara/Dhauwurd Wurrung country, and for some years I've lived on Gadigal country.

All of this land was stolen and has never been ceded, and the legacy of that foundational crime lives on all around us, every day. Always Was, Always Will Be.